THE SIKHS AND THE SIKH WARS.

THE SIKHS

AND

THE SIKH WARS:

THE RISE, CONQUEST, AND ANNEXATION OF THE PUNJAB STATE.

BY

GEN. SIR CHARLES GOUGH, V.C., G.C.B.,

AND

ARTHUR D. INNES, M.A.,

AUTHOR OF "BRITAIN AND HER RIVALS IN THE EIGHTEENTH CENTURY."

GYAN

Published by

GYAN

Gyan Publishing House
5, Ansari Road
Daryaganj, New Delhi-110002
Phone: 011-47034999, 9811692060
E-mail: books@gyanbooks.com

Distribution Network
gyanbooks.com
India, USA, Canada, UK, Australia, France

ISBN: 978-81-212-0029-5 (HB)

Reprint in India, 2024
First Published, 2013

Printed at: Gyan Press, Delhi.

The Sikhs and the Sikh Wars:
The Rise, Conquest and Annexation of the Punjab State
Author: Gen. Sir Charles Gough, Arthur D. Innes

PREFACE.

THE authors of this work have endeavoured to leave no source of information neglected. Various portions of the subject with which it deals have been treated in the works of Captain J. D. Cunningham, Sir W. W. Hunter, Mr. Marshman, Sir Herbert Edwardes, and others; and in such biographies of the principal figures in the story as have been published from Ranjit Singh to the Lawrences. Blue-books and dispatches are necessary to the historian, though not always consulted by the picturesque story-teller. At the time of the two great campaigns, numerous letters and articles appeared in the press and the magazines, the work, occasionally, of men who knew more than they told, but not less often of men who told more than they knew.

That some erroneous ideas on the whole subject should have become prevalent, and threaten to be stereotyped is, perhaps, natural; the more so, no doubt, because Lord Gough made a point, not only of refusing to answer his critics in the press, but of forbidding his friends to do it for him.

In addition, however, to the published matter already referred to, the authors have had access (1) by the courtesy of the present officers, to the regimental records of all the British regiments engaged; (2) to the unpublished notes and diaries of officers who took part in the campaigns, notably of Sir Arthur Borton, through Lady Borton's kindness; (3) to the diary and memoranda of Lord Gough, in the possession of the Gough family; (4) to personal communication with men who were eye-witnesses of many of the events narrated; among whom their thanks are more especially due to Field-Marshal Sir Frederick Haines.

On one point they have to express their regret. It has been found to be a sheer impossibility to adopt any uniform principle in spelling. Wherever it can reasonably be maintained that one way of spelling a name is more generally recognised than another, they have used that form. In other cases, they have fallen back on the spelling of the old blue-books and dispatches. But when the published books speak variously of one single place as Ferozeshah, Feerozshah, Firozshah, Firozeshahar, Ferozeshur, and P'heerooshuhur; of another as Tricca, Trickhur, Truckhur, and Tirkha; it will be admitted that, with the best intentions, uniformity of principle is a little difficult of attainment.

Of the accuracy of the facts as here set forth, the authors believe there can be no question. As to the soundness of the opinions and inferences derived from those facts, the impartial reader must judge for himself.

C. G.
A. D. I.

CONTENTS.

BOOK I.

INTRODUCTORY: BEFORE 1808.

CHAPTER I.

PRELIMINARY.

CHAPTER II.

THE MOGUL EMPIRE AND THE BRITISH ADVANCE.

CHAPTER III.

THE GROWTH OF THE SIKHS.

CHAPTER IV.

Ferozeshah—Second Day: Dec. 22.

CHAPTER V.

Budhowal and Aliwal: Dec. 23–Jan. 28.

CHAPTER VI.

Sobraon: Feb. 10.

CHAPTER VII.

Survey of the Campaign.

BOOK IV.

FROM THE TREATY OF LAHORE TO SHERE SINGH'S REVOLT: MARCH, 1845–SEPT., 1848.

CHAPTER I.

The Lahore Treaty: March–Dec., 1846.

BOOK V.

THE CONQUEST OF THE SIKHS 1848–9.

CHAPTER I.

THE SIKH RISING: AUG., 1848–JAN., 1849.

CHAPTER II.

SECOND SIEGE OF MULTAN: SEPT.–JAN., 1849.

CHAPTER III.

THE CROSSING OF THE CHENAB: NOV.–DEC. 4, 1848.

CHAPTER IV.

CHILLIANWALLA: DEC. 4–JAN. 13, 1849.

CHAPTER V.

After Chillianwalla : Jan. 14–Feb. 21.

CHAPTER VI.

Gujerat and the End of the Campaign : Feb. 21.

CHAPTER VII.

Summary and Conclusions as to the Sikh Wars.

BOOK VI.

THE ANNEXATION.

CHAPTER I.

The New Administration.

CHAPTER II.

The Work of the Governing Board.

CHAPTER III.

Epilogue.

APPENDICES.

LIST OF MAPS AND PLANS.

struggles and feuds; and the strength of the Sikh confederacy was gradually increasing. At the same time the British Power was steadily advancing. In the early years of the nineteenth century, the great Maharajah Ranjit or Runjeet Singh of Lahore consolidated the Sikh Power north of the Sutlej, gradually extending its sway down to Multan, the south-western corner of the triangle, up to Peshawur on the north, and over Jammu and Kashmir on the north-east; while the British had broken down the power of the Mahratta chiefs in Central India, absorbed Delhi, and taken under their protection the Sikhs of Malwa, who were not minded to accept the domination of Ranjit Singh. That astute prince, greedy as he was of dominion, yet knew thoroughly the measure of his own powers, and was determined in no case to come into collision with the British, with whom he remained in complete amity throughout his reign.

In the chapters immediately ensuing, a brief account will be given of the development of the Sikhs from a religious fraternity into a military brotherhood, and from a military brotherhood into an organised Power; preceded by a sketch of the contemporary Mogul Empire, and of the advance of the British until their dominions reached the Sutlej, which became the border between them and the realms over which Ranjit Singh held sway.

CHAPTER II.

THE MOGUL EMPIRE AND THE BRITISH ADVANCE

Mussulman invasions of India—The Great Moguls—Disintegration of their empire—French and British—Conquest of Bengal—Warren Hastings—Subsidiary alliances—The constitution of 1784—Conquest of Mysore—And of the Mahrattas.

In the early centuries of the Christian era, the religion prevailing over the Indian Peninsula was Hinduism; that is, a form of Brahminism, modified by Buddhism, and embodying, at least among the lower castes, relics of more primitive forms of worship. On the rise of the militant faith of Mohammed, there followed a series of irruptions through the north-western passes of Afghan, Turcoman, or Tartar disciples of the prophet, who overran the whole country from north to south, and from west to east; neither establishing, nor attempting to establish, universal empire, but setting up, wherever they went, Mussulman dynasties resting on the power of the sword, alien in religion and customs to the populations over which they held sway; dynasties unstable in their nature, and liable to be overthrown either by fresh invaders, the opposition of the more warlike Hindu tribes, or military intrigues. The antagonism between Hindu and Mussulman is active at the present day, and had no small share in counteracting that tendency of Orientals as such to recognise kinship with each other in opposition to the wholly alien European, which made the Mutiny of 1857 so formidable.

Early in the sixteenth century, Baber, the descendant of Timur the Tartar, invaded India through the north-west, and founded the Mogul dynasty in the Ganges basin, after winning the first battle of Paniput. But the resistance of the Mussulman monarchs of the Lower Ganges proved too strong for his son Humayun; who was driven from the throne, to be restored not long before his death by the second victory of Paniput, where his young son Akbar was in nominal command. Akbar, whose long and glorious reign corresponded in time with that of our own Queen Elizabeth, was sufficiently conspicuous as a conqueror, but far more as a ruler. Throwing off the militant propagandism of Islam, he adopted a policy of toleration and conciliation, seeking to weld together the discordant elements of his vast dominion, treating Hindus and Mohammedans as on an equal footing. Something of the same spirit marked the rule of his successors, Jehangir and Shah Jehan; but they held the reins of government with a less vigorous hand; and while the Empire was extended southwards, the fanaticism of the Mussulman chiefs was less firmly curbed, and the opposition of the rival faiths became more active. Aurungzebe, the last great monarch of his line, who reigned throughout the last half of the seventeenth century, dying in 1707, was himself a fanatical Mussulman who wholly threw aside the tolerant policy of his great ancestor. He succeeded in adding the greater part of Southern India to his dominions; but in so doing, he not only swelled the bounds of the Empire beyond all possibility of adequate central control, but provided an incentive to a new militant Hinduism which gave birth to the great Mahratta confederacy in Southern and Central India, and imposed a military form on the Sikh brotherhood of the north-west.

Aurungzebe had sown the seeds of disintegration; from the time of his death, the Mogul Empire rapidly broke up. The series of puppet Moguls residing in their head-quarters at Delhi lost all control. The rulers of the great provinces

intrigue was on foot at the Nawab's court to get rid of him, and establish Meer Jaffier in his place; the conspirators invoked British assistance; Clive, with a small body of troops, routed Suraj-ud-daula at Plassey; Meer Jaffier was made Nawab, and found himself simply a puppet in the hands of the English, whose small but effective army made resistance to their will impossible. Clive's last work before he finally left India, in 1765, was to organise the administration of Bengal on the only possible working basis—the sole alternative being unmitigated anarchy—namely, the acceptance by the East India Company of the responsibilities of government, retaining the Nawab as a merely nominal figure-head, and professing allegiance to the Mogul at Delhi. At the same time he made a treaty with Oude, the province on the western border, with a view to establishing it as a firm buffer-state against invasion, whether by marauding hosts from the north-west, or by the advancing Mahrattas.

But this practical acquisition by a trading company of a vast new territory—rendering them in effect sovereigns of Bengal and Behar, the two great provinces of the Lower Ganges, while they held also a dominant influence among the states of Southern India—compelled the interference of the Parliament at Westminster. Until the retirement of Warren Hastings in 1785, an attempt was made to carry on the government under the highly unsatisfactory system established by Lord North's Regulating Acts of 1773. Warren Hastings succeeded in laying the foundations of a strong system of administration; but, to a great extent in spite of himself, he was compelled to plunge into active war. It was no part of his policy to extend dominion, nor were the possessions of the British materially added to during his rule. He was dragged into collision with the Mahrattas by the injudicious action of the Bombay Government, and in the south he was obliged to do battle with Hyder Ali of Mysore, whom the Madras Government irritated into hostilities which threatened to result in the annihilation of the British in the Carnatic. Broadly speaking, however, the nett results of his governor-generalship were that the administration of Bengal was consolidated, Hyder Ali was successfully resisted, the Mahrattas learned to recognise the British as a dangerous and presumably aggressive Power—since all strong Powers in India were presumably aggressive—and the very important policy of subsidiary alliances was instituted in Oude.

This system of subsidiary alliances plays so important a part in the history of Indian politics that it demands a brief explanation. Warren Hastings did not wish to extend territory; but he did wish the provinces on our borders to be effective barriers against aggression from beyond; and he wanted money for government and for dividends. To secure the first object it was necessary that the border provinces should be strong enough to resist invasion, and should yet not be in a position either to turn actively hostile on their own account, or to ally themselves with the enemy beyond. This could only be effected by bringing their military forces up to an efficient standard, and at the same time keeping them under British control. This might have been done by employing an army of occupation, but then the problem of money came in, as well as the practical difficulty of avoiding responsibility for government under such conditions. The plan devised, therefore, was to treat the army as being provided for the defence of the state and the maintenance of the throne—as a boon to the ally, in short—and to require in return that it should be paid for by the state assisted. Thus, in the specific case of Oude, the arrangement amounted to this: that the Vizier was to be protected against either invasion or rebellion by the Company's troops permanently quartered in his country; and was in return to hand over to the Company revenues adequate to the maintenance of those troops, with a profit on the transaction. A subsequent development arose when such allies found a difficulty in producing a sufficient revenue, and as a result handed over a district in lieu of cash; a plan which was largely resorted to when the British had become less chary of accumulating territory.

By the India Bill of 1784, Pitt and Dundas placed the government of India on the basis which it occupied until the Mutiny of 1857 caused the abolition of the Company and the transfer of the government direct to the Crown. The institution of a Parliamentary Board of Control made the Parliament at Westminster ultimately responsible for the government of India, while general instructions were issued by the London directors; but the Governor-General in Council could act habitually without direct reference to England, and the Governor-General himself had powers of action on emergency which made him virtually an autocrat whenever he chose.

As the century drew to its close, the outbreak of the Napoleonic wars in Europe introduced fresh complications into Indian politics. The British dominion over the seas, and the resulting impossibility of France lending any material assistance to native Powers in a struggle with England, were recognised insufficiently by the British themselves, and not at all by Tippu Sultan in Mysore. That prince was not less bellicose than his father, while he wholly lacked Hyder Ali's exceptional political sagacity. By seeking an aggressive alliance with Napoleon, he made war with the English inevitable; although he had once already challenged a conflict which had resulted in curtailment of his revenues and of his territory. Lord Mornington, afterwards Marquess of Wellesley, who arrived as Governor-General in 1798, was entirely free from his predecessors' aversion to extending dominion. He formed a subsidiary alliance with the Nizam of Hyderabad, and persuaded the Mahrattas to join in a league against Tippu. The war which followed was decisive. Tippu was slain. Part of

Mysore was restored to the Hindu dynasty whom Hyder Ali had ejected; the rest was divided between the Mahrattas, the Nizam, and the British.

Now, therefore, a formidable enemy had been removed from the south; the Deccan had been brought into the same condition of nominal independence accompanied by practical military subordination, as Oude in the north. In effect, therefore, there were now, at the beginning of the nineteenth century, two Powers, the British and the Mahrattas, dividing between them, if not the sovereignty, at any rate the practical control of all India from the eastern seas as far west as the Delhi districts where the Mogul was now wholly under Mahratta control, and Rajputana.

From time immemorial, conquest had, in India, been the first business of every state which had been strong enough to attempt it. The idea that any Power should have a positive preference for not extending its territories was almost inconceivable. Moreover, though the British profession in this respect had been entirely honest, though it could be demonstrated that every step forward had been taken only after provocation which left no alternative, the fact remained that in hardly more than half a century this would-be peaceable and unaggressive Power had extended its sway from three or four mercantile factories over nearly half the peninsula. Moreover, Wellesley's idea of not being aggressive was coupled with an active policy of pressing for subsidiary alliances, which native rulers could not but regard as merely a more insidious method of extending dominion, calculated to enable the British to assert actual sovereignty whenever they had a mind. Wellesley, with Napoleon still in view as the real enemy, felt that ascendency at the courts of the Mahratta chiefs was still a necessity; the Mahratta chiefs took a different view, and were disposed, by preference, to a trial of strength with the British. But their mutual rivalries and jealousies drove one of them, the Peshwa of

Poonah, to accept the protection of the British. Of the four remaining chiefs of the confederacy, the Rajah of Berar combined with Sindiah of Gwalior; while the other two, Holkar of Indore, and the Gaikwar of Baroda, stood by. The forces of Sindiah and his ally were shattered at Assaye, Argaon, and Laswaree. The result was that Delhi and the Mogul were delivered to the British, and both Sindiah and the Berar Rajah were obliged to hand over immense territories, on the south side of the Ganges and on the east coast, which very effectively crippled their power and greatly strengthened the British. When his rivals had been beaten, Holkar attempted to take up the struggle single-handed; but the attempt was futile, and he was forced to make peace on terms strictly analogous to those which had been dictated to his brother chiefs.

Thus in 1805, when Lord Wellesley left India, the whole of the basins, both of the Ganges and the Jumna (with the exception of Oude), the eastern coast from the Ganges to the Carnatic, and all India south of the Deccan, except the diminished Mysore, were actually British territory. Oude and Mysore, and the Nizam's dominions, were under British protection; while the Mahratta chiefs who still retained dominion did so by leave of the British without power of effective independent opposition.

We shall now turn to the origin and development of the Sikh body which was going on during the same three centuries—the sixteenth, seventeenth, and eighteenth.

CHAPTER III.

THE GROWTH OF THE SIKHS

Hinduism—Nanuk's reformation—The successors of Nanuk—Govind and the Khalsa—The Sikh outlawry—Formation of the Misls or Sikh confederacies—Development of Sikh dominion—Appearance of Ranjit Singh.

THE country over which the Sikh religion spread comprises, as we have noted, two great districts—that between the Jumna and the Sutlej, known as Malwa and also as Sirhind; and that beyond the Sutlej, known with more or less accuracy as the Punjab. In these districts the population consisted of Jats and Rajputs, chiefly Hindu, but sometimes Mohammedan; Pathans, all Mohammedan; and the numerous and mixed descendants of conquered races; belonging generally to the lowest Hindu caste (called Sudras). In the fifteenth century, such government as there was bore some resemblance to that of the Scottish Highlands, local chiefs doing pretty much what they thought fit, fighting and robbing at large without organisation, and paying tribute to the last invader who had proved himself able to enforce it.

Owing to the essential intolerance of Mohammedanism, there was a constant feud between Mussulmans and Hindus, the former regarding the latter as infidels and idolators. Whatever the esoteric doctrines of the Brahmins are, Hinduism in its practical, popular form is Polytheistic, idolatrous in the natural interpretation of that term, and overladen with forms and observances. The religious tenet of most vital consequence is the doctrine of transmigration; that is, the belief that, before ultimate purification and emancipation, the soul passes through a series of incarnations, each new life being conditioned by the conduct of the soul in its past life.

Its fundamental institution, resting on religious sanction, is that of caste. Caste may be generally described as the theory and practice of hereditary social distinctions carried to the extremest limits and confirmed by the sanction of religion. The spirit of it is more or less present in most societies which have attained a high organisation. But, carried to an extreme, it is a barrier to all progress, since it is in effect an enormous system of privilege. Among the Hindus there are four great castes, each with innumerable subdivisions: the Brahmins, or priestly caste; the military; the agricultural; and the Sudras, or semi-servile. Even among the subdivisions of these greater castes, sometimes territorial in character, sometimes depending on occupation, intermarriage is forbidden, or greatly restricted, under religious as well as social penalties, and social intercourse limited; while in the relations of the four great castes, a rough analogy may be observed to the mediæval distinction between clerics, knights, yeomanry, and villeins—with the important difference that the priestly caste, like all others, is hereditary, while the European class-divisions are mainly social.

Besides this great institution, there prevailed a large number of binding observances of sacred import to the pious Hindu.

Nanuk, the founder of the Sikh sect, was born in 1469, in the neighbourhood of Lahore. A seeker after truth from his earliest years, he tried study, solitary meditation, travel, and intercourse with his neighbours, but failed to find either in Islam or in the current Hinduism the satisfaction which his soul desired; but he penetrated beneath the crust of observances and conventions, and found the root of the matter in the Unity of God and the equality of men before Him. He made no attempt to formulate his religious teaching scientifically, nor did he attempt to frame a creed; but, if it is legitimate to apply an exceedingly modern terminology to what was in effect his doctrine, it might be said that he found salvation in good deeds as the fruit of a good will. He set himself to teach men the way of salvation, not as a ruler, but as a servant of God to whom the light had been shown, coming to bring not strife among men but peace.

Nanuk is remarkable as being, not only a really great reformer but one who seems to have inspired singularly little animosity. He appears to have remained on excellent terms alike with Hindus and Mohammedans, insomuch that when he died a dispute arose as to whether his body should be buried as a Mussulman's or burned as a Hindu's, since he acknowledged Mohammed as well as the Hindu "incarnations" as among the prophets of God. The secret of the personal favour in which he was held seems to have lain not merely in the gentleness of his disposition and the charm of his character, but also in the manner in which he put forth his claims, and the total absence of any pretensions for himself which could be interpreted as arrogant or impious. When he denied the religious importance of caste, he did not denounce the Brahmins, while to the Mohammedans he appeared as a Hindu who was almost persuaded to be a Mohammedan. The unostentatious virtue of his own life, the absence of austerity combined with the practice of the moral principles which he preached, appealed to the humanity of those with whom he came in contact. Since he preached no crusade against conventions, he did not excite the wrath of those who were attached to them; while the fundamental principles on which he laid vital stress were such as must always, in virtue of their "sweet reasonableness," appeal to every religious mind, and most of all to those large classes who found in orthodox Hinduism but little consolation in the next world for the sorrows of the present.

Thus did Nanuk found the religious sect or brotherhood who called themselves Sikhs, or "disciples"; a sect entirely religious, without any political aim or organisation, based on two fundamental principles: the Unity of God and the Brotherhood of Man, without distinction of race, caste, or creed. His teaching is embodied in the book known as the "Granth."

The torch of Nanuk was handed on through a series of successors bearing the title of guru, which is perhaps best rendered by the term prophet. The guru being recognised as the head of the sect, it was inevitable, under the pressure of quasi-feudal custom, that his followers should acquire something of the character of feudal retainers. The fifth guru, Arjun, is the first in whom the germ of a political leadership comes to be recognised; in the sixth, Hur Govind, it developes. Hur Govind, in addition to his office as the religious light of the Sikhs, was forced by circumstances to adopt a military training, and, being naturally fitted thereto, he gave his following a decidedly martial character. The rules of virtuous living were relaxed, and it would scarcely seem unjust to say that an active sectarian spirit was regarded as a sufficient equivalent, at any rate if accompanied by sound fighting qualities. Hur Govind and his followers fought with distinction in the armies of Jehangir and of Shah Jehan; but in what may be called his baronial character he came into frequent collision with the Mogul's officers in the Punjab—the central district of which had now become the Sikh headquarters, Amritsir having been established as a sacred city.

By this time, then, *i.e.* towards the middle of the seventeenth century, the guru and his Sikhs still retained the character of a spiritual leader and his disciples, but on to this was grafted that of a baron and his retainers; with this special peculiarity: that they were bound together, not only by the common feudal tie, but also by their religious separation from others, religious equality among themselves rendering them at once all brothers in arms and brothers in the Faith.

This military character of the brotherhood naturally progressed under the successors of Hur Govind, and new members were added in great numbers to the band of disciples. The tenth in the guru succession, Govind Singh, grandson of Hur Govind, set the seal upon the new policy, gave the Sikhs a definite organisation, and marked out Mohammedanism as the special object of hostility.

Govind Singh succeeded his father Tegh Bahadur in 1675, when Aurungzebe was Mogul. Whether the Sikhs had already adopted an attitude towards the Emperor which justified Aurungzebe in treating the guru as a rebel, is not quite clear; but there is no doubt that Tegh Bahadur was summoned to Delhi, and that he was there in effect executed by the Mogul's orders. Hence the mind of the young Govind was filled with fierce animosity towards the great monarchy of Delhi. Able, high-minded, and ambitious, he was a religious enthusiast with a mission, and a son with a murdered father to avenge. His followers were inspired with his own enthusiasm. They believed him to be the special favourite of Heaven. He proclaimed the Faith anew; he announced a new initiation. Henceforth the Sikhs were to be bound together by a closer tie. Salvation—the passage of the soul to bliss, freed from the necessity of incarnation after incarnation—was given to all faithful members of the Khalsa, the army of the Free; and all who received the Pahal, *i.e.* underwent a new ceremony of baptism, received the surname of Singh, signifying "Lion," and were admitted to the Khalsa. He introduced the curiously distinctive custom of not cutting the hair or beard, and prohibited the use of tobacco—apparently as outward signs by which the Sikhs should be recognised as such. Under no circumstances, not even to save his life in fever, will a Sikh allow his hair to be cut. He declared himself the last of the gurus in whom individually the spirit of their great founder Nanuk should reside; from thenceforth the spirit of the guru would live in the body of the Khalsa; wheresoever five Singhs were gathered together, there would he be present in their midst. Sudra and Brahmin, warrior and husbandmen, all alike were brethren and comrades in the Khalsa. The sacred places of the Hindus remained sacred, but their ceremonials and observances must be abandoned. Above all, the Khalsa was essentially two things—an army and a religious brotherhood, united against the Moslem power as the common enemy. Henceforth the name of the Khalsa and the title of Singh became words of power.

Govind Singh's attitude to the Mogul Empire was assumed at a favourable moment. Aurungzebe was in the south, his energies absorbed in the endless effort to crush the Mussulman kings of the Deccan and the newly born Mahratta power. Govind had only minor lieutenants to deal with, and it was his policy to build up a strong military basis in the Punjab rather than to advance against the forces of the Empire; but that the Empire rather than Islam was the object of his animosity is shown by his readiness to make use of the services of Pathan mercenaries. His career was by no means uniformly successful; at one time it seemed that his power was altogether broken; but the spirit of the Khalsa was strong, and the Sikhs rallied to him. When Aurungzebe died, the new Mogul, Bahadur Shah, thought it politic to treat Govind with favour, and Govind doubtless felt that it would be no less politic on his own part to disarm suspicion by accepting the favour. Being summoned to appear at the court of the Mogul, then held at Aurungabad in the Deccan, he accepted the invitation, remaining there until, in 1708, he was assassinated by two Pathans whose father he had himself slain. He lies buried at Nadeir, not far from Aurungabad, where a small Sikh colony maintain his tomb in veneration.

By the energy of the great Guru, the Khalsa had been

developed into a far from contemptible military force; differing from that of ordinary chiefs in its extraordinary recuperative capacity, since the rallying power remained so long as the Faith survived. It would be misleading to speak of a body so loosely organized as a "State;" perhaps the most correct idea will be maintained by describing the Sikhs as forming from this time a commonwealth, military in character, and based on religion.

Now, however, this newly-born commonwealth was fallen upon evil days. When Govind died, he named as the new leader of his people a devoted follower named Bunda. Bunda was a zealot of considerable ability and great daring; but he was lacking in popular qualities, and in political judgment. He led the Sikhs in open rebellion against the town of Sirhind in Malwa; but the Mogul's officers were too strong for him; and though he maintained the struggle for some years, he was crushed and put to death in 1716. For the next thirty years the Sikhs were unable to form an effective combination, and lived to a great extent the life of scattered and persecuted outlaws.

But the Empire was falling to pieces. In 1738 Nadir Shah sacked Delhi. The Sikhs began to raise their heads. Nine years later came Ahmed Shah the Abdallee. From this time the Moslem governors at Lahore (the chief city of the Punjab) began to own an allegiance divided according to convenience between the monarchs of Afghanistan and Delhi. Intrigues were rife. The army of the Khalsa revived, not without secret encouragement from one or another of the great officers. One of these had thoughts of becoming an independent sovereign by the help of the Sikhs, but the scheme came to nothing. Then came Ahmed Shah's most important invasion, and the great Mahratta check at Paniput in 1761. The Mogul power had already ceased to count, and there was now no effective controlling force throughout the Sikh districts.

From the time when the invasions began, the

reconstruction of the Sikh commonwealth began also; the chiefs drawing together for joint action in local groups or "Misls," while the idea of the whole Khalsa as a united army revived. There was no recognised head; but the Misls now began to act with a certain degree of concert; though the Sikhs of the Punjab and of Malwa were hardly united, the Powers which threatened the latter being mainly to the east and south, while the danger to the former came from Afghanistan. But since all owned a fervent allegiance to the Khalsa, each chief felt a general readiness to assist his neighbour's schemes of conquest, for the good of the Khalsa, and for the sake of a legitimate share in the spoils. Consequently it was no long time before one Misl or another had spread Sikh dominion over the greater part alike of Malwa and the Punjab. And this progress was distinctly assisted by the policy of Ahmed Shah, who had no objection to recognising a Sikh chief and bestowing on him the title of Rajah, finding this a practical method of dominion quite as convenient as setting up lieutenants of his own in distant provinces. By this means, the whole of Malwa became subject to the "Phulkia" Misl, which recognised as its head the Rajah of Patiala, who held his title from Ahmed Shah.

North of the Sutlej, the Misls which acquired the greatest power, and were roughly recognised as the leading confederacies of the great Sikh body, were the Banghis, Ramgharias, and Aluwalias, all of them having their head-quarters in the district lying between the Sutlej and the Chenab, known as Manjha. It is to be observed that while Ahmed Shah lived, the Sikhs feared his name greatly; and though they attacked and routed his lieutenants, they gave way before the approach of the great Durani himself. But after Ahmed Shah's death in 1773, they commonly met the Afghan armies on equal terms; and, during the closing years of the century, despite the loose organisation of the whole general body, the leaders of the various sections of the Khalsa had acquired among them something like complete predominance over the greater part of the Punjab, with such occasional submissions to the Afghan monarchs as proved expedient from time to time; the intrigues of Afghan chiefs usually making it necessary for the Afghan king to return to his own country within a very short time, whenever he had left it with aggressive movements in view.

The Misls then had fulfilled their function. They had served to enable the Sikhs to act together for the common advantage; yet they had been so far independent of each other that the temporary ruin of one did not mean the ruin of the whole body; and a process went on by which each sirdar or baron, to return to the feudal illustration, endeavoured to acquire direct lordship, or, at any rate, recognised leadership, over a gradually extending area within the Sikh dominions. When the nineteenth century opened, the young Ranjit Singh—he was born only in 1780—was already proving himself one of the most astute and pushing of the sirdars. Supported by the friendship of Futteh Singh "Aluwalia," a chief with a large following, who, while of no mean abilities, lacked the personal ambition and the vigorous initiative powers of the great Maharajah, Ranjit Singh established himself at Lahore; crushed or attached to himself one after another of the greater chiefs; and by the year 1808, seemed likely to bring the entire Sikh body under his sway, having obtained the title of Maharajah from the Afghan king.

But by this time the Southern Power of the Mahrattas had been broken by the English; Delhi was in their hands; the formation of an organised military state spreading over Malwa was an idea which they could not contemplate with entire equanimity; they were encouraged to interfere by the appeal of the Malwa Sikhs, who had no mind to be forced into submission to the Maharajah; and so direct relations were established between the British and Ranjit Singh.

BOOK II.

SIKH DOMINION

CHAPTER I.

RANJIT SINGH CREATES THE LAHORE STATE

Geography—Character of the Sikh body—Character of Ranjit Singh—Malwa—British policy—Establishment of friendly relations—Shah Shujah and the Barukzais—Ranjit Singh's overtures—Collision with Futteh Khan—Acquisition of Multan and Kashmir—And of Peshawur.

BEFORE proceeding to an account of the great Maharajah Ranjit Singh, it will be well for the reader who is unfamiliar with the north-west of India to form a clear idea of the meaning of certain geographical expressions, and of the position of the more important places which are likely to be mentioned.

The Five Rivers * join the Indus at Mithenkote, which may be taken as the south-western point of the Punjab. South of this point, the Indus flows through Scinde; west of Scinde lies Beluchistan.

Parallel to the Indus from south to north run the mountains which border Afghanistan. Well to the north, at the entrance of the passes leading up to Kabul, the Afghan capital, stands Peshawur.

Crossing the Indus eastwards, at the south-western end of the Plain of the Five Rivers, stands Multan. At this

* It will have been observed that, counting the Indus, there are six rivers. The weight of authority omits the Indus as being the border, not one of the five; other authorities include the Indus but omit the Sutlej; while others, again, omit the Ravi as only an insignificant stream.

time, Peshawur and Multan were both under governors appointed from Kabul. The greater part of the plain of the Punjab, having for its political centre Lahore, and for its sacred city, Amritsir, was under Sikh control, which, north and west of the Sutlej, was coming rapidly to mean the sway of Ranjit Singh; and might virtually be called the kingdom of Lahore.

North-east of the Punjab plain, running from north-west to south-east, lie the mountains of Kashmir, Jammu, and Kangra, as yet independent of the Sikhs, while Kashmir was controlled by the Afghans.

Across the Sutlej, from that river to the Jumna, on which Delhi stands, and which was as yet accounted the limit of British territory, were the Sikhs of Malwa, of whom the Patiala Rajah was the head. Close to the Sutlej are two places which shortly became important British military posts, Ludhiana and Ferozepore.

The rise of the Lahore kingdom is a remarkable phenomenon, worthy of careful consideration.

When Ranjit Singh began to assume the place of the Sikh chief *par excellence*, the *machinery* of the Sikh confederacy was by no means of the best, but the *material* on which he had to work was of very fine quality. Any effective fighting machine must have a single controlling head, whereas the Sikh doctrines of brotherhood and equality made every chief kick at the idea of subordination. It may be observed generally that wherever there is theoretical equality the individual interprets that as meaning that *he* is as good as his neighbour, but his neighbour is not as good as he. So the chiefs had their followers, but every chief was reluctant to own a superior. Therefore the members of the "Misls" were hard fighters, very difficult to cope with individually, but at the same time very difficult to organise collectively.

Hence, in order to raise the armed Sikhs into a formidable state, it was imperative that they should be induced to recognise some one head. It was absolutely necessary that any man seeking such recognition for himself should by force of character compel an acknowledgment of his personal superiority; in other words, he must show that he had a longer head and a stronger arm than any rival. But having a theoretical brotherhood to deal with, it was necessary to do a good deal more. Among the great mass of the Sikhs, equality of a kind, at least, was an essential article in a strongly held creed; and this could only be overcome if the would-be leader succeeded in inspiring strong personal enthusiasm.

Ranjit Singh possessed precisely the necessary qualities. His prowess in battle was beyond question; the vigour and shrewdness of his judgment were conspicuous; his promptitude of action was obvious. And he struck a note to which the heart of the Sikh people vibrated, by proclaiming himself always as the servant of Guru Govind, and acting always in the name of Govind and to the glory of the Khalsa; in other words, he made it his business to pose as a national hero, whether he was leading his Sikhs against the Moslem, upsetting a Sikh rival, appropriating the estates of a dead chief's heirs, or diplomatising with the British. By these means he won recognition, until by degrees the Maharajah of Lahore had consolidated the Punjab into the Lahore kingdom.

But he did a great deal more than this. Ranjit Singh possessed in a very high degree one particular kingly quality not usually conspicuous in Oriental monarchs: he always knew exactly how far he could go. However large and far-reaching his ultimate designs might be, his immediate measures were always practicable. The progress of his arms was steady and stubborn; but each step was part of his large design, and he made each step secure before he took the next, never challenging an enemy till he felt that the chances of a contest would be in his favour. He saw with complete insight how tremendous the power of the British had come to be, and he made up his mind at an early stage that their goodwill must be retained at all costs, that he must entertain no project which he was assured would alienate them, or make a rupture with them probable. So he began life as a Lahore chieftain, and ended it the lord of all the lands north and west of the Sutlej, from Multan to Peshawur, and from Peshawur to Jammu.

Already, in 1808, Ranjit Singh was recognised north of the Sutlej as the leader of the Khalsa; and it was on his claim to that position that he began also to base and to assert his title, not only to estates south of the Sutlej, which he had annexed, but to lordship over Malwa, as Sikh territory and consequently subject to the Khalsa. The Malwa chiefs, on the other hand, were more alive to the danger of political subjection than to the advantage of political unity; not feeling moved by the hope of extending the power of the Khalsa. In fact, seeing that they were bordered by the British Power, there was no prospect of any Imperial extension from which they would derive benefit; while they would gain security by enlisting British sympathies in their behalf.

Now, the British at this time had no intention or desire to annex dominions beyond the Jumna, but their attitude was liable to be affected by suspicions of the designs of France. It was not yet fifty years since the hand-to-hand struggle for a footing in India had been decided in favour of the British. Only five and twenty years ago the skill and valour of Suffren had brought us within measurable distance of a renewal of that struggle. The invasion of India had been an avowed design of Buonaparte's, until his plans were wrecked by Nelson's victory of the Nile. The whole of Lord Wellesley's administration had been dominated by the idea that France was the real enemy to be kept in view even in India. The idea of an overland invasion through Persia, which would receive considerable assistance from native states, was in the air. The British, consequently, felt it to be of considerable importance that the Malwa Sikhs should be friendly, as the defence of the Sutlej would be thereby rendered easier. On the other hand, judging by the previous action of the Mahrattas and of Tippu Sultan of Mysore, a great independent Sikh state, occupying both the Punjab and Malwa, was likely enough, if invasion threatened, to side with the French; in which case the difficulty of resistance would be greatly increased. Policy therefore demanded, in the first place, that the Malwa Sikhs should be kept apart, and friendly; and in the second that, provided this condition were fulfilled, the trans-Sutlej Sikhs should also be kept friendly.

On the other hand, Ranjit Singh was particularly long-headed. The English power was present and palpable. The French power was distant, and there were no means of measuring its available effectiveness. It was perfectly clear to the astute Maharajah that, unless some one was ready to back him with overwhelming strength, a collision with the British would wreck him, as he had seen Holkar wrecked. A hypothetical French army which might never arrive was not worth taking into consideration, in the light of recent Mahratta experiences. Collision with the British was, therefore, by all means to be avoided. The hypothetical French might be dexterously worked into negotiations, but did not form a serious factor in his policy.

Hence, when the Malwa Sikhs appealed to the British for protection against Ranjit Sinjh, the British were strongly disposed to grant their request; while Ranjit Singh had no notion of pressing his claim further than judicious diplomacy warranted. It was much more to his interest to get our moral support on his own side of the Sutlej than to be driven out of Malwa by force, and get nothing but animosity and suspicion for his pains.

Thus, in the beginning of 1809, a rough settlement, satisfactory to all parties, was arrived at. Ranjit Singh might do very much as he chose beyond the Sutlej, provided that he showed no hostility to the British. South of the Sutlej he might retain the estates he already held, but under the same conditions as the other Sikh chiefs of Malwa, with whom he was not to interfere. In case of any aggression, the British would defend the Malwa Sikhs—which very soon came to mean that they would insist on the Malwa Sikhs abstaining from aggression against each other.

The Maharajah was quite sufficiently acute to perceive that the British reluctance to interfere with affairs beyond the Sutlej was perfectly genuine, and that, so long as he aroused no mistrust of his own intentions, he would be allowed a free hand. In this acuteness of perception he was almost unique; since it may be considered an axiom of Oriental monarchies that every Power aims at extension of dominion whenever opportunity occurs, each habitually judging the action of every other Power on that hypothesis. Ranjit Singh's shrewd appreciation of the British attitude clearly marks the statesmanlike qualities of his mind. He even realised that they would prefer a strong state in the Punjab to a weak one, provided only its friendliness were assured.

Having thus settled his relations with the British, Ranjit Singh turned his attention to the systematic extension and consolidation of his power beyond the Sutlej—a process which involved operations against minor chiefs within the line of the Indus, and against Afghan governors at Multan and from Peshawur to Kashmir.

With respect to the Sikh and other minor chiefs, the Maharajah's method was simple. He worked partly by steady pressure on individuals, partly by confiscating for his own benefit the estates of the more important men who died and left heirs who were not in a position to defend their own interests.

With respect to the gradual acquisition of Multan, Peshawur, and Kashmir, more detail is necessary.

Afghanistan had arrived at the usual condition of Oriental monarchies. Two brothers, Shah Zeman and Shah Shujah, were dethroned in turn; and in 1810 a third brother, Shah Mehmud, was king in Kabul. The real power, however, lay in the hands of the Vizier Futteh Khan, and half the most important governorships were held by groups of the Barukzai brothers, of whom he was the chief. Those of whom we shall hear most were Mohammed Azim, Yar Mohammed, Sultan Mohammed, and Dost Mohammed.

When Shah Shujah was driven out in 1810 he was very much disposed to try to get himself reinstated by whatever assistance he could procure. To Ranjit Singh it at once became evident that Shah Shujah might be made use of as a tool for his own profit, while he was further impressed with the possibility that the ex-king—unless he interfered—might go further and get British help. Such a proceeding would contain serious elements of danger. An Afghan king maintained on his throne by British bayonets would give the British an interest in the territories which lay between their own borders and Afghanistan of a kind which might prove exceedingly inconvenient to the Maharajah. He therefore decided to offer Shah Shujah his friendship, and to use him for his own ends.

His projects at first were not particularly successful. Shah Shujah did not put himself in the Maharajah's power, and the Governor of Multan stoutly refused to admit either of them within his walls, maintaining a professed allegiance to the *de facto* king at Kabul. On the other hand, Shah Shujah did succeed in recovering Peshawur, but was unable to hold it, and was then made a prisoner and carried off to Kashmir by his own nominal followers who continued to act in his name.

Meantime, Ranjit Singh, with Kashmir as his ultimate objective, was reducing the hill Rajahs of Jammu and the neighbouring districts. Now, however, Futteh Khan the Vizier appeared on the scenes—also with the recovery of

Kashmir as his object; and Futteh Khan was a man of intelligence, who was quite aware that if Ranjit Singh opposed him he was fairly certain to fail. Consequently the two came to terms. They were to reconquer Kashmir in concert, and then to punish the Governor of Multan, whose professed allegiance to the king at Kabul went no further than bidding defiance to the exiled brother.

The alliance between Ranjit Singh and Futteh Khan merely meant that each wanted to make a tool of the other. The Vizier managed to capture Kashmir without Sikh assistance, and immediately declared that under these circumstances the Sikhs had no claim to the spoils. Ranjit Singh countered by getting possession of Attok, a fort lying near the confluence of the Kabul river and the Indus on the way from Peshawur to Kashmir. The result was a fight between the Sikh troops and the Afghans, in which the former were victorious. The most important point, however, gained by the Maharajah in this contest was the possession of the person of Shah Shujah—an advantage which he very shortly afterwards lost; since the unlucky ex-king found his position at Lahore so equivocal that he made his escape across the Sutlej, and took refuge at Ludhiana, now occupied by the troops of the British in their character of guardians of Malwa. In 1814 Ranjit Singh's further attempt to conquer Kashmir was frustrated by Mohammed Azim (Futteh Khan's brother), who had been left there as governor.

As soon as the Maharajah perceived that the conquest of Kashmir was likely to demand a more thorough organisation and larger resources than he as yet had at his disposal, he made up his mind to defer that particular scheme, and directed his attention to completing the subjection of the still independent Rajahs of the hills and outlying districts of the Punjab itself; to the organisation of his territories; and then, in 1818, to the capture of Multan. There the governor, who had been aiming at virtual independence, paid the penalty of isolation; and in spite of a splendidly stubborn resistance, the fort was captured after a siege of four months by a sudden and furious assault carried out almost on the spur of the moment without any special plan or preparation.

The Maharajah's patience was duly rewarded. Futteh Khan was put to death at Herat in 1818; Mohammed Azim hastened from Kashmir to Kabul, to put a fresh puppet on the throne in place of Shah Mehmud, who still held Herat, and to secure the practical predominance of the Barukzai family. He was quite sufficiently occupied in making himself master of Kabul and Kandahar. The Sikhs invaded Kashmir in the summer of 1819; the Afghan troops left in possession made no long resistance, and Kashmir was annexed to the Lahore kingdom. In the following year the remaining dependencies of Kabul east of the Indus were also brought into subjection.

By this time Mohammed Azim seemed to have made his position sufficiently secure to begin preparing for reprisals. Ranjit Singh, however, now meant to assert himself, and sent to Peshawur to demand tribute from the governor, Yar Mohammed, brother of Mohammed Azim. The tribute was given. Early in 1829 Azim marched to Peshawur to remedy this state of things. Yar Mohammed fled. Ranjit Singh determined to have Peshawur for himself. On both sides the contest partook of the character of a religious war, Sikh fanaticism on the one side, and Moslem fanaticism on the other, having been violently aroused against the "infidel." The Sikhs crossed the Indus, the Afghan tribes came over from Peshawur, and there was a very great fight. Ranjit Singh was victorious, Mohammed Azim fled, and Peshawur was sacked. The Maharajah, however, was shrewd enough to know that for his Sikh soldiery to hold such a place as Peshawur in the midst of a hostile Mussulman population would be an exceedingly difficult task. Therefore, when Yar Mohammed offered submission, he cheerfully accepted the proposal, and Peshawur became tributary to Lahore under a Barukzai governor, while the governor's brother was Vizier at Kabul.

It was not long, however, before Mohammed Azim himself died; and then the divisions and rivalries among the Barukzai brothers became worse than before, while the Durani kings, ex-kings, and would-be kings were taken up or dropped, according to temporary exigencies, after a fashion not less confusing than that period of perpetual topsy-turvy in English history known as the "Wars of the Roses."

CHAPTER II.

LATER YEARS OF RANJIT SINGH: 1819-1839

Ahmed Shah—Ranjit Singh's designs on Scinde—Attitude to the British Commercial Theory—Shah Shujah attempts to return to Kabul—Dost Mohammed fails to recover Peshawur—Death of Ranjit Singh—Nature of his rule—His army—His sagacity.

RANJIT SINGH'S acquisition of Peshawur did not place him in peaceful and permanent possession of that province, which in some respects was rather to his advantage than otherwise. The essentially military character of the Khalsa which he so carefully protected for his own ends, made it necessary that the Sikhs should be constantly occupied with fighting of one sort or another; and Peshawur and the Mussulman districts of the north were sufficiently restless to provide the needed occupation. Had it not been so, the Maharajah would have found it difficult to refrain from schemes of conquest which might have seriously endangered his relations with the British.

It was not long before there arose a Mohammedan fanatic named Ahmed Shah, who gathered round him a very considerable following of Mussulman tribes, set himself up as Commander of the Faithful, and preached a *jehad*, or religious war against the Sikhs. Ahmed quarrelled with Yar Mohammed, who though a Mussulman, held Peshawur as a tributary of Ranjit Singh. Yar Mohammed was killed, and succeeded in office by his brother Sultan Mohammed, who was subsequently beaten out of Peshawur by Ahmed. It was not till 1831 that the Mussulman prophet was finally vanquished and slain by the soldiers of the Khalsa; while Sultan Mohammed was reinstated as a tributary governor.

Having the entire Punjab under his sway, and needing further outlets for expansion, the Maharajah was exceedingly anxious to turn his attention to Scinde. In this direction, however, his projects were not at all in accord with the objects which the British Government at the time had in view. The Sikh monarch's action in the matter was eminently characteristic of the man, and caused no little dissatisfaction among his most hot-headed followers; while that of the British—constantly liable to misinterpretation—aroused that distrust of their ostensible motives which is a potential factor in Oriental diplomacy habitually and dangerously overlooked in England, and sometimes underrated by Governors-General, with serious results.

The British had no idea of conquering Scinde, of attacking the Punjab, or of actively interfering with Afghanistan. But their minds were bent on commercial development, and the notion had been formed at headquarters that a fine field for commercial enterprise would be opened up, if only the Indus could be guaranteed, like the Ganges, as an open waterway. But that a mighty military power should view mere commerce as an end in itself, without ulterior designs of conquest, is a conception quite foreign to the Oriental mind. The mere knowledge that the Indus was being, so to speak, officially investigated, aroused in the minds of the Punjab and other chiefs suspicions to which the whole history of the Honourable East India Company gave a good deal of colour. The establishment of British merchants had, as a matter of fact, been invariably followed sooner or later by the establishment of a British Protectorate, if not direct British dominion. The British might affirm that the first step had not been taken with a view to the second; that the second had only been forced on them time after time by the wanton misconduct of native states. There remained the incontrovertible facts that the second step always had followed the first, whatever the explanation might be; and that no

Oriental state would have dreamed of taking the first step unless it had the second in view.

Ranjit Singh, however, was an exceptional man. He recognised the truth of the British assumption that they never had set about conquering until they had received provocation which they honestly regarded as leaving them no option; he did not suspect them of wishing to conquer either Scinde or the Punjab; but he knew that if he provoked an attack from them, his Sikhs, with all their fine qualities, would be shattered as the Mahrattas had been before them. Therefore he had no mind to defy them, however anxious he might feel to extend his own dominions southwards. He contented himself, therefore, with impressing upon them that he very much wanted to go to Shikarpore; that his desire was exceedingly reasonable and feasible; and that he only abstained out of consideration for his highly esteemed allies who really were treating him rather shabbily, when he might make himself extremely inconvenient to them if he were so disposed.

An additional complication was introduced into the Scinde question by the proceedings of the ever-restless Shah Shujah. Roughly speaking, from Shikarpore north, the territories now held by the Scinde Amirs had been in possession of Afghanistan until the death of Mohammed Azim. Shah Shujah bethought himself that if he could get the assistance of the Scinde Amirs by resigning his claims in this quarter, and of Ranjit Singh by formally ceding Peshawur, he might recover the throne of Kabul. The British had no objection to his making the attempt, but the support he received from Ranjit Singh was at best half-hearted—since that monarch was inclined to believe that if the Shah did get back to Kabul, he would probably repudiate his promises; and if he did not his cession of Peshawur would be worth nothing. The Amirs of Scinde, on the other hand, distrusted Shah Shujah equally, and came to blows with him on his way through their country and when he did get fairly into Afghanistan, Dost Mohammed defeated him and forced him to retire.

This, however, was merely an interlude of interest as far as concerned Scinde, for the reason that it gave colour to Ranjit Singh's theory that all he wanted was lands which were not properly speaking in Scinde territory, but were outside of any existing legitimate jurisdiction. In fact, the marauding practices of the tribes in these districts did give his officers at Multan a fair excuse for military operations, ending in the establishment of the Sikhs at Rojhan, some way below Mithenkote. The British, however, maintained their argument that they were bent on securing the free navigation of the Indus; that war between the Scinde Amirs and the Lahore state would frustrate that desire; and, therefore, that if Ranjit Singh persisted in quarrelling with the Amirs, they would be obliged to regard his action as distinctly unfriendly. Ranjit Singh submitted with a tolerably good grace, but he took care to make the most of the favour he was rendering, and of the want of consideration for him which the British were showing.

If the Maharajah's designs upon Scinde were checked, there was still occupation for him in the Peshawur district. Important movements were taking place beyond the Afghan border, which were very shortly to result in a total reversal of the policy of non-interference hitherto pursued by the British in Afghanistan, of which it will be necessary to speak subsequently. For the moment it is sufficient to remark that Dost Mohammed, who had succeeded his brother Mohammed Azim as practical ruler of Kabul, and as the most important of the Barukzai brothers, was, among his other projects, exceedingly anxious to recover Peshawur. But his brother, Sultan Mohammed, on the whole preferred his status as Ranjit Singh's tributary to the uncertain position which would result if he submitted to Dost Mohammed instead. The Sikhs were prepared to do battle for their dependency, and showed their real military power in the contest which followed; for a great fight took place in which the Sikhs were indeed ultimately routed, and their gallant leader Hari Singh was slain; but the Afghans failed to take Peshawur; reinforcements were brought up with a speed and vigour which reflected great credit on the Sikh organisation; the Afghans were obliged to retire; and Peshawur itself was placed directly under the command of a lieutenant appointed from Lahore, in place of the Barukzai governor, whose position was felt to be no longer compatible with the real security of the place.

But the days of the great monarch were numbered. Before he died, the British had already initiated their new policy, and were advancing on Afghanistan to eject Dost Mohammed, and replace the long-exiled Shah Shujah on the throne, in alliance with the Lahore Maharajah. But the project was one for which Ranjit Singh had no liking; he only entered upon it lest a worse thing should happen to him; and he died in June, 1739, shortly after the expedition had started.

The Lahore state which Ranjit Singh built up, and which ceased to exist nine years after his death, is a unique phenomenon in history. Perhaps the nearest parallel is the military commonwealth of England under the Protector Cromwell, which indeed offers several points of resemblance, though plenty of essential differences are equally discoverable.

For Ranjit Singh was not a great conqueror in the ordinary Oriental sense of the term. He was not, like Baber, an adventurer who annexed an empire; nor, like Akbar, did he construct an imperial system. But within the limits of the Punjab proper he found a congeries of Sikh chiefs holding dominion; he welded that loose confederacy into a single solid army, and extended its sway to Kashmir, Peshawur, and Multan. He enlarged his borders, but he did not hurl his armies over distant provinces, to return laden with spoils, or to remain under the command of viceroys ready to throw off their allegiance at a moment's notice.

The fundamental characteristic of his polity was not the supremacy of a dynasty, but the supremacy and the unity of the army of the Khalsa. He rested his own power not on the mercenary troops which hope of plunder or promise of pay brought into his service, but on the armed brotherhood of the Sikhs. His administrative and organising talents were not turned to beneficent legislation, to the spread of commerce, to the introduction of the arts of peace; but to developing the Khalsa into the most efficient fighting machine that ever an Indian potentate had at his command. How successful he was in that effort, the later chapters in this volume will testify. It has been said—and the words undoubtedly contain a general truth—that among non-European peoples the most successful opponents of the British arms have been those who, like Hyder Ali and Holkar, made no attempt to adopt alien methods of fighting, but held to their own native habits, conducting a guerilla warfare on a huge scale, avoiding pitched battles, and easily rallying their forces after a contest. Nevertheless, tho struggle with the Sikhs seems to present an exception to the rule. Never did a native army having so relatively slight an advantage in numbers fight a battle with the British in which the issue was so doubtful as at Ferozeshah; and if the victory was decisive, opinion remains divided as to what the result might have been if the Sikh troops had found commanders with sufficient capacity to give their qualities full opportunity. It is indeed true that Lall Singh and Tej Singh have both been charged (though no evidence is adduced) with something worse than incapacity; but neither ascertained facts nor partial hypotheses vitiate the truth that the Sikh soldiery fought with a discipline and a stubbornness unequalled in our experience of native warfare; and their doing so was largely due to the methods introduced by Ranjit Singh. The Maharajah had recognised that as against ordinary native levies, British troops might fairly be called invincible. He strove to discover the secret of this invincibility; he found it in their use of artillery and their employment of large masses of disciplined infantry. He conceived that by the adoption of like methods he could make the Sikhs, whom he knew to be magnificent material, second to none except the British themselves. He never supposed that he would make them a match for the British; when his hot-headed chiefs urged him to resist British demands, he only shook his head and asked what had become of the 200,000 spearmen of the Mahrattas. When a lad whom he had sent to study the wisdom of the English returned to Lahore and showed him the Government maps, he asked "what all those red circles meant?" "British dominions," was the answer. "Ah," he exclaimed, kicking the sheet from him in an outburst of prescient disgust, "it will be all red soon." In fact, the principle which guided him was that no native state relying on its own resources and its own methods could in any case hold out against the British; but that by adopting for his own purposes the British methods in lieu of native practices, he could produce a machine more effective, at any rate against native Powers, than any known army except that of the British.

The result proved that he was right, because he knew the material on which he had to work. The Sikhs were better adapted to learn and to assimilate the European methods of fighting than any other native population. Ranjit Singh studied the ways of the English, and applied the knowledge which he obtained; he supplemented that by employing able European officers—Allard, Ventura, Avitabile, and others—who had learned in the school of the Napoleonic wars; and the result, as we have said, was that the Sikh army was the most efficient, the hardest to overcome, that we have ever faced in India.

CHAPTER III.

AFTER RANJIT SINGH: 1838-1843

State of *Afghanistan:* Dost Mohammed—Persia and Russia—A buffer-state—British resolve to restore Shah Shujah—Defence of Herat against the Persians—Restoration of Shah Shujah—Annihilation of the British force at Kabul—Disastrous effect on the native mind—Annexation of Scinde—Maharajpore—*Punjab:* the reputed sons of Ranjit Singh—The Jammu brothers—The Sikh army and the Punchayets—Dhian Singh and Shere Singh—Insubordination of the Khalsa—Murder of Maharajah Shere Singh and Dhian Singh.

It has been made sufficiently clear by the foregoing narrative that Afghanistan proper in the "thirties" was in a condition of very grave disorder.

This had been the case from the time when the great Barukzai, Futteh Khan, was murdered by order of Kamran, the heir of the throne, at Herat. Since that time Kamran had maintained himself in the governorship of Herat. At Kabul, Mohammed Azim, and after his death his brother Dost Mohammed, had established themselves as the real heads of Afghanistan. Another group of the Barukzai brothers ruled Kandahar, while another couple governed Peshawur, paying tribute to Kabul or to Lahore as circumstances demanded. As Dost Mohammed gradually emerged into the leading position amongst the brothers, he attempted to assert a more definite supremacy, adopted for himself the title of Amir, and attempted, unsuccessfully, as has been related, to wrest Peshawur from the grip of Ranjit Singh. The Amir, however, was virtually the head of the main part of the Afghan state, while Kamran, the lineal descendant of Ahmed Shah, and nephew of the exile Shah Shujah, reigned at Herat.

It was during the thirties that the shadow of Russian advance in Central Asia began to fall upon the political prospect as viewed by Indian statesmen. The indifference —to use no stronger term—of the rulers of the British Empire at Westminster, had allowed Persia to enter unsupported on a conflict with Russia, with the result that the Shah found promise of greater advantage to himself in alliance with that power than in dependence on backing from Great Britain. Dreams began to be formed of another great Mussulman invasion, under the ægis of Russia. The Shah, in the eyes of a vast body of Mohammedans, is the head of Islam. If Afghanistan fell under his sway, he would be at the gates of India; the Mussulmans of the Peninsula would rise at his call. The Hindus might very well seize the opportunity to fling off the yoke of their Western masters and take their chance of preventing a complete Mussulman domination to follow; and with Russia behind to back them up, the thing looked as if it might be worth trying for, at any rate. That appeared to be the Persian point of view.

Russia certainly encouraged the Shah's dreams; certainly, also, she made considerable efforts to obtain for herself the favour, and for the British the disfavour, of Dost Mohammed. Whether, as a matter of fact, she had India in view for herself is a question of minor importance. She may merely have desired to keep the British in a state of convenient embarrassment while she prosecuted other designs of extension. Whatever her real ultimate intentions were, her actions were at any rate calculated to rouse serious suspicions, to cause grave uneasiness, and to considerably disturb the mental equilibrium both of the Eastern Mussulman world and of the British governors of so many Mussulman subjects. That anything in the nature of an actual Russian invasion was quite impracticable did not remove the present source of danger, which was that of a Mohammedan upheaval encouraged by the expectation, however vain, of Russian support. Then, as now, the real danger from Russia was not the fear of Cossack invaders, but of the influence on the native mind created by the belief that in case of invasion or rebellion Russia would throw her weight into the scale against the British.

Thus the rulers of India had to decide whether they were to allow the whole of the country beyond the passes to be in the hands of hostile governments; relying on the Lahore state—friendly and definitely anti-Mussulman as it was under Ranjit Singh—to check any aggressive movement; or whether they should not rather secure the co-operation, in the character of a buffer, of the Afghans; thus retaining a large and, from a military point of view, important section of Mohammedans on their own side. The decision was that Afghanistan should be secured as a buffer-state.

It appears quite certain that this programme would have found an adherent in Dost Mohammed. The Amir showed quite plainly that he would prefer a British to a Russian alliance, and had no inclination to recognise Persia as paramount. His quarrel with Ranjit Singh about Peshawur was, *primâ facie*, a serious matter, since the Punjab would have to be included in any alliance; but the Dost seemed willing to accept, as the price of British support, an arrangement which would have satisfied the Maharajah. Yet, for whatever reason, the Indian Government refused to trust Dost Mohammed, and came to the conclusion that the most effective plan would be to restore Shah Shujah to the throne of Kabul by Ranjit Singh's assistance. The theory appears to have been that Shah Shujah would be much more completely under British control than the Dost was likely to be; and that Ranjit Singh would get a more agreeable bargain out of him.

Three objections to this plan were overlooked. The

Maharajah wanted nothing more than the Amir was prepared to concede. If Peshawur was held as tributary to him, that suited him rather better than having to garrison it as an outpost of his own, because the Sikh soldiers loathed the place. Secondly, he did not want an Afghan king who should merely be a puppet of the British Power. Thirdly, the question how Shah Shujah was to be kept on the throne when he had been put there was left out of count. A fourth consideration may be added, that Shah Shujah wanted to be reinstated, but not by British arms.

While the expedition was being decided upon, and Ranjit Singh's unwilling concurrence obtained, the Persians descended upon Herat (1838). Chiefly owing to the exertions and enterprise of a young Englishman, Eldred Pottinger, who succeeded in obtaining virtual control of the operations, the defence was brilliantly conducted; a grand assault was triumphantly driven back; and, in spite of the assistance of Russian officers, and the energetic encouragement of the Russian minister at Teheran, Herat continued to hold out, until the Shah and his troops took fright at the rumour of a great British invasion, made terms, and withdrew.

When the siege of Herat was raised, the popular scare of a great Mohammedan invasion disappeared, and the idea that Russia for the present meant to do anything more than make a catspaw of Persia was removed. But the feeling remained that a repetition of similar proceedings must be guarded against, and the plan of reinstating Shah Shujah was persisted with. Ranjit Singh drew the line at allowing a large British army to march through his territories, and the main expedition had to go by way of Scinde and Beluchistan. There were plenty of difficulties in the way of commissariat, but none of importance in the way of fighting; Kandahar and Ghuzni were taken, and Shah Shujah was set up in Kabul. Dost Mohammed could offer no resistance, being very generally deserted; and, after having been victorious in a skirmish, the Amir felt that he could surrender with honour, and did so in preference to carrying on a struggle which he saw was hopeless.

Now, however, it became clear that Shah Shujah had been restored by British bayonets, and that nothing but British bayonets would keep him on his throne. The disastrous termination of the great expedition need not here detain us. It is enough to say that with every month of our occupation of Kabul the discontent of the Afghans, and their hatred of the English, rose higher and higher. There is no word to be said in palliation of the flagrant mismanagement of the British officers. At last the natives rose; several prominent Englishmen were murdered, and it may roughly be said that the great Kabul garrison was annihilated. At Kandahar and at Jellalabad the honour of the British arms was maintained, and Pollock's brilliant conduct of the relieving force went far to retrieve the British reputation. But it is impossible to escape the fact that the most notable characteristic of the attempt to reinstate Shah Shujah—who, it may be mentioned incidentally, was murdered in the course of the proceedings—was gross mismanagement of an ill-conceived policy; and the chief result that followed was an immediate loss of prestige, and a revival in the native mind, and—which most affects us in this narrative—in the Sikh mind in particular, of the belief that the British were by no means invincible after all; that Ranjit Singh, now dead, had exaggerated the power of England.

Happily, at the time, the Sikh Government still adhered loyally to the British alliance, and not only allowed a free passage to Pollock's force through the Punjab to the Khyber, but furnished a contingent of troops which aided us to force the Pass itself; and further permitted the return of the British troops by the same route to Ferozepore.

Had the Sikh army turned against us whilst Pollock was still in the Afghan passes, the situation would indeed have been critical. Good fortune, not wisdom or forethought, saved our Indian Empire from disaster.

It is, in fact, by no means easy to gauge the extent of the dangers due to that most disastrous episode. An impetus was given to the idea that, after all, the British advance might be stayed, and the British mastery overthrown, which might easily have led to a very serious native combination. The Punjab, released from the strong hand of its great chief, was becoming restive; anti-British feeling was rapidly increasing in the army, and the army would not be long in learning that it could control the state. Outside the Punjab, the Scinde Amirs were suspected of anti-British designs; and although no tolerable colour for the charge was ever produced, it served as a pretext for one of the few inexcusable acts of aggression in our career in India, and Scinde in the beginning of 1843 was conquered, annexed, and at any rate put out of the way of doing any mischief. Later in the same year, a short, sharp, and decisive campaign was happily precipitated by the conduct of the rulers of the Mahratta state of Gwalior—happily, for the Sikhs had not yet made up their minds to a war. The Gwalior army was anything but contemptible; the Mahrattas were Hindus, and no religious questions would have complicated a coalition between them and the Sikhs if the outbreak had been delayed. The Gwalior army, however, elected to challenge the British while it stood alone; and ceased to be a dangerous element in the situation after the decisive fight of Maharajpore.* But it is doubtful whether either Mahrattas or Sikhs could have challenged us, had it not been for the disaster of Kabul; it is certain that the successful issue of the Sikh War, when it came, would have been most gravely jeopardised if the Gwalior army had not rushed upon its own destruction two years earlier.

With all Ranjit Singh's abilities, the great Punjab State

* See Appendix I.

which he constructed was left by his death in the common condition of Oriental kingdoms when a brilliant chief has died. He left no successor capable of controlling the turbulent elements which had been held in check under his vigorous government.

It would hardly be unjust to say that the Lahore Court had always been somewhat conspicuously licentious; with the careless licence of a rough warlike people, rather than the elaborate sensuality of the effete courts of the Ganges states. One result in Ranjit Singh's own case was peculiar: he had a good many reputed sons, but out of them all one only, Kharak Singh, was probably in truth his offspring. At any rate, being the only one as to whose relationship to himself Ranjit Singh was really satisfied, Kharak Singh was naturally recognised as the successor to the throne. He was himself almost imbecile, but Nao Nihal Singh, the heir apparent, was a youth of very considerable promise. It was, however, certain that another reputed son of the dead Maharajah, Shere Singh, was inclined to assert claims to the throne if opportunity offered.

It is probable, however, that the most powerful man in the state was the late monarch's minister, Dhian Singh. Dhian Singh and his brother Gholab Singh were not Sikhs, but Rajputs, who had found favour in Ranjit Singh's eyes, and had risen in his service. They had received from him large grants of land, and had been made by him jointly Rajahs of Jammu; in consequence of which they are commonly referred to as "the Jammu brothers." It is probable that these two designed to share the rule of the whole Punjab between them, the plan being that Gholab Singh was to acquire the whole of Jammu, Kashmir, and the north-east generally; while Dhian Singh should rule at Lahore. There was also a third brother, Suchet Singh.

The third great factor in the situation was the Sikh army, of which the special peculiarity was its democratic character; in fact, it may, perhaps, be most easily realised by the analogy of a trade-union. Apart from the military organisation of officers and men, there was a system of what were called Panchayets, or committees of five chosen by the men, for companies, regiments, and battalions, deriving their form from the prevalent customs of village government. These committees guided the united action of the soldiery, were able to dictate to their officers, and later on found themselves able to appear as representing the Khalsa in arms, and to dictate to the "Durbar," or Court, itself. As yet, however, they did not know their own power. The political aspirants were already aware of the advantage to be derived from having the army with them, but the army itself did not for some time begin to take the initiative. When the army did assert itself, it did so in the name of the Khalsa, and the position presents a closer resemblance to the days when in England the army of the Parliament dictated to the Government, than to any other.

Kharak Singh was accepted as his father's successor; but the control exercised over him by a favourite made Dhian Singh uneasy, and was also eminently unsatisfactory to the heir apparent, Nao Nihal Singh. These two, therefore, to begin with, made common cause, and with the support of Gholab Singh, they put the favourite to death in his master's presence, and virtually established Nao Nihal Singh as chief of the state, with Dhian Singh as minister. This, however, was not a condition of affairs calculated to last long. Nao Nihal considered that the power of the Jammu brothers was too great, and was bent on breaking it. Kharak Singh died; Nao Nihal became Maharajah, but on the day of his accession he met with a fatal accident which the Jammu brothers were very strongly suspected of having deliberately designed.

There was only one man who could reasonably be placed on the vacant throne, and this was Shere Singh, the reputed son of Ranjit Singh. The widow of Kharak Singh, however, asserted her right to the position of regent in the name of a hypothetical unborn son of Nao Nihal's, and this somewhat curious arrangement was sanctioned. Still Dhian Singh was accepted as minister, while Shere Singh assumed for the time most of the functions, and shortly afterwards the title, of Maharajah. At the same time a party of Sikh chiefs, known as the Sindhanwala family, who were connected ancestrally with Ranjit Singh, stood out as supporters of Kharak Singh's widow.

Meanwhile, the attitude of the army was becoming steadily more aggressive; they were under no efficient control, the rulers not venturing to treat them with a strong hand; and the regiments began mutinying and deposing their officers. These disorderly proceedings were brought somewhat emphatically under notice of the British, when, in 1841, Major Broadfoot was escorting the wives and families of Shah Shujah and his brother Zeman Shah across the Punjab from Ludhiana to Kabul, some months before the rising against the British took place in the Afghan capital. This was, no doubt, in part the cause of the mistaken estimate formed at British head-quarters about this time of the real efficiency of the Sikh troops. It does not seem to have been perceived that their mutinous attitude did not signify incapacity for united action, or for the display of thorough discipline in the field. Consequently, the idea appears to have become prevalent that the Sikh soldiery were disorderly and of no great account from a military point of view, though it obviously lay in their power to produce anarchy in the administration of the Punjab; and it was supposed that they were not fully competent to face Afghans, or the Jammu hill-men.

On the other hand, this same soldiery was rapidly becoming by no means well-inclined towards the British, whose proceedings in Afghanistan meant, in the popular judgment, that they were aiming at extension of empire, would presently encircle the Punjab, and would finally fall upon the Sikhs themselves. The tremendous disaster at

Kabul, and the subsequent evacuation of Afghanistan after the honour of the British arms was deemed to have been sufficiently vindicated, did not wholly efface the popular suspicion, while it went far to encourage a disbelief in that British invincibility which had been a cardinal point in the political creed of Ranjit Singh.

Nevertheless, while Shere Singh's power lasted, he maintained his favourable attitude to the British, and rendered them effective assistance when the final Kabul campaign was in progress. The Sindhanwala chiefs, however, whose support of Kharak Singh's widow had placed them in a very precarious position, were restored to favour partly in consequence of the interposition of the British in their behalf. They resolved to get the government into their own hands, and entrapped Dhian Singh, first into a plot for the assassination of Shere Singh, which was carried out, and then into their own power, when they put him to death as well. This double murder opens the last chapter of the Sikh anarchy; which led directly to the war with the British, of which the first stage is known as the Sutlej Campaign.

CHAPTER IV.

THE SIKH ANARCHY

Dhulip Singh and the Rani—Hira Singh and the army—Hostility to the British—Fall of Hira Singh—Designs of the Rani—Policy of Sir Henry Hardinge—Domination of the Panchayets—Increasing animosity towards the British—Crossing of the Sutlej.

It has already been observed that, in addition to his one undoubted son, Kharak Singh, Ranjit Singh had several reputed sons as well. One of these, the infant Dhulip Singh, was born after the great Maharajah's death. His mother, the Rani Jindan, was young and beautiful, and her character was such that Henry Lawrence named her "the Messalina of the Punjab." There were, at least, very strong grounds for doubting whether Ranjit Singh was really the young Dhulip's father; still, it had already been decided while Shere Singh was ruling at Lahore, that the infant was to be regarded as heir to the throne. The plot between Dhian Singh and the Sindhanwala chiefs had been formed on the hypothesis that Shere Singh was to be removed, and Dhulip Singh to be proclaimed Maharajah—when the minister considered that the absolute necessity of retaining him as practical head of the state would immediately become apparent. The Sindhanwala chiefs, however, had other plans in view, and, as related, followed up the assassination of Shere Singh by that of the minister himself.

Dhian Singh, however, had a son, Hira Singh, a youth of very considerable promise, and some personal popularity, despite the fact that the Sikhs, the people as well as the chiefs, disliked the power of the Jammu brothers. On hearing of the murder, Hira Singh promptly appealed to the army, making effective use of the argument that the Sindhanwala faction looked to the British for support, and would increase British influence in the Punjab. The army at once marched to Lahore, seized and put to death those of the Sindhanwala family who were there, proclaimed their allegiance to Dhulip Singh, and made Hira Singh Vizier.

Hira Singh, then, was in a very difficult position. The army had placed him in power, and he could not afford to quarrel with them. He had used their anti-British feeling to secure their support, and so was committed to an anti-British policy. Yet, unless he was to be a mere puppet, that army must be brought under control, and its power diminished. At the same time he could not rely upon support from the Sikh chiefs, who were set as a body against the ascendency of the Jammu family, while the Rani Jindan wanted to reign herself through her lovers and her brother Jawahir Singh.

Now, not only was the power of the army very apparent; it was also rapidly bringing the finances of the state into a very awkward condition, as in order to secure its good-will the men's demands for increased pay had to be favourably received. It became clear to Hira Singh and to Pandit Jalla, the finance minister, who largely guided his policy, that the expenditure on the troops would have to be diminished; and that then it would probably become necessary to let them attack the British—a policy which would have the double advantage of gratifying them to begin with, and then, either breaking their power or renewing the prestige of the Government, which stood to win in either event. Movements of troops towards the Sutlej frontier were therefore made which excited the apprehension of the British Government, already perturbed by the obvious weakness of the Punjab rulers, and expectant of a collapse of the great Lahore State. Responsible British officers were rapidly becoming convinced that it would be no long time before a conquest of the Punjab might become necessary, since a strong government from the Passes to the Sutlej was needed; and if the Sikh state went to pieces, the only alternative to annexation would be the establishment of a Mohammedan power, which it was felt could not be permitted.

Hira Singh's difficulties were increased by the fact that his uncle, Suchet Singh, the third of the Jammu brothers—Gholab Singh avoided Lahore, devoting his attention to the North Eastern Provinces, which he wished to turn into a separate kingdom for himself—was jealous of his power. Suchet Singh encouraged two more reputed or adopted sons of Ranjit Singh to revolt, but was himself killed in attempting to win over the army, and so displace his nephew.

Out of this revolt arose two matters which the anti-British party in the Punjab were able to seize upon and turn to account in fomenting hostile feeling. One of the Sindhanwala chiefs, who had taken refuge in British territory, was allowed to return over the frontier to join the revolting sons of Ranjit Singh—an improper proceeding, of which the Lahore Government was quite justified in complaining. Also, Suchet Singh had left a considerable treasure in the protected states; and the decision of the British Government as to the disposition of this treasure, though proper enough according to English notions of inheritance, was unsatisfactory to the Punjab "Durbar" or Court, which held that the property ought to be confiscated to the state.

Hira Singh appears to have brought sufficient skill and energy to the problem before him to have effected considerable improvement in the subordination of the army; but his progress was not sufficiently rapid for his financial requirements. He was obliged to summon the officers and point out to them the necessity for a reduction in expenditure; and the position was so clear that they were compelled to admit the need. The Rani, however, went not to the officers but to the men, and roused their disaffection. The crisis came when some 500 men were discharged in a body. The Rani sent messages to the soldiery, charging Hira Singh and his party with treasonous designs, and throwing herself and the boy Maharajah on their protection. The men declared themselves on her side. Hira Singh and Pandit Jalla, seeing that as far as Lahore was concerned the game was already lost, at any rate for a time, fled in the direction of Jammu, probably hoping to reinstate themselves by the aid of the hill troops and Gholab Singh; but before they had gone far they were overtaken and slain, fighting desperately.

The fall of Hira Singh left the Rani Jindan and her favourites without personal rivals for the time being: her brother Jawahir Singh, a drunken debauchee, was appointed Vizier. But from this time the army scarcely made any pretence of owning allegiance to the Court. The Panchayets gave it to be understood that the Khalsa was supreme, that the Government must obey orders, and that the Rani, and even the Maharajah were where they were merely by grace of the soldiery. It became, therefore, the policy of the Court, which felt itself powerless in the hands of the Panchayets, to devise means of destroying, or else satisfying the army itself; and the plan adopted was that foreshadowed by Pandit Jalla. The Khalsa was to be urged to challenge the British. If it were shattered, the Court would be rid of its masters; if triumphant, the Court would claim the credit.

There were, indeed, some few of the Sikh Sirdars who were alive to the danger of the programme. They had appreciated the wisdom of Ranjit Singh, and could understand the obvious truth that if the army marched against the British and was beaten, the British could scarcely help assuming the government themselves, and there would be an end of the Sikh State.

Anxious as was the British Government to avoid creating needless suspicions, which would only hasten a *dénouement* which it was desired, if possible, to escape; the condition of the Sikh frontier made it absolutely imperative that Ludhiana and Ferozepore should be prepared for an emergency, and that everything should be in train for the advance of troops in case of a crisis. Nothing, indeed, was done which the circumstances did not positively demand in the judgment of the military authorities; and far less than they considered (justifiably enough, as the event proved) requisite for security; nevertheless, exaggerated reports did reach the Sikhs, who were already quite prepared to believe that the British were designing an invasion. On the other hand, the proceedings of the Sikh army were such that a very heavy demand was made on the moderation and caution of the Governor-General, and of Major Broadfoot, the political Agent, to stave off an outbreak. The Sikhs claimed that the presence of so large a body of British troops as was stationed at Ludhiana and Ferozepore was a menace to them, and, was a breach of the true relations between the states; on the ground that the Cis-Sutlej estates of the Maharajah (which in our view, and in Ranjit Singh's practice, had been hitherto held not as part of the Lahore state, but in just the same way as other protected states of Malwa) were only under British control so far as was necessary for what may be called police purposes; and a right was asserted to send Sikh troops thither, which Ranjit Singh had himself not pressed. Whereas it was maintained by us that if Sikh troops crossed the Sutlej in arms on any pretence, they must either be accounted as rebels against the Lahore Government, or as committing an act of war on behalf of that Government.

A temporary relief was afforded early in 1845 by the withdrawal of Sikh troops from the Sutlej to march against Jammu, the intentions of the Rajah Gholab Singh being regarded with suspicion by the Court, while the Jammu family influence had long been viewed with disfavour by the Khalsa. When the troops reached the neighbourhood of Jammu, the Panchayets took matters into their own hands and formulated their own demands. Gholab Singh, conscious that in a military point of view he could offer no resistance, avowed himself the servant not of the Court but of the Khalsa, and placed himself unreservedly in their hands. He was brought down to Lahore, virtually a prisoner, and used his opportunities to conciliate the men, and at the same time to fan their hostility to Jawahir Singh.

Then Peshora Singh, one of those reputed sons of Ranjit Singh who had revolted before, revolted again, and the army were very much inclined to support him. Roughly speaking, from the month of July, 1845, onwards, the army used Peshora Singh and his claims as a means of compelling the Court to accede to any demands they might feel inclined to make; and it appears almost certain that the boy Dhulip Singh would have been ejected, if not killed, and Peshora Singh made Maharajah, if the British had not made it thoroughly clear that they would not recognise any such change of government effected by force.

Gholab Singh judiciously persuaded the soldiers to allow him to return to Jammu, from whence he sent offers to the British of co-operation to enable them to march on Lahore, if they would guarantee him the North Eastern Provinces as an independent ruler. The British, however, declined to consider the proposal, being honestly desirous of maintaining the effort to establish a strong Sikh Government throughout the Punjab, rather than of annexing it themselves. At the same time the gravity of the situation was increased by the fear that the very high rate of pay which the Sikh soldiery had extracted for themselves, and the general success which had attended their insubordination, was having an injurious effect on the *morale* of the sepoys in the British army.

In September, Peshora Singh was murdered—as every one believed, by Jawahir Singh's order. The army were in consequence much enraged against the Vizier, who felt that the only available method of self-defence was to turn their attention to the British instead of to himself as the object of wrath. Before the end of the month, however, the Panchayets formally assumed the Government, declared the Vizier guilty of the murder of Peshora Singh, put him to death, and offered the Viziership to Gholab Singh—an offer which the Rajah was much too astute to accept, remarking that he wished to live more than six months. The office was nominally bestowed upon Lall Singh, the Rani's favourite.

The army now controlled the policy of the state; and its feeling was vehemently anti-British and favourable to a war. This feeling was fostered and encouraged by the Durbar, which hoped to profit by war, in any event, since it could claim credit for success, while the army would be broken up by defeat. On the other hand, most of the Sirdars feared the power of the army, disliked both the Durbar and the British, but believed that a war would be disastrous; still if war was forced on them they were prepared to fight valiantly enough.

Now that the Panchayets had assumed formally the reins of Government, neither Sir Henry Hardinge the Governor-General nor the Agent Broadfoot had much hope that any working system would be established; yet they were inclined to believe that the unpardonable act of aggression—the crossing of the Sutlej by the Khalsa—would not yet take place. The tone and attitude of the army were menacing in the extreme, but there was a possibility of its stopping short of that irrevocable step. By the end of November, however, the probability that the more ardent spirits would frighten the more cautious into compliance with their design became more marked. Gholab Singh sent a messenger affirming positively that the Sikhs were determined on war, and offering to throw in his own lot with the British.

Then came reports that the army was advancing towards the Sutlej.

On the 13th December Sir Henry Hardinge received the intelligence that the body of the Sikh army had crossed the Sutlej on the 11th; and he then issued the proclamation which was the virtual Declaration of War.

BOOK III.

THE SUTLEJ CAMPAIGN

BOOK III.

THE SUTLEJ CAMPAIGN: DEC., 1845–*MARCH*, 1846

CHAPTER I.

OPENING OF THE CAMPAIGN: DECEMBER

The Sikh force—Ferozepore and Ludhiana—Umballa and Meerut—Europeans and sepoys—Deficiency of troops on the frontier—Explanation—Sir Henry Hardinge on the frontier—Rapid collection of the available forces—Advance on Moodkee.

THE crossing of the Sutlej by the Sikhs constituted an act of war, and opened the Sutlej Campaign. The next division of the narrative here set forth is almost exclusively military; and it is to military details that our attention must now be turned.

Information as to the Sikh army is not quite as precise as might be desired. But there are certain facts with regard to it which are quite definitely known.

It was under the leadership of Tej Singh, a Sikh Sirdar of some position and repute, who was probably in touch with the Court party, and certainly believed that nothing but disaster would come of the war. Associated with him in the leadership was Rajah Lall Singh, the favourite of the Rani Jindan, and nominal Vizier. It must, however, be observed that there is no evidence in support of the assertion which has been made that these chiefs were guilty of treachery.

The army itself was filled with a vehemently hostile

feeling towards the British, and a strong sense of self-confidence and of loyalty to the Khalsa. Loyalty to the Durbar it had none; its vows were to the Sikh brotherhood, very much as our Covenanters gave their allegiance to the Covenant. But this turbulent and insubordinate body, recklessly democratic in its political treatment of the Government, was fully alive to the impossibility of democratic methods in the field; and the Panchayets now laid aside their assumed control, formally accepting the purely military organisation for purely military purposes.

The component parts of the regular army had been wholly reorganised by Ranjit Singh. In the old days of the Misls the vast bulk of the Sikhs had been horsemen; infantry and artillery were contemned or misunderstood. Ranjit Singh, not without valuable help from his European officers — Allard, Ventura, Avitabile, and others — had educated his people into preferring the infantry to the cavalry service, and into becoming first-class artillerymen. Consequently, in 1845, the regular army was composed somewhat as follows: artillery, which could bring 200 guns into the field and serve them admirably; 35 foot regiments of 1000 men each; and 15,000 cavalry, known as "Ghorchurras." But in addition to these regulars, who, when it came to fighting, showed splendid discipline, an immense force could be brought into action, consisting of the private levies of the Sirdars. Neither in armament nor in discipline were these men at all on a level with the regular army, but both in infantry and cavalry they are estimated to have numbered nearly double of the trained troops.

According to information received by Major Broadfoot late in November, the plan of the Lahore Durbar was to send five out of the seven divisions of the regulars against the British. Allowing for the artillery, this would seem to mean a body of from 40,000 to 50,000 men. If the Sirdar's contingents be added to these, it is probable that the whole Sikh force destined to do battle with the British troops did not fall short of 100,000. No such force, however, was ever collected at one time against the British. It should, perhaps, be noted that Captain Cunningham, in his "History of the Sikhs," places the numbers very much lower. It is not, indeed, clear from his narrative how numerous he reckoned the Sikh army which crossed the Sutlej to have been; but he seems to put it at between 30,000 and 40,000 regulars, with half the number of irregulars. While giving due weight to his opinion, however, it must be remembered that he wrote always as an enthusiastic admirer of the Sikhs, with a strong inclination to give the benefit of every doubt in their favour.

As regards our own troops, the reader to-day should perhaps be reminded that in the year 1845 the British army in India was armed entirely with the old "Brown Bess" of the Peninsular War, the fire of which was not effective much beyond 300 yards, disciplined troops rarely firing a shot till within half that distance from the enemy. The effective range of field artillery was about 800 yards for round shot and shell; about 300 for "grape." The Sikh artillery was as good as our own; their guns were more numerous; and the infantry muskets were the same as ours.

In order to follow the movements of the armies with any accuracy, it will now be necessary to give considerable attention to the map of the "theatre of the war" which is here given, as well as the map at the beginning of the volume.

It will be obvious that the first objective of the force invading from Lahore would be Ferozepore, in the immediate neighbourhood of the point on the Sutlej where the troops would naturally cross.

Ferozepore, as will readily be seen, was the most advanced of the British military stations, being the westernmost post on the Sutlej. Here, and at Ludhiana, also very near the Sutlej, 80 miles to the east of Ferozepore, Sir

Henry Hardinge, the Governor-General, and Sir Hugh Gough, the Commander-in-Chief, had throughout 1845 been steadily and quietly increasing the garrisons; also a large number of boats adapted for building pontoons had been collected.

Ferozepore itself was an open cantonment, without any attempt at fortification; though in view of the threatening attitude of the Sikh army, Major-General Sir John Littler, an experienced and trustworthy officer who commanded, had thrown up some shelter trenches and light field works to aid in the defence. It was garrisoned by two troops of Horse Artillery, and two light field batteries of 6 guns each; H.M.'s 62nd Foot, the 12th, 14th, 27th, 33rd, 44th, 54th, and 63rd Regiments Native Infantry; the 8th Native Light Cavalry, and the 3rd Irregulars—numbering altogether about 7000 fighting men, taking the infantry regiments at 700 and the cavalry at 300. The composition of the force was, as can be seen, almost entirely native—a great disadvantage, considering its very exposed position; but as there was no barrack accommodation for another British regiment the reinforcement had been postponed.

At Ludhiana, about 80 miles almost due east of Ferozepore, also on the banks of the Sutlej which was about 10 miles distant, there was a small fort. It was held by a force under Brigadier H. M. Wheeler, at that time a very able and reliable officer (subsequently so unhappily connected with the great Cawnpore disaster in 1857), consisting of H.M.'s 50th Foot, the 11th, 26th, 42nd, 48th, and 73rd Regiments Native Infantry, one regiment Native Cavalry, and two troops Horse Artillery—about 5000 fighting men, with 12 guns.

These two cantonments were situated within the Sikh Protected States.

Umballa, the principal station in support of the two advanced posts, was about 80 miles from Ludhiana and 160 from Ferozepore by the most direct routes. The country between was a dead flat, very sandy and dusty; the roads being mere tracks, and extremely heavy either to march over or for carts, but better suited for camels, which were principally used by the people. There were very few villages, and little or no water except from wells dug by the villagers; while, for the most part, the country was overgrown with camel-thorn and low jungle trees without any undergrowth—a very different country to what it is now.

Umballa was held by a fairly strong garrison under a most able and gallant soldier, Major-General Walter Raleigh Gilbert. It consisted of H.M.'s 9th, 31st, and 80th Regiments of Infantry; the 16th, 24th, 41st, 45th, and 47th Regiments of Native Infantry; the 3rd Light Dragoons, 4th and 5th Regiments Light Cavalry, and the Governor-General's body-guard formed the cavalry; and, in addition to these, there were the 29th Foot at Kassauli, and the 1st Bengal European Regiment at Subathu, both in the hills. This whole force would amount to about 10,000 fighting men, good men and true, efficient and fit for anything, and held ready to move, literally, at a moment's notice.

These troops—Ferozepore, 7000; Ludhiana, 5000; Umballa, with Kassauli and Subathu, 10,000—were all that were available to meet any sudden emergency; for Meerut, the next large station—too far off to appear in the map—was about 130 miles by road, nor could large bodies of troops be put in motion, equipped for a campaign, without some delay. A certain amount of transport was kept up ready for immediate use at each station, but beyond that transport animals, mostly camels, had to be requisitioned or and got in by the civil authorities. The Commissariat Department, though it may have worked expensively, was, however, very efficient, and supplies of all sorts were generally fully and rapidly obtained.

At Meerut there was a force of about 9000 men and

26 guns, viz. 9th and 16th Lancers, 3rd Light Cavalry, H.M.'s 10th Foot (save one company), the corps of sappers and miners, and several regiments of native infantry, which could be pushed forward in support, and might come into the field later on.

There were also two Goorkha regiments, the Nusseeree Battalion near Simla, and the Sirmoor Battalion at Deyrah Dhoon, which were available at a comparatively short notice.

The backbone of the Indian army consisted of the British troops; but, unfortunately, there were very few of them, and too much reliance was placed in those days on the sepoys. These, on the whole, did well, sometimes very well, led by British officers, and encouraged by the presence and example of the British regiments. Sir Henry Hardinge considered that they were about on a par with the Portuguese troops, with whom he had served during the Peninsular War, and that, like them, they had their "fighting" days. But they were not made of the same stuff as Englishmen; and this was well known to the Sikhs, who invariably concentrated their fire and attention on the English regiments, feeling confident that if they could only stop them the others would soon give way.

Sir Hugh Gough, the Commander-in-Chief, had been fully alive to the insecurity of Ferozepore, situated as it was within such easy striking distance of the Sikh frontier, and so far from all support. Being responsible for the military safety of the frontier, he earnestly wished to take all precautionary measures to meet the possible contingency of a war, and to bring up the troops from Meerut and Cawnpore; but for political reasons, already set forth, the Governor-General did not consider it advisable. The fact is, the Government of India did not think the Sikh army would ever actually cross the Sutlej. In January, 1845, they had prepared to move to the Sutlej, but the troops were withdrawn again, partly owing to the remonstrances of the political Agent; and the Government, presumably, expected much the same thing to occur again. The Governor-General was most anxious to avoid not only giving the Sikh Government any pretext for alarm, but also taking any step which might precipitate a war without ample cause for making it. Looking back on events that did occur, it cannot be doubted that he carried his prudence too far, and ran a much greater risk by neglecting the precaution of ordering up the Meerut troops. Nevertheless, he had greatly increased the strength of our forces on the frontier since his assumption of the Governor-Generalship. We were far more ready to meet a sudden emergency than we had been previous to his arrival; and all the available frontier troops, from Ferozepore to Umballa, were fully prepared for movement the moment the order should be given.

In these arrangements Sir Henry Hardinge and Sir Hugh acted together in perfect harmony.

On the 20th November Major Broadfoot wrote to Sir Hugh Gough, reporting that he had received Lahore letters, dated the 18th, stating that the Durbar had ordered in writing the following plan of operations: Sikh army to be divided into seven divisions, of which one was to remain at Lahore, one to proceed to Peshawur, and five were to invade British India. Each division to be of from 8000 to 12,000 men. On this Sir Hugh Gough took on himself to order up some of the Meerut troops, and on the 25th a force of nearly 3000 men left Meerut for Umballa. He at the same time wrote to Sir Henry Hardinge, forwarding his order for confirmation or otherwise, as the Governor-General thought fit. The Governor-General was, as already stated, most averse to giving the Sikh Durbar any cause for apprehension; and as the next moment the aspect of affairs looked more peaceful, the order was countermanded, and the troops were ordered back to Meerut, where they arrived on the 30th November. This was unfortunate, as had they been allowed to proceed they would have been up in time to join in the advance on Moodkee; but great pressure was put on the Governor-General by the Court of Directors to avoid all cause of offence, and not to interfere with the Punjab unless actual aggression was first perpetrated by the Sikhs; so that no further steps were taken to meet the coming storm. Meantime the Sikhs were endeavouring to tamper with the Hindostani sepoys, and many discharged sepoys, having been taken into the Sikh service, were employed in tempting our men to desert, using the high rate of pay as an incentive. A few instances occurred, but the fidelity of the native army stood the strain.

The plan of operations of the Sikh leaders on crossing the Sutlej seems to have been far from badly laid. Part of the force was to cut off Sir John Littler at Ferozepore, while, if possible, the Ludhiana force was to be met and crushed by the main body before the Umballa troops should have effected a junction; the theory being that the danger of Ferozepore would compel the Ludhiana force to advance at once in the hope of effecting a relief. The design, however, was frustrated, as will be seen, by the great marching achievement of the Umballa regiments.

At the beginning of December, the Governor-General, Sir Henry Hardinge, himself a very distinguished soldier, who had won the high approbation of the Duke of Wellington in the Peninsula, was near Ludhiana; the Commander-in-Chief being at Umballa. Sir Henry Hardinge's position was indeed a dangerously exposed one, considering the office he held, for his escort, consisting of only one regiment of native infantry besides his body-guard, could hardly have secured him from capture, had the Sikh cavalry possessed the enterprise to make the attempt. No such attempt was made, however, and accordingly he rode into Ludhiana in order to personally inspect the position and the fort. Seeing that this could be held by a small body, he desired Brigadier H. M. Wheeler to hold himself in readiness to march at the shortest notice, leaving the defence of the fort in the hands of the sick and weakly. On the 8th December he heard from Major Broadfoot, his political Agent, that there was no longer any doubt whatever that the Sikhs were making preparations on a large scale to cross the Sutlej, and the following day he sent the too-long-deferred orders to the Commander-in-Chief for the immediate advance of troops from Umballa, Meerut, and elsewhere towards the frontier. On the 12th he heard of the actual crossing by the Sikhs, and on the 13th he issued his proclamation declaring war, dated from his camp about 25 miles from Ludhiana.

So complete had been the preparations for an advance that on the 12th the Commander-in-Chief and the Umballa force marched 16 miles to Rajpura; on the 13th to Sirhind, 18 miles; on the 14th to Isru, 20 miles; on the 15th to Lattala, about 30 miles; and on the 16th to Wadni, 30 miles; overtaking the Governor-General, who with the Ludhiana troops had already marched to Bussean on their way to Ferozepore. Bussean was of great importance, as it was here that Major Broadfoot had stored the supplies which it had devolved upon him to collect (most successfully) by the most strenuous exertions at the shortest notice.

On the 17th the Governor-General and the Commander-in-Chief marched with the now united columns of Ludhiana and Umballa to Charrak—a comparatively short stage—to give some rest to weary men and beasts; for the whole march up from Umballa had been exceptionally rapid, and through an exceedingly trying country. On the 18th they advanced 21 miles to Moodkee.

This march has been described in the diary of an officer, Captain Borton, of H.M.'s 9th Foot, afterwards General Sir Arthur Borton, as throughout most harassing; at one time over heavy ploughed land, then through low, thorny jungle, breaking all order, then again over heavy sand. The dust surpassed all the writer's previous experience; the soldiers were sometimes the whole day without food, and when their meat rations were served out it often happened there were no means of cooking them, as the cooking-utensils had not come up. Yet, the troops marched bravely, though often straggling fearfully from fatigue and heat and dust.

On approaching Moodkee a patrol of the 9th Irregulars with Major Broadfoot reported it occupied by the Sikhs; and the British, formed in order of battle, marched in at noon, the small Sikh picquets retiring.

Thus about 150 miles had been covered by the troops in seven days over tracks heavy with sand, under clouds of dust which almost smothered the men in column, with little or no water or regular food, and under a sun which was hot and oppressive in the day. This extraordinarily rapid march of all available troops towards the frontier had been necessitated by the Sikh army, which for so long had been threatening an invasion, having at length crossed the Sutlej. Ferozepore, though held by a fairly strong garrison of about 7000 men, was more than 150 miles by the most direct route from the nearest support, and the sudden irruption of an army of 100,000 Sikhs with a powerful artillery was a source of danger which could not be ignored. It was perhaps also felt that forbearance had been carried already too far; that the Sikhs had been allowed to gain an advantage which nothing but very prompt and decisive measures could remedy. The Governor-General and the Commander-in-Chief were most anxious to get near enough to Ferozepore to insure a combined movement with Littler's force and to relieve it from the pressure of the Sikhs. Within 24 hours of the receipt of orders the Umballa force was on the march, and Moodkee, about 20 miles from Ferozepore, was reached on the afternoon of the 18th.

CHAPTER II.

THE ENGAGEMENT AT MOODKEE, AND AFTER: DEC. 18–21

Order of British troops—Flank movements of cavalry—Rout by the infantry—Losses—Cruelty of the Sikhs—Their generosity to Lieut. Biddulph—Discomfort in camp—Reinforcements from Kassauli and Subathu—Their march—Considerate action of Sir H. Hardinge—Hospital at Moodkee—Sir Hugh Gough's plan for a junction—Sir H. Hardinge appointed second in command—With Sir John Littler—Littler's forces and movements at Ferozepore.

THE country round Moodkee was a plain, with here and there slight risings, covered almost entirely with low, thorny jungle, the soil being heavy and sandy, so that the slightest movement of any body of men created an almost impenetrable dust.

Wearied with long and incessant marching, the troops were enjoying a well-earned rest when reports came in from the cavalry patrols that a large force of Sikhs, preceded by clouds of dust, was advancing upon them. Orders were at once issued to fall in, and in a very few minutes the force was formed in line of battle, the time being now about four o'clock in the afternoon.

The cavalry, together with the horse artillery, immediately advanced under Sir Hugh Gough's personal direction, and formed line in front of the Sikh position, the guns occupying the centre, flanked on the left by Brigadier Mactier, with the 9th Irregular Cavalry and a portion of the 4th Lancers, and on the right by Brigadiers Gough and White, with the rest of the cavalry.

The infantry formed up in second line and moved forward; Wheeler's brigade, of H.M.'s 50th, the 42nd and 48th

Native Infantry, on the extreme right, having Brigadier Bolton, with H.M.'s 31st and the 24th and 47th Native Infantry on their left, these regiments forming Sir Harry Smith's Division. Gilbert's Division, still incomplete, since the British regiments composing it had not yet joined, was only represented by one brigade of native troops: the 2nd and 16th Grenadiers and 45th Native Infantry. These formed the centre, McCaskill's Division—H.M.'s 9th Foot, the 26th Native Infantry, the 73rd Native Infantry, and H.M.'s 80th Foot, under Brigadier Wallace—being on the extreme left.

The field batteries having joined the Horse Artillery, a smart cannonade was opened. Then, in order to complete the infantry dispositions, the cavalry, first on the right and then also on the left, were ordered to make flank movements, turning the enemy's flank if possible, more especially because their line, extending beyond ours on either side, threatened to turn our left and right. Accordingly Brigadiers Gough and White, with the 3rd Light Dragoons, the Body-guard, the 3rd Light Cavalry, and a portion of the 4th Lancers, swept out to the right, and fell upon the enemy's left flank. The Sikh horse at once fled, and the British and native cavalry swept down along the rear of the Sikh infantry, disconcerting the latter, and silencing their guns. While this manœuvre was being brilliantly accomplished, Brigadier Mactier, sweeping to the left, fell upon the Sikh right in similar style, and with like success, completely averting all danger of the British line being outflanked. But for the jungle, the cavalry would have done even more complete execution.

Meantime the infantry, their front now uncovered, advanced upon the Sikh line in an echelon of brigades from the right, Sir Harry Smith's Division leading, and by their heavy fire soon convincing the Sikhs that they had met more than they expected; the artillery pushing on to close quarters, and maintaining an effective fire in support. The Sikh infantry and guns stood resolutely, fighting well and with great determination; but were steadily driven back by the British infantry, until they were forced to give way, and fled in great disorder. Darkness put an end to the pursuit, but the conflict was maintained in an irregular manner for another hour, clouds of dust still further obscuring every object.

Night saved the Sikh army from further disaster. Their loss was very severe, the ground being covered with their dead and wounded; and 17 guns were captured on the field. The troops did not get back to camp till midnight, fatigued and worn out by their arduous day's work and the severe fight; a sharp battle which foreshadowed the nature of the coming struggle with the Sikh army. Successful as it was, it was attended with very severe loss, particularly among the leaders and most distinguished officers of the army. Sir Robert Sale, Quartermaster-General of the British troops, was struck by a grape-shot which shattered his thigh, from the effects of which he died shortly afterwards. Sir John McCaskill was shot through the heart leading his division to the attack; and Brigadier Bolton, of H.M.'s 31st, received his death-wound at the head of the first brigade of Sir Harry Smith's Division; whilst Brigadiers Mactier and Wheeler were severely wounded, as also were Lieutenant-Colonel Byrne, commanding H.M.'s 31st Foot, and Major Pat Grant, Deputy-Adjutant-General of the army. The brunt of the fighting had fallen upon Sir Harry Smith's Division. The native infantry fought fairly well, but did not keep up with the European troops, and in the darkness that fell before the action was over some of our troops suffered from the fire of friends as well as foes.

The grand total of losses was:—

Killed	13 officers,	2 native officers,		200 men	=	215
Wounded	39 ,,	9 ,,	,,	600 ,,	=	657
			All ranks killed and wounded			872

Of the head-quarters' staff, 3 officers were killed and 3 wounded. The artillery lost 2 officers and 21 men killed, 4 officers, 1 native officer, and 42 men wounded, 45 horses killed and 25 wounded.

In the Cavalry Division, the 3rd Light Dragoons, who took 497 men into action, suffered most severely, losing 101 of all ranks killed and wounded, and no less than 120 horses; the Native Cavalry lost 1 officer and 20 men killed, 6 officers, 1 native officer, and 43 men wounded. In Sir Harry Smith's Division the 31st Foot lost 175 all ranks killed and wounded; the 50th Regiment 125; the native corps, 1 officer 13 men killed; 7 officers 115 men wounded.

General Gilbert's Division lost 4 officers wounded, 1 native officer, 17 men killed; 5 native officers, 91 men wounded.

In Sir John McCaskill's Division, the only officer killed was its commander, and the loss generally was inconsiderable, but in proportion much heavier amongst the European than the native troops.

The returns published with despatches do not show the regimental losses, which have therefore been compiled from the regimental records.

In the despatches, the Sikh army was estimated at from 20,000 to 30,000 men, horse and foot, with 40 guns. It is most probable they advanced to attack the British under the supposition they would meet only the Ludhiana force, and that they were not aware that the Umballa force had already effected a junction. Other reports put the numbers as low as 2000 infantry, 10,000 horse, and 22 guns. The losses were never ascertained.

This was the first great combat with the Sikhs. Their gallantry and discipline in the fight evoked the admiration of their enemies, but their savage and barbarous treatment of the unfortunate wounded that happened to fall into their hands roused the most revengeful feelings on the part of

British officers and men; for not only were the wounded horribly mutilated and slaughtered, but so treacherous and fanatical were they that even when their own lives had been spared by the order of officers, they were known in several instances to have fired on their deliverers, as soon as their backs were turned, and some fine gallant soldiers fell victims to their own generosity. So strong was the indignation excited in the 3rd Light Dragoons, who were horrified to find their comrades, who had fallen wounded in their splendid charge, cruelly murdered, that "Remember Moodkee," became a cry with them when they met the Sikhs again, and many were ruthlessly slain who would otherwise have been spared.

Mercy in the field of battle is not a thing understood by Orientals. One instance, however, deserves to be recorded to the credit of the Sikhs. About the time that the Sutlej was crossed, an officer, Lieutenant Biddulph, on his way to join his regiment at Ferozepore, fell into their hands, and although his life was in peril, it was spared, and he was made over to the charge of an officer of Sikh Artillery; the gunners became his friends; and, strange to say, after the Battle of Moodkee, he was allowed to return to the British camp, whither he was escorted by the artillery officer's brother. Sir Henry Hardinge very rightly would not allow Lieutenant Biddulph to take part in the subsequent battle at Ferozeshah; remarking that he owed that at least to the generous enemy who had released him. It is pleasant to be able to record occasional traits of civilisation and generosity on the part of our brave enemy, for, as a rule, their conduct on the field of battle was merciless in the extreme. Another striking act of generosity will, however, fall to be related in connection with the Battle of Ferozeshah.

The following day the force halted in order to allow reinforcements to join, being now near enough in its position at Moodkee to render assistance to Littler's force in case of any urgent need. So that the principal object of the very rapid advance had been attained. In consequence, however, of the proximity of the Sikh army, the troops remained under arms all day, ready to fall in, in case the enemy should attempt a fresh attack.

The dead were as far as possible buried, and the wounded brought in; but owing to the very rapid advance at only a few hours' notice, the arrangements for the Field Hospital were by no means complete, and the sufferings of the wounded were great, without either proper shelter or food. The medical men worked, as they always do on such emergencies, with more than zeal, and did all that was possible; but rice-water and coarse wheaten cake, prepared for the elephants, were the only "hospital comforts" available.

Meantime such reinforcements as were at all within possible reach—those, namely, from Kassauli and Subathu—were hurrying up, eager to join the Commander-in-Chief and take their share of the fighting they knew would have to take place before Ferozepore was relieved. These reinforcements consisted of H.M.'s 29th Foot, and the 1st European Light Infantry, with a division of heavy guns and some native infantry.

The 29th Foot were quartered at Kassauli, and the 1st European Light Infantry at Subathu. Both regiments had received orders to be ready to move at a moment's notice. They received the orders for the march at very nearly the same time—that is, about 10 o'clock on the evening of the 10th December. The night was a busy one for all. A hurried medical examination was held at once, and all men unfit for active service, and those in hospital, were hurriedly told off to remain at regimental headquarters, whilst the regiments were ordered to prepare for their march forthwith. Shortly before this campaign, Robert Napier (subsequently Lord Napier of Magdala) saw the 1st European Light Infantry drawn up on parade at Subathu, numbering then nearly 1000 strong, and described its appearance as "glorious." About 60 men were left at Subathu; and by 10 o'clock on the morning of the 11th December, the regiment, probably about 800 strong, was in full march to join the Commander-in-Chief. In the same prompt manner the 69th Foot at Kassauli completed all its arrangements during the night of the 10th, and early on the morning of the 11th was on the march for Kalka, each man being served with 100 rounds of balled ammunition.

There was no "mobilization scheme" in those days, yet nothing could have been more prompt and effective than the rapid and highly disciplined manner in which all these troops moved off for the war. The 29th were one march nearer Kalka, at the foot of the hills, than the 1st European Light Infantry. The former regiment arrived there, received their camp equipage and transport without any delay from the commissariat department, and resumed their march in the afternoon for Munny Majra, doing twenty-three miles that day. Here they received orders to wait for the 1st European Light Infantry, who, likewise, on arriving at Kalka, were equipped for service, and reached Munny Majra on the 12th. On the 13th the two regiments, with the heavy guns, pushed on by double marches from 20 to 35 miles a day. On the 18th, late in the evening, the sound of heavy firing in front announced that the war had begun in earnest. The troops struggled on to reach the field, but it was not possible, eager as they were; nor was it till the following evening, the 19th December, that they were able to join. They were sorely disappointed at not having been up in time for the first brush, but they had done all that could be done, and had covered nearly 200 miles in nine days' marching. Sir Henry Hardinge, always considerate for the soldiers, sent his own private elephants to help to bring the regiments in; a string of camels with fresh water was sent for the relief of the thirsty; whilst the bands of the regiments that had fought the battle of Moodkee the day before were sent out to march them in, so warmly were they welcomed, so fully were their efforts to join recognised by the Governor-General, the Commander-in-Chief, and their comrades.

On the 20th, preparations were made to attack the enemy. No further reinforcements could possibly reach for weeks. The army could not remain in front of the Sikhs, waiting for them to come up. Ferozepore was partly invested, and open to an attack from the whole Sikh army; and it was necessary to relieve it and drive the Sikhs across the Sutlej. Accordingly sixty rounds of balled ammunition was served out to each man, and two days' cooked rations ordered to be carried with the troops, each man carrying all he could in his haversack, besides a bottle covered with leather slung over his shoulders for water. They were clothed in their ordinary scarlet uniform and blue trousers, and wore forage caps covered with white cloth, and a curtain hanging down behind for the protection of the head and neck; great coats were not carried.

There were no means of moving the large number of wounded, and consequently they were placed in a small fort at Moodkee. Two regiments of native infantry were all that could be spared for their protection, each regiment being ordered to detail one officer and a small party of men for their assistance.

Ferozepore was about 20 miles distant north-west from Moodkee, but the Sikh army, under Lall Singh, lay between the two. It might be possible to get Littler's force out by the south, and, effecting a junction with the Commander-in-Chief, to make a combined attack upon Lall Singh. The British Force all told would then be about 18,000 men; but Littler had only one European Regiment, the 62nd Foot, and it was quite possible that he might not be able to get away from Ferozepore without the knowledge of Tej Singh, who was lying before it; so that the junction could not be calculated on as a certainty. The Commander-in-Chief, therefore, had to decide on his plan of operations in view of Littler not being able to join. He could not march round by the south and throw himself into Ferozepore, as that would have left the whole country open to the Sikh army, and his wounded at Moodkee, as to whose safety he was honourably solicitous, would have been at the cruel mercy of the Sikhs. Moreover, the armies of Lall Singh and Tej Singh, now known to be separated, would certainly have united and become more formidable than they were at present. Clearly, then, it would be advantageous to deal with Lall Singh whilst separate from Tej Singh, and to attack him—with the aid of Littler's force, if possible; if not, without. Accordingly secret and trustworthy messengers were sent to Sir John Littler, with orders for endeavouring to march out with as large a force as he could bring, consistently with the safety of Ferozepore, and without detection by the Sikhs; and so effecting a junction with the Commander-in-Chief.

On this day also Sir Henry Hardinge, Governor-General of India, placed his services as a general officer at the disposal of the Commander-in-Chief. Whether right or wrong in his position, it was a noble and chivalrous act. He was a soldier of great experience and of the highest reputation, and had already, at Moodkee, shared the honour and the danger of battle with the army. His offer was accepted by Sir Hugh Gough with a full acknowledgment of its value, and he was appointed second in command.

Ferozepore was threatened on the north-east side by Rajah Tej Singh, with a force of all arms, immediately after the passage of the Sutlej. Sir John Littler told his force off into brigades; one cavalry brigade, under Brigadier Harriott, consisting of the 8th Native Light Cavalry, and the 3rd Irregular Cavalry, each numbering about 300 men; the infantry in two brigades, of which H.M.'s 62nd, the 12th, and 14th Regiments Native Infantry, formed one under Brigadier Reid, of H.M.'s 62nd; while the other consisted of three native infantry regiments, the 33rd, 44th, and 54th, under Brigadier the Honourable T. Ashburnham, of the 62nd; and artillery, one European and one Native troop Horse Artillery, one field battery European, and one Native gunners, under Lieut.-Colonel Huthwaite, of the Artillery. The 63rd Regiment Native Infantry occupied the entrenchment, into which all the ladies, women, children, and sick of the station were sent; the 27th Native Infantry occupied and covered the city; while half a battery of artillery, and a squadron of irregular cavalry watched the ford at Koonda Ghat, to the north-west of the station.

A position was taken up by Sir John Littler to the north-east of cantonments, and he drew his small force up in order of battle on the 13th; Tej Singh, however, declined to make the attack, and Littler pitched his camp so as to cover the cantonments and the native city, the Sikh army having their camp within a short distance, and their outposts close up. The Sikhs made demonstrations threatening an attack on the 15th, 16th, and 17th; but though Littler drew out his force in the open, neither side precipitated a combat, for Littler, acting under particular instructions received from the Commander-in-Chief, would not be drawn away from his post, and whilst showing himself ready to engage, acted strictly on the defensive. On the evening of the 17th the approach of the Umballa force under the Commander-in-Chief was reported, and was followed by intelligence of the battle of Moodkee and the repulse of the Sikh army. At midnight on the 20th Sir John Littler received his orders to move out the following morning in order to effect a junction with the Commander-in-Chief. He arranged to move at 8 o'clock the following morning with the artillery, the cavalry brigade, and the two infantry brigades made up as described above, leaving the defence of the cantonments to the 63rd

Regiment Native Infantry, under Lieut.-Colonel Wilkinson, and that of the town to the 27th Native Infantry, with half a field battery in the town, and a battery of heavy guns in the cantonments, which was strengthened by entrenchments.

CHAPTER III.

FEROZESHAH—THE ATTACK: DEC. 21

The start from Moodkee—Composition of Sir H. Gough's force—Position of Tej Singh and Lall Singh—Sir Hugh's plan of action—Forbidden by the Governor-General—Junction with Littler—Disposition for attack—Commencement of attack—Littler's advance—Repulsed—Losses of his division—Advance of Gilbert's Division—Taylor's Brigade—McLaran's Brigade—Charge of the 3rd Light Dragoons—Wallace's Division—Sir H. Smith's Division—Within the Sikh entrenchments—Dispositions for the night—Danger of the situation—Prince Waldemar—Events of the night.

THE force at Moodkee, under the immediate orders of Sir Hugh Gough, was called to arms in perfect silence at 2 a.m. on the 21st December; by 3 a.m. the camp had been struck and packed on camels, and by 4 a.m. the whole formed up in a line of columns preparatory to the march—four hours before Littler made his start from Ferozepore. Camp equipage and all heavy baggage were left behind at Moodkee. In consequence of the arrival of the reinforcements, the previous distribution in brigades and divisions was modified. They now stood as follows:—

Cavalry and *Artillery* the same as at Moodkee.

Infantry: First Division, under Major-General Sir Harry Smith; H.M.'s 31st Foot, the 24th and 47th Regiments Native Infantry, under Brigadier Hicks; the 2nd Brigade, H.M.'s 50th Foot, the 42nd and 48th Regiments Native Infantry, now commanded by Brigadier Ryan, of the 50th, *vice* Wheeler severely wounded at Moodkee. Second Division, under Major-General Walter Raleigh

Gilbert (a descendant of Sir Walter Raleigh, and worthy of his ancestor); H.M.'s 29th Foot, the 80th Foot, and the 41st Native Infantry, under Brigadier Taylor, of H.M.'s 29th; and the 1st European Light Infantry, with the 16th Native Grenadiers and the 45th Native Infantry, under Brigadier McLaran. Third Division, now commanded by Brigadier Wallace, *vice* Sir John McCaskill; consisting of H.M.'s 9th Foot, the 2nd Native Grenadiers, the 26th and 73rd Regiments Native Infantry.

The army advanced for about four miles in a line of columns, ready to deploy into line in case the Sikhs should be met with; but when it was ascertained that the enemy had concentrated about his entrenched position at Ferozeshah, they moved in a column of route, left in front.

The advance was necessarily slow, owing to the broad front of the army, the darkness, and the rough nature of the country; the road being a mere track through the jungle. At about half-past ten the Sikh position was approached; and the troops halted, and were allowed to rest awhile and get a scratch breakfast from their haversacks, whilst the Commander-in-Chief rode forward to make a personal reconnaissance. Littler's force had not yet joined, but it was ascertained that he was on his way, and his junction was secure.

The Sikh army was in two divisions. One under Tej Singh lay on the north of Ferozepore, facing Sir John Littler's cantonments. The second, and larger, under Lall Singh, had occupied a position at the village of Ferozeshah, between Moodkee and Ferozepore, some two miles on the northern side of the line of march. Here they had formed batteries, and thrown up entrenchments (within which was the village), shaped roughly like a horseshoe. The toe, or central front, faced towards the south, and lay more or less parallel to the British line of march. The right wing faced westward, in the direction of Ferozepore; and the left eastward, in the direction of Ludhiana. Thus, Sir

John Littler, starting from Ferozepore, would march out in a south-easterly direction, leaving Tej Singh on the north and east of his cantonments. The force under the Commander-in-Chief, arriving from Moodkee, might either give battle to Lall Singh or march on towards Ferozepore; but this, of course, would leave the whole country eastwards, including Moodkee, open to the advance of Lall Singh.

While the troops were breakfasting, the Commander-in-Chief rode forward to make a personal reconnaissance, as the result of which he formed the following plan of action. Knowing definitely that Littler's force was on the way, and was secure of effecting the junction, he resolved to leave it the duty of acting as a reserve, and to himself at once attack the position at Ferozeshah with the whole of his three divisions, without waiting for Sir John. The arguments in favour of this plan of action were strong. By making the attack early in the day the troops would be able to do their work while fairly fresh; and in Sir Hugh's judgment, supported by the event, they might then be relied on to carry the entrenchments and drive the Sikhs back. Meantime, if Tej Singh advanced from Ferozepore, Littler would hold him in check, or if he did not advance would be able to fall on Lall Singh's engaged army and effect a complete rout. On the other hand, delay would mean that the day might close before the engagement was decisively at an end, and would be accompanied by the risk of Tej Singh's arrival at a critical time.

The Commander-in-Chief explained his plan of action to the Governor-General, who was also second in command in the field; but Sir Henry was flatly and resolutely opposed to it. In his view, the issue at stake was so serious, and the Sikhs had already at Moodkee shown such high fighting qualities, that he considered it imperative to wait till the junction with Littler was accomplished before proceeding to the attack.

Now, Sir Henry Hardinge, as things stood, occupied a

very anomalous position. As Governor-General, he was responsible for the safety of the British dominion in India, but as a matter of course a civilian Governor-General cannot be held responsible for military operations. On the other hand, previous military Governors-General had combined that office with the Commander-in-Chiefship. There was no precedent for his position. An experienced military officer, he had a very strong opinion as to the military necessities of the position which was in flat contradiction to that of his Commander-in-Chief, whose view was equally strong. Sir Hugh Gough could not surrender his judgment in favour of that of his subordinate in the field; Sir Henry could not escape his own sense of responsibility. Taking this view, there was only one course open—as Governor-General, he must overrule the Commander-in-Chief on the very field of battle, and in the presence of the enemy.

The affair must have been painful enough for both; but it is clear that the responsibility for the serious results which followed this historic incident falls entirely upon Sir Henry Hardinge. The Commander-in-Chief had no option in the matter; Sir Henry could and did simply overrule him. But, to his honour, it can be said that no man ever more resolutely and loyally carried out the Governor-General's wishes than did Sir Hugh Gough; and from this moment, throughout the critical events which immediately followed, no trace or hint appears of the vexation which he might legitimately have felt.

When, after considerable discussion, this decision had been arrived at, the troops were ordered to move to their left, and at about one o'clock the junction with Littler was effected, at the village of Shukur, close to Misreewalla, some 3000 yards south-west of the enemy's extended position. Sir John had accomplished his withdrawal from Ferozepore with great skill, and entire success. Leaving his camp standing, and his picquets out as usual, he had thoroughly deceived Tej Singh, and had marched out on the southern side at about eight o'clock in the morning, without arousing a suspicion in the mind of the Sikhs—who remained watching the empty shell while the army went on its way to join the forces from Moodkee.

By waiting for the actual junction, valuable time had been lost; for it must be remembered that the day was December 21st, the shortest in the year. The arrival of the fresh column, moving in another direction, involved further delay before the troops could be got into position; and it was close upon four o'clock before the attack commenced. By this time, the force that marched from Moodkee had been already nearly fourteen hours under arms; that from Ferozepore nearly eight hours, under a hot sun, and marching over a heavy sandy country in clouds of dust, with scarcely a drop of water.

The army then was drawn up fronting the southern and western faces of the Sikh position, with Littler's division on the left, Wallace's in the centre, and Gilbert's on the right, Sir Harry Smith's forming in reserve. A powerful battery, including the heavy guns, was placed between the divisions of Gilbert and Wallace, and batteries of horse artillery on the flanks. White's Cavalry Brigade, 3rd Light Dragoons and 4th Bengal Lancers, protected the right, whilst Gough's Brigade, consisting of the Governor-General's Body-guard and 5th Cavalry, was in support of Wallace; and Harriott's Brigade, 8th Light Cavalry and 3rd Irregulars, supported Littler's Division, he having also with him the artillery from Ferozepore.

By four o'clock the action had commenced, and the first gun was fired. The British artillery came into action within effective range all along the front, and poured their fire on the Sikh position, our infantry being ordered to lie down. The enemy's artillery, however, responded vigorously, and, after heavy pounding on both sides, it became apparent that our guns were quite unable to gain the mastery of the Sikhs, who had a considerable superiority both in number

THE BRITISH ARMY

as drawn up at the commencement of the

BATTLE OF FEROZSHAH

at 3½ P.M. on the 21st December, 1845.

Fought under the personal command of H.E. Genl. Sir Hugh Gough Bt., G.C.B. Commander in Chief

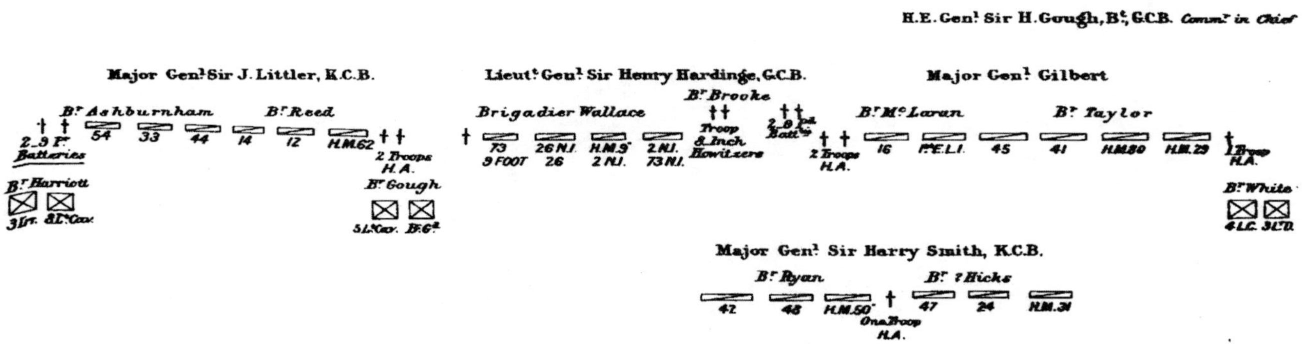

London; Stanford's Geogl. Estabt.

of guns and weight of metal; while the day was drawing to a close. Our artillery therefore advanced to closer quarters, supported by the infantry.

Littler's division somewhat prematurely advanced to the attack, on the Sikh right or westerly front, under a most galling fire; and, to quote his description, "the casualties were awful." Brigadier Reid led the right brigade, the 62nd Foot and 12th Native Infantry in first line, the 14th Native Infantry in support. The advance was conducted with perfect steadiness, notwithstanding that the nature of the country made occasional breaks in the line. As they approached the entrenchments the ground became more open and the enemy's fire increased to a storm of grape. The line approached the enemy's battery to within about one hundred and fifty yards, when the prize seemed to be within their grasp; but it chanced to be the strongest part of the position, defended by numerous guns of heavy calibre, although the entrenchments were no stronger than elsewhere. The native infantry regiments had, to a certain extent, melted away, and the 62nd was assailed by a terrific fire. Sir John Littler, Brigadier Reid, and all the officers cheered and encouraged the men; but, unable to advance, the 62nd were brought to a stand. So fierce was the firing that, within a few minutes, 7 officers and 97 men were killed, and 11 officers and 184 men wounded. Lieutenants Gubbins and Kelly fell from sabre cuts, close to the entrenchments, and many individuals distinguished themselves in setting a brilliant example of courage. But the regiment was almost alone and unsupported; the Sikh cavalry were threatening their left; and Brigadier Reid at length, to save the regiment from further useless destruction, ordered them to retire, seeing the hopelessness of carrying the enemy's works. This movement was executed in good order and with deliberation, the men, in fact, being so exhausted as to be scarcely able to put one foot before the other, till they came upon H.M.'s 9th Foot and the 26th

Native Infantry who were formed in reserve. The Divisional Staff lost 1 officer killed and 1 wounded, and Brigadier Reid and 1 officer of the Brigade Staff were wounded. The 12th Native Infantry, which advanced with the 62nd, lost 4 officers wounded, and the 14th Native Infantry 5. The other losses of the native infantry regiments amounted to 3 native officers and 47 men killed, 5 native officers and 164 men wounded. As far as can be ascertained from the returns of casualties, the second brigade, on the extreme left, commanded by Brigadier Ashburnham, and consisting of three native infantry regiments, suffered no loss whatever, and cannot have afforded any support to Brigadier Reid. The Sikhs paid all their attention to the European troops; and Ferozeshah was unfortunately not one of the sepoy's "fighting days." As a matter of fact, the Hindostani sepoys of those times had not the stamina to stand the long and hard day's work, and were far more exhausted than the European troops.

The news of Littler's repulse went down the line before the attack of the centre and right was made. It was announced by wild shouts of triumph among the Sikhs, whose hopes of victory were greatly raised by it, but it in no way affected the Moodkee force, unless perhaps it made them even more determined to succeed. The assault was ordered in direct echelon from the right, Brigadier Taylor leading with H.M.'s 29th in advance, closely and vigorously supported by H.M.'s 80th, and after them the 41st Regiment Native Infantry; under the direct personal leading of the Commander-in-Chief, who took the right of the line, whilst Sir Henry Hardinge took command of the centre. Covered by a line of skirmishers, the 29th advanced in quick time with the utmost steadiness, notwithstanding the heavy fire it was exposed to, which swept away sometimes whole sections; Brigadier Taylor, himself being grazed by a round shot in the side, was removed from the field, suffering much from the shock. The 80th, eager to bear their full share of the honour and danger of the fight, pressed on so close as almost to form in prolongation of the 29th. The two regiments cheered each other as they advanced. Unflinchingly, and pouring in a heavy fire, Taylor's brigade charged up the entrenchments, but only to find on crossing them that though they had got the guns, the Sikh infantry stood unsubdued behind them. The men, however, pushed gallantly and resolutely on, driving the enemy back at the point of the bayonet, and entered the Sikh camp. Here the 80th came upon a number of the enemy clad in chain armour, who suddenly rushed upon the regiment and inflicted considerable loss before they were bayoneted.

Brigadier Taylor's attack was rapidly followed by Brigadier McLaran with the 1st Bengal European Light Infantry, and the 16th and 45th Regiments Native Infantry. Major Birrell commanding the 1st, wisely ordered the regiment to reserve their fire until they came to close quarters with the enemy. As the line advanced the fire from the Sikh guns increased in intensity, the round shot and shell tearing through the ranks. Many officers and men fell; but the brigade, led by the 1st Europeans, continued its steady advance. As they approached close to the enemy's battery, the order was given to charge, and in a few minutes the regiment was right under the batteries, the smoke being so dense that it was almost as dark as night. The Sikhs had thrown down branches of trees to form a sort of entanglement. Surmounting these, the men were soon amongst the guns. The Sikh gunners, fighting desperately, were bayoneted to a man; behind them the Khalsa Infantry was drawn up, and their camp stood visible in rear. The infantry, dropping on one knee as if to receive cavalry, opened a galling fire; but with a cheer McLaran's Brigade, the 1st leading, charged. The Sikhs fired a wild volley and broke; many drew their swords and fought to the death, compact bodies again and again dashing at the colours. At length, however, they gave way, seeking cover amidst their tents; though hard work still remained, as will presently be told.

Thus Gilbert's Division had been completely successful in its assault, which was followed almost immediately by a magnificent charge by the glorious 3rd Light Dragoons. Led by White, and accompanied by a troop of Horse Artillery, they had followed up the attack of the right. Now, advancing through a most destructive fire of grape and musketry, their leaders falling in numbers, they charged undismayed over the Sikh entrenchments with loud huzzas, dashed through the Sikh infantry, silenced their guns, cut down the gunners, swept right through the enemy's camp, and finally emerged among their friends with numbers thinned, but, as it was said at the time, "covered with imperishable glory."

Wallace's Division next followed, and was directed partly against the portion of the enemy's position from which Littler's Division had been already repulsed, *i.e.* the left central face. The four regiments of which the division was composed were being temporarily formed in two brigades—that on the left consisting of the 9th Foot and 26th Native Infantry, led by Colonel Taylor of the 9th; the 2nd and 73rd Regiments Native Infantry being on the right. The smoke and dust combined were so thick that it was impossible to see the exact position of the enemy's guns; the left wing of the 9th found itself immediately in front of the muzzles, and suffered terribly, Colonel Taylor and many officers and men being killed. So severe was the fire that a portion of the regiment was for a time thrown into confusion; but, although himself very severely wounded by a grape shot in the right arm, Captain Borton, the senior officer on the spot, rallied them; and the right pressing on with great dash, the guns were captured at the point of the bayonet. Here, in the increasing darkness, the Grenadier company under Lieutenant Daunt, with part of the right wing of the 9th under Major Burnewell, got separated from the remainder of the regiment, and falling in with a party separated from McLaran's Brigade, which formed the left of Gilbert's Division in their movement to their left, advanced with them upon the village of Ferozeshah; which was found to have been captured by Sir Harry Smith, who, having been placed in reserve, had been ordered by the Commander-in-Chief to follow up Gilbert's attack, in view of the severe fighting on the right. With this force that portion of the 9th remained till next day.

Sir Harry Smith had formed in rear of the centre of the line, his right brigade led by Brigadier Hicks, and his left by Brigadier Ryan. As they advanced they came under a heavy fire, and passing through a gap in the first line, charged the entrenchments, cheered on by Sir Harry, who shouted, "Into them, my lads; the day is your own!" Here fell Major Broadfoot, the Governor-General's political Agent, shot through the heart, having already been once knocked off his horse by another shot —a brave and invaluable officer, whose thorough knowledge of frontier affairs was most useful to the Governor-General. Smith pressed with Ryan's (the left) Brigade into the Sikh camp, driving all before him, and then coming upon the village of Ferozeshah, stormed and captured it; but in the confusion and darkness which was fast falling, his right brigade, under Brigadier Hicks, was separated from him, adhering to Gilbert's Division.

After carrying the entrenchment, as narrated, Gilbert's Division had been involved in a further struggle. His left brigade (McLaran's), with the 1st European Light Infantry leading, had wheeled to their left, and were charging along the line of the Sikh entrenchments, capturing and spiking many guns, when orders were received to secure the village of Ferozeshah. Towards this they now bent their way, but before they had gone more than 200 yards the men were suddenly scattered by the explosion of a large magazine of powder, the air being filled with smoke and fire, which, as it cleared away, exposed to view a number of gallant soldiers lying frightfully mutilated. This fearful explosion in the rapidly approaching darkness scattered the regiment so much that scarcely 150 men remained with the colours of the 1st Europeans, whilst the fire spread, causing other and smaller explosions, all adding to the confusion. McLaran's Brigade, however, now greatly reduced in numbers, continued its advance on the village; but finding it already in possession of Sir Harry Smith, returned towards the line of the entrenchments.

A number of men of the 1st Europeans, scattered by the explosions, were collected by their officers, and, falling in, as related, with a portion of the 9th Foot, joined Sir Harry Smith in the village of Ferozeshah. Parched with thirst, the men, seeing some wells near by, sought for water, when the Sikhs from the camp suddenly opened fire on them. Lieutenant Greville of the 1st, the senior officer on the spot, led his men against the Sikhs, but was met by so severe a fire from a barricade the enemy had built up that they were forced back. Lieutenant Moxon, carrying one of the colours, was killed immediately in front of the barricade, when Lieutenant Percy Innes, seeing the colour lying on the ground, rushed back alone and brought it off amidst the cheers of the men. Lieutenant Greville, leading a second charge, succeeded in driving off the Sikhs and capturing the barricade.

Darkness was now rapidly increasing, and with it confusion. The Sikh camp was on fire, and frequent explosions were taking place; there became a danger of the troops firing into each other. The Commander-in-Chief therefore wisely decided to withdraw the scattered troops from the Sikh camp, and to form a bivouac in the open space about 300 yards from the entrenchments. The assembly, with the various regimental calls, was sounded. At length, after much search, the regiments, which had got considerably mixed, were collected and formed up.

It will indeed be obvious that the confusion was very great. Sir Harry Smith, with Brigadier Ryan's Brigade and detachments of various regiments, principally the 9th and 1st European Light Infantry from Taylor's and McLaran's Brigades respectively, with scattered bodies of sepoys, remained in the village, but without knowing the position occupied by any other troops. Owing to the sudden arrival of the darkness, the day being the shortest of the year, they were enveloped in its shades before Sir Harry Smith had means of ascertaining the whereabouts of the rest of the force, or of communicating his own position to the Commander-in-Chief. He formed up the 50th in a square on the eastern side of the village, the detachment of the other corps forming another square, irregular, but effective. These retained their position all through the night, although harassed by the enemy's fire and by parties of Sikhs prowling round in the darkness.

Littler's repulsed brigades had drawn up westwards, near Misreewalla, but this was not known to the other divisions.

In this position the British troops, with the Commander-in-Chief and the Governor-General of India in their midst, passed the night of the 21st December. The attack had been on the point of success when night put an end to the conflict. It was impossible to say exactly what was the position of the troops, but it was certain that the losses had been very severe. Littler's Division had been repulsed, and its position was unknown, while Sir Harry Smith, with a portion of his brigade, was missing. The men and officers were all worn out with fatigue, having been at work since 2 a.m.; hungry and without food, parched with thirst and without a drop of water, bitterly cold, without great-coats or any shelter, and unable to light fires without bringing down the fire of the enemy; and all this after a terribly severe struggle, while the Sikhs still maintained an incessant fire, and made the darkness more hideous with their shouts and clamour.

That night, when, as it has well been said, "the fate of India trembled in the balance," was a truly awful one for all; most so for the Commander-in-Chief and the Governor-General, while it tried the nerve of the most resolute and intrepid.

The Commander-in-Chief did not, indeed, disguise from himself the critical nature of affairs; but he never for one moment wavered. Sternly and firmly he remained fixed to his decision to fight it out in the morning, fully relying on the discipline, courage, and tenacity of his British regiments. There were, indeed, those who would have counselled retreat; to one such he replied, "Better that our bones should bleach honourably on the field of battle, than retire." Sir Henry Hardinge was equally resolved, and entirely supported the chief; and their courageous determination proved the highest wisdom. No troops in the world could have behaved better than the Englishmen. Fatigue, hunger, thirst, the bitter cold, the losses they had suffered, the groans of their wounded comrades, the yells and incessant firing of the enemy—all these failed to shake their nerve. Animated and encouraged by the noble example of their commanders, and placing full reliance on their leading, they faced the worst with stern resolve to drive the enemy out in the morning. But even brave and experienced officers were forced afterwards to admit that they had the most gloomy anticipations; knowing that the attack was to be renewed in the morning, they had uneasy doubts as to the result, for the native troops were much disheartened and unnerved by the carnage of the two preceding fights. The stern valour of the English troops and their indomitable courage was felt to be the sole and only resource.

Up to this time a gallant and distinguished officer, Prince Waldemar of Prussia, a member of the royal family, had accompanied the Governor-General through all this severe fighting, attended by some of his own friends, one of whom had already met a soldier's death upon the field. But now Sir Henry Hardinge felt it would not be right to allow him to risk his valuable life in a cause not his own, and, to his great disappointment and vexation, Sir Henry insisted upon Prince Waldemar leaving the field and proceeding to Ferozepore. The prince was filled with regret at not being allowed to remain with the comrades he had learnt to love and respect, and to share their dangers to the end. He was, however, allowed subsequently to rejoin, and came in for further fighting at Sobraon.

The Sikhs had also suffered terrible losses, had been driven from their entrenchments, and, though much shattered, and to a considerable extent demoralised by the combat, still clung to the interior of the position. But when they found that the British force had evacuated the entrenchments, they reoccupied them, and opened fire upon the British bivouac. One gun causing especial annoyance, Sir Henry Hardinge at length called on H.M's 80th, with the 1st Europeans, to "Silence that gun." They responded gallantly, Colonel Bunbury leading with the 80th, assisted by Lieut.-Colonel Wood, an aide-de-camp to the Governor-General, and supported by the 1st, under Major Birrell. In perfect silence they advanced straight upon the gun till within a short distance, when they charged, bayoneting the gunners, spiking the gun, and completely dispersing the enemy. This gallant and very decisive episode showed the Sikhs beyond any doubt that they had not yet done with the English army, and gave a comparative peace to the weary troops for the remainder of the night.

Whilst this, the main portion of the army, consisting of the divisions of Gilbert and Wallace, and part of Smith's, together with the artillery and most of the cavalry, were lying outside to the south of the Sikh entrenchments, Sir Harry Smith, with his one brigade, held on to the village of Ferozeshah, in the centre of the Sikh position. To them also it was a terribly trying night, nor could they ascertain what had become of the rest of the army, nor whether they were conquerors or conquered. In this state of isolation, and without any apparent support, Sir Harry Smith decided to evacuate the village before daylight, and to rejoin the rest of the army as best he could. Accordingly, at 3 a.m. he withdrew his troops by the south-west corner, and, guided by the lights of a bivouac, effected a junction with Sir John Littler, who after his repulse had drawn up his force in the neighbourhood of Misreewalla.

CHAPTER IV.

FEROZESHAH—SECOND DAY: DEC. 22

Renewal of the attack—Flight of the Sikhs—Approach of Tej Singh—His attack repulsed—Gallantry of Sir Hugh Gough—Retreat of Tej Singh—Generosity of a Sikh soldier—Losses at Ferozeshah—Comment of the Duke of Wellington—Discussion of Sir H. Hardinge's action on the previous day, and its effect.

So closed the memorable night of the 21st December; though not, for some hours yet, the Battle of Ferozeshah.

At the first appearance of the dawn, that portion of the army under the immediate orders of the Commander-in-Chief, formed line to renew the attack. Sir Hugh Gough placed himself at the head of the right, and Sir Henry Hardinge at the left of the line; Gilbert and Wallace at the head of their respective divisions. H.M.'s 31st, with the remains of the native corps attached to it, were on the extreme right. The Horse Artillery occupied the flanks, the heavy guns and a rocket battery the centre. These opened as effective a fire as they could pour in upon the Sikhs; under cover of which the infantry advanced in magnificent style unchecked by the enemy's fire, till the charge was sounded. Thereupon the whole line rushed upon the Sikhs, driving them in headlong flight at the point of the bayonet; then changed front to their left, swept the camp, and dislodged the enemy from their whole position. The line then halted, and drew up victorious on that well-fought battle-field, receiving both Sir Hugh Gough and Sir Henry Hardinge with loud and prolonged cheers, as they rode together down the line. The division of Sir John Littler, with Sir Harry

Smith's 2nd brigade, now rejoining, the whole army was concentrated in the Sikh position.

The troops which had been over twenty-four hours under the severest physical and nervous strain, with scarcely any food, and but little water, were fairly exhausted; but at last it seemed as if their labour was over, and they might get water and refreshments from the village and the camp. They were in the highest spirits, and already congratulating each other over their hard-won victory, when intelligence was sent back by the cavalry following up the retreat, to the north, of the defeated Sikhs that a fresh Sikh force was approaching from the direction of Ferozepore. The approach of these new-comers was presently heralded by huge clouds of dust. Tej Singh had spent the whole of the previous day watching, as he thought, Littler's force. Hearing the heavy fire in the evening, and probably finding that Littler had moved out, he had marched in the early morning of the 22nd to the assistance of Lall Singh; and now arrived upon the scene with some 30,000 cavalry and infantry and a large field of artillery. It is impossible to say whether he expected to find Lall Singh still in possession of his entrenched position; but it must soon have been made clear to him that the British were now entire masters of the field, and that the Sikhs had fled.

Our position, however, was now most critical. There was a perfectly fresh army to face; our men had had no opportunity for rest or refreshment; the ammunition was all but exhausted; the cavalry horses were so worn out by the long-continued work and want of food that many of them could hardly raise a trot. On the other hand, the Sikhs, brave and stubborn as they showed themselves in defence, never displayed equal capacity in the attack, owing, no doubt, in part, to want of training and ability in their leaders. Moreover, they were ignorant of the straits in which we were; whilst they plainly realised that our army had driven Lall Singh from his entrenchments, and were now clearly determined to hold them.

Tej Singh drew up his army, sending his artillery to the front, and opening a heavy fire which was maintained with great vigour. An energetic attempt was made to turn our left flank, which was repulsed; this was followed by a similar attack and repulse on the right; and then the Sikhs began to fall back. It has been believed by many that Tej Singh took alarm at a movement on the part of the bulk of our cavalry and horse artillery, which had been ordered by an officer of the head-quarters staff to proceed to Ferozepore. That order has never been explained—it was wholly unauthorised; and the officer who gave it (who is said to have been suffering from sunstroke) was subsequently removed from his appointment, and severely reprimanded. But Tej Singh, unable to account for this curious movement, appears to have jumped to the conclusion that it was intended to attack him in the rear. At any rate, he began to fall back, when a bold dash of a squadron of the 3rd Light Dragoons, supported by a portion of the 4th Bengal Lancers, into the middle of the horde of Sikh cavalry, sent them flying. This charge was led by Brigadier White in person, and as they galloped past Gilbert's Division in their attack, that fine old soldier rode up and joined in the charge.

The second Sikh attack, and the fire of their heavy artillery, had been a great strain on the endurance, discipline, and pluck of our troops, and occasioned considerable loss; amongst others, Brigadier Wallace of H.M.'s 9th Foot, commanding the 3rd Division, was killed by a round shot. During this cannonade, Sir Hugh Gough was so deeply moved at seeing his brave infantry, soldiers who had fought so nobly, subjected to the severe fire, that he rode out to the flank of the force, accompanied by one aide-de-camp, and placed himself in a conspicuous position, in order to draw the fire of the Sikh guns away from his men. The shot struck all round him, but neither Sir Hugh nor his gallant steed moved, nor were even touched, though His Excellency had had one horse struck by a round shot in the earlier part of the battle.

Tej Singh had now become aware of the tremendous carnage which had taken place in the course of expelling Lall Singh's troops from their entrenchments. From this knowledge he appears to have derived a conviction that it would be utterly useless to attempt dislodging from those entrenchments the men who had carried them with such manifest valour in the face of a resistance so conspicuously stubborn. Accordingly, he now withdrew, suddenly and entirely, and commenced a hasty retreat northward and towards the Sutlej. Detractors have affirmed that he merely wished for a plausible pretext; but the defence given is the one he himself subsequently alleged for his action; nor does it appear unreasonable. He did not know how exhausted our men were, nor that ammunition was failing; he did know that the troops before him were behind entrenchments out of which they had thrashed the flower of the Sikh army, while his own troops were chiefly irregulars. Had he been inspired with the enthusiasm of the Khalsa, he might have acted differently; but there is no real ground for questioning the honesty of his explanation.

Whatever Tej Singh's motive was, the sight of his army in hurried retreat was singularly welcome to the British troops. They had now been under arms for upwards of forty hours; they had had neither food nor water since the previous morning; they had been ceaselessly exposed to the most fatiguing work; the additional strain of anxiety, during the past night especially, had been intense; and for a great part of the time they had been engaged in actual hard fighting with a powerful and most stubborn foe. Now at last the weary troops, completely tired out and exhausted by their two days' sanguinary contest, and the want of food and water, could seek shelter and refreshment.

Fortunately the Sikh camp and village of Ferozeshah afforded both, large stores of grain having been collected by the enemy; besides which several bullocks were found and promptly killed.

The wounded, many of whom had been lying for twenty-four hours on the ground untended, were now looked after. Their sufferings had been terrible, and many had fallen victims to the merciless cruelty of the Sikhs; but it is again gratifying to be able to give one instance of humanity on the part of the enemy. Lieutenant Sievwright, an officer of H.M.'s 9th Foot, had been desperately wounded in front of the Sikh battery, and lay all that night in dreadful anguish on the field with a shattered leg, helpless and unable to move. At daylight, finding that the Sikhs were cutting up the unprotected wounded, he managed with incredible difficulty to drag himself some short way further off. Seeing a Sikh soldier approaching, Sievwright grasped his pistol and challenged him; to his relief, the Sikh replied, "Salaam, sahib." Seeing that he was clearly kindly disposed, Sievwright called him up; the man sat down beside him, and after some conversation it was arranged that the Sikh soldier should carry him to the nearest succour. This good Samaritan took his wounded foe on his back, and carried him, at the peril of his own life, some two miles to the rear, where he met a dooli, in which Sievwright was placed, and conveyed into Ferozepore. Acts of kindness between enemies have often been heard of on a battle-field, but never one that could surpass this. The Sikh remained with Lieutenant Sievwright, and tended him in hospital; but it is melancholy to relate that the gallant young officer himself died only a week after from the effects of his wound, which necessitated the amputation of his leg above the knee. Records do not show what became of the brave and kind-hearted Sikh, but it may be certain that his generous humanity did not pass unrewarded.

The list of casualties in this great battle shows not only

how stubborn was the fighting, but also how entirely the brunt of it was borne by the European troops. Sir Hugh Gough himself had one horse killed under him, and one of his personal staff, Lieutenant—now Field-Marshal Sir Frederick—Haines severely wounded. The Governor-General had every member of his staff disabled, and Major Broadfoot was killed. Brigadier Wallace, in command of a division, was killed. General Gilbert, commanding a division, had one horse killed and another wounded under him; and Brigadiers Harriott, White, and Taylor, were all wounded.

It is difficult to ascertain the actual strength of regiments in action. The European infantry regiments probably numbered about 5600, making up about 6000 with the grand old 3rd Light Dragoons, who had already lost nearly 100 killed and wounded at Moodkee, and cannot now have amounted to more than 400 men. On the other hand, the 15 regiments native infantry, and 5 regiments native cavalry, must have made up 10,000; but the losses were:—

Killed: officers, British, 37, native, 17; men, British, 462, native, 178; total, 694.

Wounded: officers, British, 78, native, 18; men, British, 1054, native, 571; total, 1721.

Grand total of all ranks killed and wounded, 2415.

The losses of the British regiments are given in detail in a footnote. Proud indeed may those regiments be of the part they played in the battle of Ferozeshah.*

* Losses in British Regiments—

	Killed.		Wounded.	
3rd Light Dragoons	2 officers	53 men	7 officers	86 men
H.M.'s 9th Foot...	3 „	67 „	7 „	197 „
H.M.'s 29th Foot	3 „	52 „	3 „	192 „
H.M.'s 31st Foot	2 „	59 „	6 „	96 „
H.M.'s 50th Foot	2 „	24 „	6 „	89 „
H.M.'s 62nd Foot	7 „	97 „	11 „	184 „
H.M.'s 80th Foot	4 „	39 „	4 „	73 „
1st European Light Infantry ...	4 „	51 „	4 „	164 „
Artillery, European and Native	2 „	39 „	4 „	84 „

Two officers mortally wounded are included among the killed. There is a slight discrepancy between the returns of casualties as shown by the various regiments in their records given as above and those made up somewhat hastily and forwarded to Army Head-quarters immediately after the action.

Seventy-three guns had been captured on the field; a Sikh army of over 60,000 men had been completely routed, and the enemy driven over the frontier. The Duke of Wellington, writing to Sir Hugh Gough, on receipt of his news of Ferozeshah, lamented the heavy losses, but added these words: "Long experience has taught me that such achievements cannot be performed, and such objects attained as in these operations without great loss, and that in point of fact the honour acquired by all is proportionate to the difficulties and dangers met and overcome."

Before leaving Ferozeshah, it is necessary once more to revert to the conflict of opinion between the Governor-General and the Commander-in-Chief. No one will dispute that Sir Henry Hardinge acted in a manner which must have been most distasteful to him, and under stress of a strong sense of duty, an entire conviction that the Commander-in-Chief's plan involved a risk which it was out of the question for him to sanction. For the plan which was followed, Sir Henry took the responsibility which was his and his only, although some of those who blamed the course taken have spoken as if Sir Hugh Gough was to be held accountable. Opinions may differ as to the wisdom of the course chosen; there is no room whatever for difference as to the responsibility for choosing it. On the other hand, the consequences of that choice are perfectly clear. The attack was delayed so long that night came on before the Sikhs were fairly driven from their position, the British brigades lost each other in the darkness, heavy losses were incurred, and a fresh fight with fresh troops had to be carried on through the greater part of the following day without time or opportunity for food or refreshment. It may indeed be argued that no one can tell what would have happened had the Commander-in-Chief been allowed to carry out his plan. Looking at the facts, however, it seems difficult to doubt that that plan would have met with complete success. It was opposed broadly on the ground that the Sikh position could not be carried without Sir John Littler's force; but when that force joined, one-half of it, Ashburnham's Brigade, never seems to have come fairly into action, and the other half was repulsed. The approach of night greatly increased the hurry and consequent confusion; yet before the darkness fell, the Moodkee force, and the Moodkee force alone, had carried the entrenchment, and would, it may be said with certainty, have driven the Sikhs completely out of their position—as they did the next morning—with another two hours of daylight to do it in. Had this same force made the attack at twelve o'clock instead of at four, while still comparatively fresh, the Sikhs must have been completely routed. Littler's force would have arrived early in the engagement, in time to give whatever support was required; whereas in the actual battle, from the time of its repulse, which preceded the advance of the right and centre, it rendered no assistance whatever. The plan of the Commander-in-Chief, in fact, bears a remarkable resemblance to that of Moltke at Königgrätz, when, instead of waiting for a junction to be completed, he attacked the Austrians; the second army coming up and attacking the enemy in flank during the engagement—thus achieving a decisive victory.

Even if the attack had met with an initial check, Sir John would have been in time to prevent disaster. The horror of the night of December 21st would have been escaped; the British troops would have had that food and water which were so sorely needed, and would have faced Tej Singh the next day recuperated instead of exhausted.

Still it must be remembered that with the smaller force the *possibility* of a complete repulse would have been greater, and its effects terrific. Sir Henry accounted that risk too tremendous to be incurred; very much as in 1857 General Wilson, before Delhi, could hardly be persuaded to sanction the storming, in which failure would have meant the loss of India.

Sir Henry's action may be deplored or applauded, and Sir Hugh's generalship commended or condemned, according to the judgment of the critic; but whatever view may be taken of the Governor-General's interference, his personal conduct in the presence of the crisis, the splendid example he showed of courage, of resolution, of calmness, or, in one word, of *grit*, are beyond all praise; and their effect on the spirit of the men on that night when "the fate of India trembled in the balance" can never be over-estimated.

CHAPTER V.

BUDHOWAL AND ALIWAL: DEC. 23–JAN. 28

Movements of troops—Renewed activity of Sikhs—Movements on Ludhiana—Skirmish of Budhowal, Jan. 21.—Runjoor Singh at Aliwal—Junction of Sir H. Smith and Wheeler—Advance on Aliwal—The attack—Action of cavalry—Rout of the Sikhs—British losses—Effects of the victory.

THE Sikh army, shattered, and having lost nearly 100 guns and about 5000 men, retired from Ferozeshah and recrossed the Sutlej, just ten days after the invasion; whilst the Commander-in-Chief encamped at Sultan Khan Walla, watching the frontier and awaiting the arrival of the troops which had been ordered to advance from the more distant stations of Meerut, Delhi, and Cawnpore, at the same time as those from Umballa and the hill stations. On the 27th December, Sir Hugh Gough advanced to Arufkee, and personally pushed a reconnaissance to the fords at Sobraon, where the enemy were to be seen encamped on the right bank of the river. Sir Harry Smith's Division was placed at Malowal, from which point he maintained a careful watch on the enemy.

In the meantime the Sikhs had not been idle. Short as the time was, they had already brought up a fresh supply of guns from Lahore, and were almost as well furnished with artillery as before, whilst their army was rehabilitated and reinforced by large bodies of well-trained soldiers. By the 5th January they were showing renewed signs of aggression and making predatory incursions across the Sutlej, in the direction of Ludhiana, with the intention of interfering with the advance of the British reinforcements.

On the 6th January, Sir John Grey arrived at the army head-quarters with a force of about 10,000 men, consisting of H.M.'s 9th and 16th Lancers, each over 500 strong; the 3rd Bengal Light Cavalry, the 4th Irregular Cavalry, two Batteries of Artillery (12 guns), H.M.'s 10th Foot, and three regiments of Native Infantry with a company of Sappers. Leaving Meerut between the 10th and 16th December, they had marched over the fields of Moodkee and Ferozeshah still covered with the signs of the sanguinary battles which had there been fought. Ludhiana also had been reinforced by the Sirmoor and Nusseeree Battalions of Goorkhas, the 30th Regiment Native Infantry, and one of cavalry under Brigadier Godby; whilst other troops were still on the march and closing up.

The Sikhs again assumed the initiative by crossing in a considerable body near Ludhiana for the purpose of gathering in supplies from their Jaghir states in that vicinity, and about Dhurmkote, a small fort halfway between Ferozeshah and Ludhiana, in which they had a garrison. On the 17th January, therefore, Sir Harry Smith was sent against this small fort, which was easily reduced, the garrison surrendering at discretion. But the Sikh force which had crossed the river, and which had been reinforced with all arms, now, under the Sirdar Runjoor Singh, threatened an attack on Ludhiana, and even indicated an intention of cutting our line of communication. Consequently, the Commander-in-Chief decided to utilise Sir Harry Smith's force, strengthened by H.M.'s 16th Lancers, the 3rd Light Cavalry, a troop of Horse Artillery, and H.M.'s 53rd Foot (now on its way up and near Bussean), to relieve and secure Ludhiana.

Accordingly, on the 20th, Sir H. Smith marched from Dhurmkote to Jugraon, so as to skirt round Runjoor Singh, and so move by him into Ludhiana. On the 21st he advanced from Jugraon towards Ludhiana; but on approaching Budhowal, about 11 a.m., he found that Runjoor Singh had taken up an entrenched position which flanked and commanded the road by which he was moving. Being desirous of reaching Ludhiana without fighting a battle, he decided to move on across Runjoor's front, leaving him to be dealt with when the force was consolidated; and this brought on the affair of Budhowal. The Sikhs opened a heavy fire, but Smith moved on, covering his movement with his cavalry, artillery, and the 53rd Foot. The Sikh cavalry came out and followed up, cutting off a large portion of the baggage and a portion of the rear-guard, but avoiding a conflict with our cavalry. Several European soldiers, exhausted by the long and arduous marching, were taken prisoners by the Sikhs, who, to their credit be it said, treated them fairly well, and, after the battle of Sobraon, released them and sent them back. Still, the number of killed and wounded, particularly in H.M.'s 53rd, proves that many stragglers, and probably sick men in the rear of the column, must have been mercilessly murdered. Quartermaster Cornes, who with a party of 1 sergeant, and 30 men of H.M.'s 53rd, was in charge of the regimental baggage, finding his party cut off from the main body, rallied round him a small detachment of the 16th Lancers and a party of sepoys, making in all 2 officers and 80 men; and succeeded in saving a considerable portion of the baggage, and making good his retreat on Jugraon, in the face of about 1000 Sikhs with a field-gun, who threatened to attack him, but were held in check by his bold front and steady discipline.

There are no official details of this affair; this account is taken principally from what can be gathered from regimental records. Sir Harry Smith, although he succeeded in passing by Runjoor Singh without fighting a general action, suffered a considerable loss in men and baggage, and marched into Ludhiana that evening, with his troops greatly exhausted. The 16th Lancers lost 2 men killed, and 1 wounded. H.M.'s 31st Regiment lost 21 men killed and wounded, and 19 taken prisoners. H.M.'s 53rd Regiment lost 36 men killed, and 12 wounded. There is no means of ascertaining the loss of native troops. The Sikhs seem to have derived considerable encouragement from this skirmish; some highly exaggerated language about defeat and disaster was used by people who ought to have known better.

The Commander-in-Chief also despatched the 2nd Brigade of Sir Harry Smith's Division on the 22nd January to reinforce him; the expulsion of the Sikhs from the Ludhiana neighbourhood being regarded as very important. Brigadier Wheeler, now recovered from the wound received at Moodkee, had resumed the command and reached Dhurmkote that evening, not having heard of the affair which had occurred at Budhowal on the previous day. On the 23rd he continued his march direct on Ludhiana, but on arriving at Sidham he gained information that a large Sikh force was on the road, and between him and the rest of the division. He therefore decided to return to Dhurmkote, and move round a circuitous way by Jugraon, his troops being fairly fagged out by their hard day's march of over 30 miles through heavy sand and under a hot sun. On the other hand, Runjoor Singh, hearing of Wheeler's advance, and feeling that he might be attacked both from Dhurmkote and Ludhiana, made haste to evacuate his threatening position at Budhowal, and fell back on Aliwal close to the banks of the Sutlej. On the 24th Wheeler moved to Jugraon; on the 25th Sir Harry Smith advanced from Ludhiana to Budhowal, where he was joined by Wheeler, and his whole force concentrated.

On the 26th, then, Sir Harry's whole force was made up as follows:—Artillery: 22 guns Horse Artillery, and 6 guns Field Artillery, under Major Lawrence. Cavalry—1st Brigade, under Brigadier McDowell: H.M.'s 16th Lancers, 530 strong; 3rd Light Cavalry, 372; 4th Irregulars, 398

= 1300 men. 2nd Brigade, under Brigadier Stedman: Governor-General's Body-guard, 351; 1st Light Cavalry, 422; 5th Light Cavalry, 402 = 1107 men. Cavalry of the Shekawatti Brigade, 631 men, under Major Forster; the whole cavalry force, under Brigadier Cureton of H.M.'s 16th Lancers, numbering 3038. Infantry—1st Brigade, Brigadier Hicks commanding: H.M.'s 31st Regiment, now reduced to 544 men; 24th Regiment Native Infantry, 481 men; 36th Regiment Native Infantry, 571 men = 1596. 2nd Brigade (Brigadier Wheeler): H.M.'s 50th Regiment, 494 men only (sad results of Moodkee and Ferozeshah); 48th Native Infantry, 857 men; and the Sirmoor Goorkhas, 781 men = 2132. 3rd Brigade, under Brigadier Wilson: H.M.'s 53rd Regiment, 699; 30th Native Infantry, 824; Shekawatti Battalion, 625. 4th Brigade, under Brigadier Godby: 47th Native Infantry, 713; the Nusseeree Battalion Goorkhas, 586 = 1299. Total infantry, 7175.

Sir Harry Smith's total force, therefore, amounted to more than 10,000 fighting men, with 28 field guns, and two 8-inch howitzers.

Sirdar Runjoor Singh, whose troops at Budhowal had been chiefly irregular levies, had also received a reinforcement of 4000 regular troops and 12 guns, on the 26th.

Sir Harry Smith's men had gone through such long marches and such hard work that he considered it advisable to give them a day's rest to recruit themselves; but at daylight on the 28th January he advanced from Budhowal to attack Runjoor, who was known to be in position at Aliwal, on the left bank of the Sutlej, about 16 miles to the north-west, having a very considerable force and some 50 guns, and with every intention of fighting.

The cavalry in the line of columns, with two troops of Horse Artillery, formed the first line, and covered Sir Harry's front, scouting the country as they advanced, infantry and artillery following. After proceeding in this order about 9 miles, the enemy were sighted in position on the west of a low ridge about a mile in front. Sir Harry Smith had received information through spies that it was Runjoor Singh's intention to move out of his position that morning either on Ludhiana, or to attack him at Budhowal; and as he approached, this rumour was confirmed by a spy, who reported that the Sikh army was actually on the march. Sir Harry, however, felt confident that whatever movements Runjoor might be contemplating, he had him in his grasp now; and his continued advance direct upon the Sikhs brought them entirely to the defensive.

Runjoor took up a position with his left on the banks of the Sutlej, along the crest of some rising ground; the village of Aliwal was held somewhat in front of his left, and the village of Boondree on his right, his guns being placed all along the line of front, the general bearing of which was south-east. Sir Harry Smith's line faced north-west. As he approached Runjoor Singh the cavalry and horse artillery wheeled outwards, and took up position on the right and left, displaying the now deployed line of infantry advancing to the attack. The batteries immediately advanced to effective range, and came into action; and the battle began.

It was now 10 o'clock, and the whole scene most striking. The morning was clear and beautiful, the country open and hard grass land—a fair field for all arms. There was no dust, and the sun shone brightly. Brigadier Stedman commanded the cavalry on the right; the 1st and 5th Regiments of Native Cavalry, the Governor-General's Body-guard, the Shekawatti cavalry, and the 4th Irregulars. Then came Godby's Brigade, the Goorkhas of the Nusseeree Battalion, and the 36th Native Infantry; next, Hicks's Brigade, H.M.'s 31st Foot, with the 24th and 47th Regiments Native Infantry; on their left and in the centre of the line the two 8-inch howitzers and a large battery of 18 guns; then Wheeler's Brigade, H.M.'s 50th, the 48th

Native Infantry, the Sirmoor Goorkhas (Brigadier Wheeler had so much confidence in his own regiment, the 48th, that he placed it in the centre of the brigade: the corps fully justified his opinion); then two batteries of artillery (12 guns); then Wilson's Brigade of H.M.'s 53rd Foot, the 30th Native Infantry, and the Shekawatti infantry; then on the extreme left H.M.'s 16th Lancers and the 3rd Light Cavalry.

Sir Harry Smith soon perceived that by bringing up his right, and carrying the village of Aliwal in front of the Sikh left, he could with great effect precipitate himself upon their left and centre, and cut off their line of retreat by the ford. He therefore brought up Godby's Brigade, and with it Hicks's. The latter was directed upon the village, which was carried in fine style, and two guns taken. At the same time the right brigade of cavalry was directed to attack the Sikh horse, and this also was most gallantly done, their cavalry being driven back upon and among their own infantry, while our right pushed on rapidly. Whilst these operations were going on on the right, Brigadier Wheeler also advanced to the attack, supported by Wilson; the guns of Alexander, Turton, Lane, Mill, Boileau, and of the Shekawatti Brigade, as also the 8-inch howitzers, pushing on continually in front of the advancing infantry. The enemy's fire fell heavily upon the right brigade—Wheeler's own—but they advanced most steadily, halting twice and lying down under the fire, to steady the men and prevent hurry, and to allow Wilson's Brigade to get forward; which was necessary, because of the enemy's position being on a curve, with the flank thrown back. In this manner the advance continued until they were close upon the Sikhs. Meanwhile that brilliant cavalry commander, Brigadier Cureton, had been following up the infantry attack, watching keenly for his opportunity; and just as Wilson was preparing to charge the Sikh infantry and guns in front of him with H.M.'s 53rd and the Goorkhas and 30th Native Infantry, a thunder of horses' hoofs was heard on their left, and H.M.'s 16th Lancers, in great strength, came sweeping by with lances lowered, and, supported by the 3rd Bengal Light Cavalry, charged right down upon the foe. The Sikh infantry hurriedly formed squares; but the squadrons of the 16th swept through and through them, and smashing up a large body of the celebrated Aieen troop, trained by General Avitabile, utterly routed the whole Sikh right. The charge of one squadron of the 16th Lancers, led by Major Smyth and Captain Pearson, upon a well-formed square of Avitabile's Regiment, deserves special notice; as, notwithstanding the steadiness of the enemy, the Lancers broke the square, charged through, reformed and charged again in splendid style—a feat very rarely accomplished. Wheeler, with his own and Wilson's Brigades, followed up rapidly, with the result of capturing the village of Boondree and many guns; the village being stormed by H.M.'s 53rd. The Sikh infantry declined to meet the charge of Wilson's Brigade; but their gunners resolutely stood their ground. They could not, however, hold the guns, which were captured at the point of the bayonet. The whole Sikh force was now driven in utter rout and confusion to the ford. Pursued by the cavalry, who made repeated charges, and pressed by the infantry, they were unable to make any attempt to rally, and flinging themselves into the river, fled to the right bank, leaving all their guns, camp equipage, baggage, and stores to fall into the hands of the victors; 67 guns were amongst the captured trophies, and many camel-guns.

Sir Harry Smith bestowed well-deserved praise on the officers and men who had fought this brilliant action. Of the artillery, he said, "Our guns and gunners, officers and men may be equalled, but cannot be excelled; no troops ever behaved more nobly, British and native, without distinction; the native cavalry vieing with H.M.'s 16th Lancers, and striving to head in the repeated charges.

Throughout the day there was no hesitation, but a bold and intrepid advance; and thus it is our loss is comparatively small." On this occasion also the Field Hospital arrangements were efficiently and well carried out, and the wounded well provided for.

Aliwal proved the utter inability of the Sikh army, even with double the number of men and guns, to make more than an honourable stand against British troops on a fair field. It showed also that the native troops, when not exhausted by hunger and fatigue, as they had been at Ferozeshah, could render invaluable support to the English regiments; and to this Sir Harry Smith in his despatches amply testified.

The loss in this well-fought battle was small, in all regiments except H.M.'s 16th Lancers; they in their brilliant charges, against guns and well-trained infantry who fought to the death, suffered heavily. There were 2 officers and 57 men killed, 6 officers and 77 men wounded—making a total of 8 officers and 134 men; 66 horses were killed, and 35 wounded. The 50th Foot also, which advanced against the Sikh central battery, suffered considerably; the native corps serving with them lost 5 officers wounded, 1 native officer and 15 men killed, 9 native officers and 75 men wounded.

The total loss of the force amounted to: killed 151, wounded 413, and missing 25 men = 580.

The immediate result of the victory was the complete submission of the whole of the Sikh territory on the left bank of the Sutlej, which was entirely evacuated by the enemy.

The news of the complete defeat of Runjoor Singh was received, as might be expected, with great joy by both Governor-General and Commander-in-Chief. The former issued a general order announcing the victory, congratulating the commander and his force, and extolling their valour, discipline, and skill, in well-deserved terms. To the cavalry especially he gave great credit. To Brigadier Cureton, who commanded the cavalry, his thanks were more markedly given for the skill and intrepidity with which he had handled his force; since the admiration of the army had been elicited by the resolute charges of H.M.'s 16th Lancers, penetrating the Sikh squares with the gallant support of the 3rd Native Light Cavalry. The guns taken in addition to those already captured at Moodkee and Ferozeshah brought the total up to 143 pieces. At Aliwal, also, the two Goorkha regiments, not yet enrolled among the regular regiments of infantry, much distinguished themselves. By order of the Governor-General a royal salute was fired from the British camp, the bands raising the National Anthem. The Sikhs on the opposite bank, not to be outdone, followed suit with both; and their bands were heard playing "God save the Queen"!

CHAPTER VI.

SOBRAON: FEB. 10

The Sikh position—Plans of attack—Final plan—The British force—Preparations for attack—Artillery duel—Advance ordered—The left attack—Smith's Division—Gilbert's Division—Rout of the Sikhs—Losses.

REINFORCEMENTS of all arms had been moving up ever since the great battle of Ferozeshah, and now the whole army was concentrated for the decisive struggle on the banks of the Sutlej. The siege-train, with ammunition for the field-guns, reached the Commander-in-Chief's camp on the 7th of February; and on the 8th Sir Harry Smith, with his victorious division, marched into camp. Meantime the Sikhs had been as busy as bees strengthening their position, and were to be seen at work every day until it had assumed quite formidable proportions. Strong earthworks with deep ditches stretched in half-circle from bank to bank; behind these the river formed a loop; and across it, in order to maintain their communications, the Sikhs had thrown a bridge of boats. There was also a ford. In order still further to protect the bridge, interior lines of earthworks had been erected in succession; the position was throughout armed with heavy guns, whilst batteries were placed on the north side of the river, more effectually to sweep the front, especially of their right, against an attack in that direction. The strongest part of the enemy's position was the centre, the weakest on their right, where the earthworks were less formidable.

The position had been most carefully reconnoitred, the proceedings of the Sikhs strictly watched, the plan of attack most deliberately thought out.

At one time a plan was considered of suddenly breaking up from before Sobraon, and endeavouring to cross the Sutlej by surprise at the Ford of Gunda Singh Walla, and then advancing upon the Sikhs; but Sir Hugh Gough, after full consideration, decided against this, as in his opinion there was little chance of effecting a surprise, the Sikhs having full information of all our movements. Moreover, even if we did cross successfully, the Sikh army might easily fall back on Lahore, thereby increasing our difficulties, owing to the hostility of the people; and the war might possibly be thus converted into one of sieges. He fully recognised the strength of the Sikh position at Sobraon; but he judged that a defeat there would be fatal to them, and would be in all probability decisive of the war; and he resolved to make it so.

Accordingly he arranged to attack the enemy's extreme right, and, having penetrated there, to roll them up.

This plan was submitted to the Governor-General, who replied in the following cautious and guarded words, "If, upon the fullest consideration, the artillery can be brought into play, I recommend you to attack; if it cannot, and you anticipate a heavy loss, I would recommend you not to attempt it." Unhesitatingly Sir Hugh Gough accepted the responsibility. On the 9th of February orders were issued for the attack, and these were fully explained to the generals commanding.

In order the better to understand the delivery of the attack, it is advisable to enumerate the force now collected, re-organised, and disposed for attack.

Major-General Sir John Littler still held Ferozepore and watched the ferry over the Sutlej. Sir John Grey, with the 8th Light Cavalry, and the 41st, 45th, and 68th Regiments Native Infantry, held Attaree, watching fords west of Sobraon. Brigadier Wheeler also took no part in the battle of Sobraon, having been left, after Aliwal, in command of a detachment of native troops, to watch the fords of the Sutlej, and cover Ludhiana.

The main body was concentrated before Sobraon with the Commander-in-Chief.

Brigadier Smith commanded the engineers; and here it is fair to mention the fact, so honourable to Brigadier Irvine, a very distinguished engineer officer, who arrived in camp on the evening of the 9th, that the command would have devolved on him as senior officer; but that, with the generosity of spirit which is always a characteristic of a true-born soldier, he declined to assume it, in order that all the credit of the work which Brigadier Smith had begun might attach to that officer. For himself, Brigadier Irvine sought only to share the perils of the field, and throughout the day he accompanied the Commander-in-Chief.

Brigadier Gowan, C.B., commanded the artillery. An endeavour had been made to rectify the inferiority of our guns in the matter of weight of metal by enlarging the bores of nine-pounders into twelve; but the number of our guns did not exceed 60.

Major-General Sir Joseph Thackwell, a distinguished Peninsula and Waterloo officer, commanded the cavalry division; Brigadier Cureton commanded the greater part of the cavalry, H.M.'s 16th Lancers, with the 3rd, 4th, and 5th Regiments of Light Cavalry—with which he was to make a show of crossing the Sutlej by the Hurreekee Ford, on the right flank of the attack, so as to draw the enemy's attention to that point.

Sir Harry Smith's Division of Infantry of two brigades, under Brigadier Penny and Brigadier Hicks respectively (the former consisting of H.M.'s 31st Foot, the 47th Native Infantry and the Nusseeree Battalion (Goorkhas); and the latter of H.M.'s 50th Foot and the 42nd Native Infantry), was to attack the enemy's extreme left; and formed on our right, supported by Campbell's Cavalry Brigade, which included H.M.'s 9th Lancers and two troops Horse Artillery.

The centre was occupied by Gilbert's Division of Infantry: 1st Brigade, under Brigadier Taylor, H.M.'s 29th Foot, the 41st and 68th Regiments Native Infantry; 2nd Brigade, the 1st European Light Infantry, the 16th Regiment Native Infantry, and the Sirmoor Battalion (Goorkhas), under Brigadier McLaran. Between him and Sir Harry Smith on the right, was placed a battery of eight heavy guns. Gilbert's Division was accompanied by No. 19 Field Battery.

On Gilbert's left was to be placed another battery of heavy guns.

On the extreme left Sir Robert Dick was to lead the attack, and his force was strengthened accordingly; it was to advance in two lines, and to have a strong reserve of both cavalry and infantry. His first line consisted of H.M.'s 10th and 53rd Regiments, with the 43rd and 59th Regiments Native Infantry, under Brigadier Stacey, accompanied by Brigadier Orchard. His second line was made up of H.M.'s 80th Foot, with the 33rd Native Infantry, under Brigadier Wilkinson; whilst in reserve were placed H.M.'s 9th Foot, the 62nd Foot, and the 26th Native Infantry, under Brigadier Hon. T. Ashburnham; and to their rear, again, Brigadier Scott's Cavalry Brigade, H.M.'s 3rd Light Dragoons, and the 3rd and 9th Irregulars, with whom were the 4th, 5th, and 73rd Regiments Native Infantry.

Fortune so far favoured the British that the river had suddenly risen owing to a storm of heavy rain which had occurred a day or two before; so much so that the ford, which was usually safe, had become extremely dangerous on the day of the attack.

At 2 a.m. the troops fell in silently, and, forming into

columns, moved quietly towards their respective positions. No sound or sign of the coming attack reached the Sikhs, and, whilst it was yet dark, the various columns had all formed accurately according to their orders for the attack. There they waited, in disciplined order and silence, for the dawn of day. When it came, a dense fog so covered the ground that nothing could be seen, and it became necessary to wait yet longer; but presently the scene changed. In the animated language of the historical records of the 1st Bengal European Light Infantry, now the Royal Munster Fusiliers, evidently written by one who was present—

> "The rising sun rapidly dispelled the fog, when a magnificent picture presented itself. The batteries of artillery were seen in position ready to open fire, and the plain covered with our troops, the fortified village of Rhoda Walla on our left rear being strongly held by our infantry. Immediately the guns opened a heavy fire. The enemy appearing suddenly to realise their danger, their drums beat the alarm, their bugles sounded to arms, and in a few minutes their batteries were manned, and pouring shot and shell upon our troops."

Thus quickly was the scene transformed from the picturesque to war in veritable earnest; and thus began the Battle of Sobraon.

For two hours the hail of shot and shell continued on both sides, and yet no decided advantage had been gained; the Sikh guns, firing from behind their field fortifications, could not be silenced. It was clear, as at Ferozeshah, that the battle could not be gained by superiority of artillery fire; the ammunition of the heavy guns was failing and their fire slackening. This was reported to the Commander-in-Chief, to whom it was evident that the issue of the struggle must be brought to "the arbitrament of musketry and the bayonet." He had the most implicit confidence in the ability and leading of his officers, and the courage and discipline of his troops. Turning to his nephew, Colonel J. B. Gough, Quartermaster-General, he directed him to convey the order to Sir Robert Dick to commence the attack. In such moments as this the spirit of the commander communicates itself like magic to his troops, and a rumour flew down the line at once "that old Gough had been told that there were only four more rounds left per gun, and says, 'Thank God! then I'll be at them with the bayonet.'" Whether he actually used those precise words or not is immaterial; the fact that the rumour went down the line is beyond any manner of doubt, and it was received with delight by the men, because they knew and felt there was not a doubt of success in their brave old leader's mind, and that he had most perfect confidence in them.

Sir Robert Dick received the order at nine o'clock, and immediately the batteries of Horsford, Fordyce, and Lane's Horse Artillery galloped to the front, and proceeded to cover the advance of Stacey's Brigade, which moved forward with the utmost steadiness, frequently halting to correct the line and prevent any hurry on the part of the men. The guns continued their advance in this manner, preceding the infantry, and taking up fresh positions till within 300 yards of the entrenchments, when a body of the enemy's cavalry moved out and threatened the left flank of the line, where H.M.'s 53rd Foot was advancing. These were soon dispersed by a well-directed fire from the flank company of the regiment, and by the discharge of some rounds of grape from one of the batteries. The 53rd immediately following up, with a cheer charged the enemy's entrenchments, being the first to enter them. During this advance the regiment was enfiladed for a time by a Sikh battery on the right bank of the river, Captain Warren being killed, and Lieutenant Lucas, carrying one of the colours, wounded. Stacey's Brigade rushed forward simultaneously, and the first line of the enemy's entrenchments was occupied. Colonel Gough, who accompanied Sir Robert Dick's attack, here fell severely wounded. Stacey's attack was ably supported by Brigadier Wilkinson, not a shot having been fired, except by the flank company, until the first line of entrenchments was carried.

Here, however, Stacey's advance was checked, and he

had to wait until Dick brought up his second line, for the Sikh batteries to the right now enfiladed our troops. These were attacked and carried by H.M.'s 10th and 80th; Sir Robert Dick meeting his death-wound about this time. The division then continued its advance, driving the enemy towards the centre; the Sikh Akhalis (fanatics corresponding to the Mussulman Ghazis) fighting most stubbornly. Here a curious form of defence had been adopted by the enemy. Large pits capable of holding 30 men had been prepared, into which they were now crowded, and, being caught like rats in a trap, were easily disposed of.

The Sikhs, seeing that their right had been broken into, commenced a rush from all parts of their position to retake it. In order to hold them in check, and to relieve the pressure on Dick's Division, the divisions of Sir Harry Smith on the right, and Gilbert in the centre, were ordered to attack at once.

In the same manner as Dick had advanced, Sir Harry Smith led on his division against the extreme left of the Sikh position; Brigadier Penny in the first line, supported closely by Brigadier Hicks, and covered by the fire of the artillery. The men, who up to this had been lying down, sprang up, formed, and advanced. But the ground immediately in front of the Sikh works was much broken by watercourses, which made it difficult for the men to keep their places; the enemy's fire was very severe, and the formidable nature of the earthworks prevented the assailants climbing up. After a desperate struggle, the first line was compelled to give way and fall back; but they were well and resolutely supported by Brigadier Hicks, who, opening the ranks to let the men through, re-formed and charged. Penny's Brigade, rapidly rallying, joined in the charge again, the soldiers being maddened by seeing the Sikhs run out and cut up their unfortunate and brave comrades who had fallen in the first attack. This time the entrenchments were carried. Brigadier Penny having been severely wounded in the first attack, Colonel Spence, of H.M.'s 31st, assumed command of the 1st Brigade.

Thus our troops had established themselves on the enemy's left flank, and were pressing on when a fire was opened on them from behind. Turning round, it was seen that some of the Sikhs had run in again on the captured guns and reopened fire; whereupon Hicks directed H.M.'s 50th to retake them, which was quickly done.

Gilbert's Division, in the centre, attacking at the same time as the first division under Smith, came upon such high earthworks that they were quite unable to scale them without ladders, and were twice forced to fall back. Not even their devoted gallantry could overcome the obstacles, and their loss was great. Gilbert himself was wounded, and Brigadier McLaran most severely. Major Fisher, of the Sirmoor battalion, was shot dead with a bullet in the brain; it is remarkable that he remained sitting on his horse for an appreciable interval before he fell. Many officers and men were struck down. Yet a third time the division was led on to the charge, on a part of the earthworks considerably to the left of the part previously attacked, where they were lower. Mounting on each other's shoulders, they gained a footing in the entrenchments, and as they increased in numbers they rushed upon the guns, which were now captured; and soon the glad news that all the troops had won their way into the Sikh position spread down the line. In this third charge fell also Brigadier Taylor, of H.M.'s 29th, struck by a bullet in the head, after he had already been wounded by a sabre-cut in the face.

H.M.'s 3rd Light Dragoons again greatly distinguished themselves by their exceptional gallantry. Following up Dick's Division, they found their way within the line of the entrenchments, and charged down among the now discomfited Sikhs; yet to the last the enemy fought bravely and doggedly, endeavouring to stem the torrent of retreat; but, pressed on all sides, they were forced headlong to the bridge. The guns now brought up opened a heavy and destructive fire; the bridge gave way under the fugitives, and no resource was left but the river, the deepened ford of which was no longer safe. Our troops, fairly infuriated by the butchery of their brave comrades massacred before their eyes, spared not, and it is calculated that the Sikh loss exceeded 10,000 men. Every gun within the position was captured, 67 guns, mostly of heavy calibre, being taken on the field, and the whole Sikh army was utterly and irretrievably defeated.

The action was completed before noon; but this great success was not achieved against a determined and resolute foe without a corresponding loss. Many brave and distinguished officers fell, foremost amongst them Sir Robert Dick, a veteran of the Peninsula and Waterloo; mortally wounded by a grape-shot in the moment of his glorious success, he died in the evening. Brigadier Taylor, of H.M.'s 29th, who had led his brigade so splendidly at Moodkee and Ferozeshah, was killed. Colonel Ryan, K.H., and Colonel Petit, both of H.M.'s 50th, were severely wounded. Colonel J. B. Gough and Colonel Barr, on the Commander-in-Chief's staff, Brigadier Penny, and Brigadier McLaran, were all severely wounded. Altogether, the killed numbered 320, and the wounded 2063.

Sir Henry Hardinge did not take any actual command on this occasion, but his fine military spirit led him into the thick of the battle, and he followed up the attack in person, encouraging the troops by his noble example.

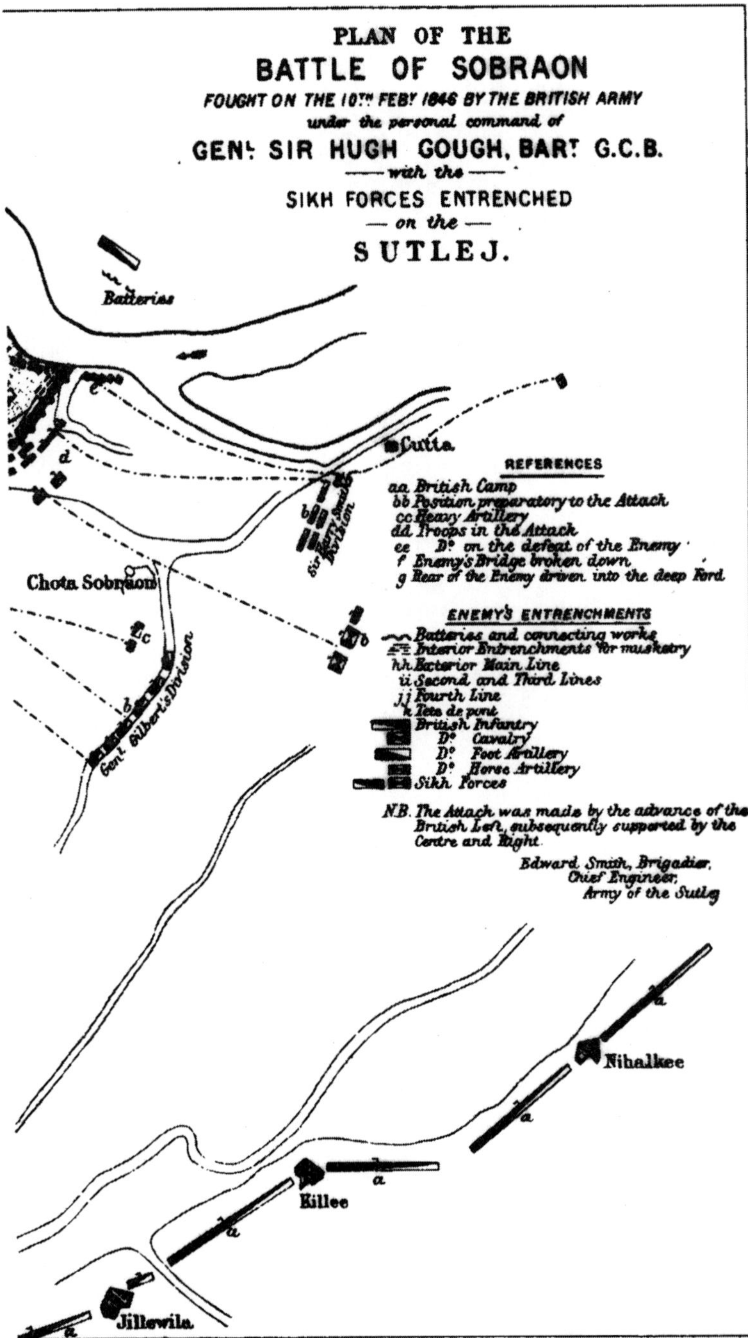

London; Stanford's Geogl. Estabt.

CHAPTER VII.

SURVEY OF THE CAMPAIGN

Quality of the Sikh army—Conduct of the British troops—Account of the European regiments engaged in the various battles—Of the Native troops—Of the officers—Merits of the Sikhs—Conclusions as to the campaign.

SOBRAON virtually terminated the war. The disaster to the Khalsa was complete and overwhelming. The Governor-General was now able to march, without meeting further resistance, upon Lahore, and there to dictate his own terms. In the next chapter we shall turn again to the political side of affairs, during the campaign and after it. Before doing so, however, we shall here pass in review certain aspects of the campaign itself.

On and about December 11th, 1845, the Sikh army crossed the Sutlej. The soldiery were the most stubborn we ever fought in India. Their guns were heavier and more numerous than ours, and were admirably served. At every stage our troops were greatly outnumbered; yet, within two months, four pitched battles were fought, and the enemy's army shattered; and another week saw the submission of Lahore to the Governor-General.

It is difficult to do even bare justice to the conduct of the troops engaged. The Umballa men were moving within 24 hours of receiving their marching orders. Over a rough country, heavy, sandy, amid clouds of dust, under a blazing sun, with little water, and often very inadequate food—for camels move slowly, and bullock-carts more slowly still, so that the cooking-utensils often arrived too late to allow of proper cooking—they marched 150 miles in seven days. They had already covered twenty miles on the day when they first came in collision with the enemy, whom they then put to rout after a stubborn resistance, capturing 17 guns. Three days later, having commenced their march at two o'clock in the morning, and having been for 14 hours already under arms, and almost without food, they stormed the Sikh entrenchments at Ferozeshah, and, despite a desperate resistance, would assuredly have carried them completely had not the fall of darkness made it necessary to draw off. The strain of the night which followed, with the bitter cold, the continued want of food and water, the incessant firing and yelling of the Sikhs, the uncertainty as to the fate of their comrades, was tremendous. Yet, when morning came, worn and exhausted as they were, they renewed the attack with undaunted courage, swept the enemy's entrenchments clear at the point of the bayonet, put them to flight, and faced without flinching the fresh army which Tej Singh led from Ferozepore.

The courage, endurance, and discipline displayed were beyond all praise. The victories of Aliwal and Sobraon were brilliant, but they were fought under far more favourable conditions. In every case, indeed, we had foemen worthy of our steel; disciplined troops, fighting behind entrenchments with dogged resolution, well armed, well supplied with artillery, and superior in numbers to our own. But at Aliwal and Sobraon we fought with a moral assurance of winning. The task was hard, but the event was never really in doubt. Whereas at Ferozeshah, from the moment when it became evident that the falling darkness must prevent the completion of the victory so nearly won, the event was very doubtful indeed. These are the conditions which put the highest military qualities to the sternest test, and our men passed the ordeal with magnificent spirit.

Ferozeshah showed emphatically the superior quality of the European troops as compared with the sepoys. There the latter, with less stamina, seemed to have lost nerve as they became exhausted, did nothing like their share of the fighting, and might have broken down but for the stubbornness of their British comrades. At Sobraon and Aliwal, where they came to their work fresh and confident, no such reproach could be laid to their charge, and they won their full mead of enthusiastic praise.

Of the British regiments which took part in this campaign, it may, indeed, be said that every one covered itself with glory. No cavalry regiment has ever surpassed the feats achieved by H.M.'s 3rd Light Dragoons. At Moodkee they entered into action 494 strong; their killed and wounded there numbered 101. Out of their diminished numbers, in their grand charge at Ferozeshah, when they swept right through the Sikh batteries and camp, they lost 148 men; altogether, just half their original strength, in the two engagements. Nor did they fail to distinguish themselves once more at Sobraon, where there fell 31 of their reduced band, and Sir Hugh Gough referred to them as a regiment "whom no obstacle usually held formidable by horse appears to check." At Moodkee, indeed, it seems likely that if they had been supported by a second and third line of such cavalry as the 9th and 16th Lancers, there would have been little left for any one else to do.

The 16th Lancers (part of the reinforcements from Meerut) won their laurels at Aliwal, where the notable achievement of the squadron which broke a Sikh square, charging clean through it, has been duly recorded. It certainly seems peculiarly unfortunate that, owing to the political exigencies before referred to, the Governor-General had found himself unable to order them to the front in time to take their part in the earlier engagements. Their losses at Aliwal were heavy: 2 officers and 57 men killed, 8 officers and 134 men wounded. At Sobraon, however, they were posted on the right, where the cavalry were not called upon to take any active part in the battle, and their losses were nil.

The 9th Foot, at Ferozeshah, after Reid's Brigade had already been repulsed, stormed and captured the same batteries, losing 265 killed and wounded out of a little over 800 of all ranks. Two distinguished old officers of the regiment, Sir John M'Caskill and Colonel Taylor, were killed at its head in the course of the war.

The 29th Foot, in spite of great exertions and hard marching, did not reach the Umballa force till after Moodkee; but at Ferozeshah, the former led the attack on the right, losing 250 of all ranks out of 758 engaged; and at Sobraon, after three desperate assaults, they again, in company with the 1st Europeans, stormed the Sikh entrenchments, losing 171 men out of the 513 which completed their muster on that morning; Colonel Taylor in command, than whom there was no better officer killed that day, fell in the third charge. When the brief campaign was over, they could scarcely turn out 350 men.

The 1st European Light Infantry, like the 29th, joined the army too late for Moodkee, after marching about 190 miles in 8 days, but were in the thick of the fight at Ferozeshah, losing 51 men killed and 164 wounded, 215 in all, out of a strength of about 650 in the field. At Sobraon they mustered not much more than 400 in the field, of whom they lost 197 killed and wounded. Brigadier McLaran, who commanded the brigade on both occasions, fell mortally wounded at their head, at Sobraon; an officer greatly beloved and respected by all who served under him. In recognition of its conspicuous gallantry and distinguished services, the regiment was granted, on the recommendation of the Commander-in-Chief, the honourable title of "1st Bengal Fusiliers," which, again, has given place to their present name, "The Royal Munster Fusiliers." So severe had been the duty, so nobly did they perform it, that, on the 11th of February, the day after Sobraon, this regiment was only able to muster 6 officers and 230 men fit for duty, a casualty roll rarely paralleled by any regiment in a successful campaign.

H.M.'s 31st and 50th Regiments served in Sir Harry Smith's Division, and were present at Moodkee, Ferozeshah, Aliwal, and Sobraon. At the first of these battles, where the brunt of the fighting fell on Smith's Division, the 31st lost 9 officers and 155 men killed or wounded out of 30 officers and 844 men taken into action. At Ferozeshah, in the two days, there fell 8 officers and 151 men more. At Budhowal 21 men more were killed or wounded, and 19 men taken prisoners by the Sikhs; these, however, were released after Sobraon. At Aliwal it lost 16 men, and at Sobraon 6 officers and 137 men, making a loss in the campaign of 503 out of a total strength of not more than 900. The 50th, a regiment of Peninsular fame, maintained its noble record. At Moodkee there fell 6 officers and 129 men; at Ferozeshah 6 officers, 113 rank and file, out of a strength of about 700 men. Although before Aliwal they were joined by a draft of 5 young officers and 90 men, they could not muster more than 494 men for that battle, where they lost 10 officers and 68 men killed and wounded; while at Sobraon there fell 197 of all ranks, including 12 officers. Colonel Ryan, who commanded the regiment with great ability throughout the campaign, fell dangerously wounded at Sobraon, dying of his wound not long after. Every one of the senior officers was disabled early in the fight, the command of the regiment devolving upon a subaltern, Lieutenant Wiley, and nearly half the men fell. To add to the mournful roll, a terrible calamity overtook this same regiment shortly after its return from the campaign, the barracks occupied by them at Ludhiana being blown down in a violent storm on the night of May 20, 1846, when 80 men, women, and children were killed, and 135 seriously wounded. During the campaign almost every officer was wounded, the total loss amounting to 565 killed and wounded of all ranks.

The 80th Regiment were engaged at Moodkee, Ferozeshah, and Sobraon. At the first action they lost 5 men killed, 1 officer and 19 men wounded; at Ferozeshah, 4 officers 32 men killed, 4 officers 73 men wounded, besides 7 privates returned "missing," who were never seen again, and were undoubtedly killed; in all 127 casualties. A detachment, 1 officer and 23 men, on the march up to join the army, took part in the Battle of Aliwal, losing 6 men killed, and 1 wounded. At Sobraon they lost 13 men killed, 4 officers 74 men wounded; during the whole campaign, 250 casualties of all ranks.

The 62nd lost heavily at Ferozeshah, 18 officers and 281 men falling in their assault upon the Sikh batteries; and at Sobraon they lost 1 officer killed, 1 officer 45 men wounded; total loss, 346. Records do not show what strength the regiment took into action, but it is probable that the number at Ferozeshah did not exceed 800 men.

The 53rd Foot did not appear on the field of battle until after Ferozeshah. They were attached to Sir Harry Smith's force, and took part in the relief of Ludhiana. At Budhowal they formed the rear-guard, and covered the movement on Ludhiana, losing 36 men killed, and 12 wounded. At Aliwal the regiment appears to have gone into action 699 strong; their small loss, 6 men killed and 8 wounded, being due to the admirable manner in which the regiment advanced upon the Sikh batteries, running forward at the double for about 100 yards, then lying down and advancing again, by which manœuvre the Sikh gunners were prevented from getting the range, and the men advanced both rapidly and steadily, without getting exhausted. At Sobraon, the loss was 1 officer and 6 men killed, 8 officers 112 men wounded; total, 189, out of a strength of about 700.

H.M.'s 10th Foot took part in the crowning victory of

Sobraon, where the extreme steadiness of its advance, under that strict disciplinarian, Colonel Franks, attracted universal notice and admiration. Their loss amounted to 10 officers 27 men killed, 2 officers 101 men wounded.

Of the native troops engaged, few remain now on the rolls of the Indian army, almost all having been swept away in the vortex of the great Mutiny of 1857; but their services in this campaign cannot be disregarded or unrecognised. It is true that neither at Moodkee nor at Ferozeshah were they equal to the occasion, but this was undoubtedly owing to the frightful exhaustion of the sepoys, who had not the same stamina and physical endurance as the British soldier. Both at Aliwal and Sobraon they fought well, and bore their fair share of the loss, affording valuable support to their European comrades. Records do not give the various losses by regiments, but simply abstracts of the loss sustained by divisions, including Europeans and natives, in one total. What the native regiments suffered can only be approximately calculated by deducting the losses of the European regiments as taken from their records.*

Sir Harry Smith spoke in warm terms of the conduct of the native troops, both cavalry and infantry, at Aliwal, and both Governor-General and Commander-in-Chief were able to applaud their conduct at Sobraon. The Goorkhas, a regiment of which, the Sirmoor battalion, is now represented by the 2nd Prince of Wales's Own Goorkhas, distinguished themselves particularly in the two last engagements, and were specially mentioned by Sir Hugh Gough at Sobraon. They were not present at Moodkee or Ferozeshah. Of the other native infantry regiments the only survivors now existing in the Indian army are the 4th Bengal Infantry

* Comparative losses at Sobraon—

				Total.
1st Infantry Division	350 Europeans	... 280 Natives	...	630
2nd " "	368 "	... 535 "	...	903
3rd " "	360 "	... 366 "	...	726

(formerly 33rd), the 5th (formerly 42nd), the 6th (formerly 43rd), the 7th (formerly 47th), the 8th (formerly 59th), and the 9th (formerly 63rd) Native Infantry.

The campaign of the Sutlej throws us back in touch with the soldiers of the Peninsula and Waterloo, many of whom were here in high command. Besides Sir Henry Hardinge and Sir Hugh Gough, both of whom gained high distinction under Wellington, Sir Harry Smith, Sir Robert Sale, Sir John McCaskill, Sir Robert Dick, Sir Joseph Thackwell, Brigadier Cureton, and Brigadier Taylor, of H.M.'s 29th, all served in the Peninsula. Of these, McCaskill, Sale, Dick, and Taylor fell gloriously for Queen and country, after long lives spent in honourable service. Amongst the most distinguished officers whose loss was to be deplored was Major Broadfoot, chief political officer to the Governor-General. General Gilbert, whose services were highly appreciated by the Commander-in-Chief, and who led his division with such intrepidity and ability, was a grand old soldier of the Indian army. He was passionately fond of riding and horses, and a distinguished performer on the pig-skin, both on the turf and in the pigsticking field. So devoted was he to this sport that during the period when the army was lying encamped in front of Sobraon, he, with a few congenial spirits, used to hunt the jungles for wild boar, riding close up to the Sikh outposts in pursuit of his game, while they never offered to molest or interfere with him. He subsequently served with equal distinction and credit, as will hereafter be related, in the second Sikh War, and it was to him that eventually the Sikh army, in 1849, surrendered and laid down their arms.

In considering the course of the whole campaign, certain points deserve special attention. Emphasis has already been laid strongly on the nature of the odds against which it was conducted. The quality of the Sikh troops was such that they showed themselves behind entrenchments hardly, if at all, inferior to average European soldiery. Insubordinate as they had been politically, their discipline and steadiness on the field were admirable. Their muskets were the same as ours, their artillery usually superior, and their fire directed with precision. Such a foe could not be beaten without heavy losses on our part. It would even seem that if they had shown the same capacity for attack as for defence, if Tej Singh had known what to do with his fresh army at Ferozeshah, the frontier force with the Governor-General and the Commander-in-Chief might have been crushed on December 22nd. It is evident that if the nature of the struggle before us had been realised, if it had not been credited that there was a real chance of averting the war altogether, and that the Sikh troops were too insubordinate to be dangerous, so small a force ought never to have been left to bear unsupported the brunt of such a contest.

But the hope that war might be avoided, coupled with the consciousness that preparations on at all a large scale, and especially any palpable increase of the frontier force, would certainly precipitate a conflict, counted for more than the urgent representations of the military authorities. When the great Sikh host crossed the Sutlej, it became absolutely necessary to make an instant advance, with all available troops, to save Ferozepore and Bussean. To wait for troops from Meerut would have meant the loss of those important places. Consequently, when the available troops got to Ferozeshah, there were not enough of them, in the Governor-General's opinion, to attack the entrenchments until Littler should arrive. Rightly or wrongly, the attack was in consequence deferred till late in the day; and further comment on the highly critical position which resulted would be superfluous, after what has been said.

Under such conditions, to have literally crumpled up the army of the Khalsa within two months of the declaration of war was no small achievement. But if the conduct of the British troops, from highest to lowest, deserves all praise, no little praise also is due to our valiant and stubborn foe. The admiration they inspired in the heart of one who knew how to appreciate their qualities may well be expressed in Sir Hugh Gough's own words, referring to the slaughter of the Sikh army at Sobraon. "Policy," he wrote, "prevented my publicly recording my sentiments of the splendid gallantry of a fallen foe, and I declare, were it not from a conviction that my country's good required the sacrifice, I could have wept to have witnessed the fearful slaughter of so devoted a body." It was indeed fortunate for us that the leaders were not worthy of the men, that Tej Singh was faint-hearted, and Lall Singh incompetent and only half trusted; that, while the chiefs were not unskilful in disposing their troops behind entrenchments, none of them had the training or the skill in manœuvring large bodies of men which would have enabled them to reap the full benefit of a temporary advantage. That is no doubt the reason why the Sikhs, in face of the British troops, invariably adopted the defensive attitude, retiring under Tej Singh before Ferozeshah, and failing to make a real attack even at Budhowal, where the consequences might well have been very serious.

But when all is said, the whole campaign shows very conclusively one fact, which always appears to be a source of astonishment to the British public—that if we have to do battle with an enemy whose army is highly disciplined, well armed, and game to fight till it can fight no longer, that army cannot be beaten without correspondingly heavy losses, and demands treatment considerably more respectful than Clive found it necessary to show for the mercenary troops of Surajah Dowlah or Chunda Sahib. Also, that it is a mistake to take for granted that "Native" opponents must be lacking in those high qualities.

BOOK IV.

BETWEEN THE SIKH WARS

BOOK IV.

FROM THE TREATY OF LAHORE TO SHERE SINGH'S REVOLT: MARCH, 1845–SEPT., 1848

CHAPTER I.

THE LAHORE TREATY: MARCH–DEC., 1846

Submission of the Durbar—Policy of annexation—Of a subsidiary alliance—Of the buffer-state—Conditions of a treaty—System of government—Triumphal march—Henry Lawrence and his problem—Early disturbances—Gholab Singh—Imam-ud-Din—Fall of Lall Singh—Request for a continued protectorate.

THERE was no question as to the completely decisive character of the great victory of Sobraon. The Sikh army was shattered, and scattered beyond possibility of an effective rally; the way to Lahore lay open to the victors. The battle was fought and won on February 10th; on the 13th the British troops were encamped in the Punjab at Kussoor; on the 20th they were at Lahore.

The war, as has been observed, was due in the first place to the enthusiastic belief in itself and its imperial destinies of the Khalsa soldiery. The Durbar—that is to say, the Rani and her immediate following—had done all in their power to foster this spirit, calculating that by means of the war they would, in the first instance, be released from the terrorising presence of the uncontrollable troops; and that secondly they could turn either victory or disaster to their own advantage. Among the Sirdars, however, who loved neither the Rani, nor the soldiery, nor the English, the majority had little hope of success at any time. They acquiesced in the war when they found that opposition to it was useless; many of them took their share of the fighting with magnificent valour; some professed enthusiasm, and were content with the profession; a few, like the astute Gholab Singh, kept out of danger, and took measures to secure friendly treatment for themselves when the British should enter the country as conquerors.

If the chiefs who had not gone to the front were doubtful of the results before the war actually commenced, their doubts were dispelled by the outcome of the first fierce struggles. The dogged faith that the tables might yet be turned on the British prevailed at the front; but at Lahore itself, the defeat of the Khalsa was now expected with confidence. The Rani and the disaffected chiefs, who recognised the Rajah of Jammu as the shrewdest among them, were merely awaiting the final overthrow to get the best terms available for themselves from the conquerors; and the British had hardly crossed the Sutlej when the emissaries of the Durbar were hurrying to meet them. On the 15th they reached Lord Hardinge's camp; on the 18th the boy Maharajah presented himself in person to the Governor-General, and accompanied him to Lahore, where the future arrangements were to be decided.

There were three main lines on which it might be possible to effect a settlement.

First, there was the obvious course of immediate annexation. But the policy of annexation was one to which the Company and the Governor-General himself were strongly averse. Moreover, in the present case, it would have been extremely difficult, if not impossible, to carry out. The Sikh army itself had indeed been thoroughly beaten in the field; but there were some 25,000 of them at Lahore and Amritsir; there were 8000 at Peshawur; and the complete subjugation of the Punjab would have involved a protracted war of sieges. For such operations the forces at the disposal of the Commander-in-Chief were quite inadequate. As we have seen, the illusory hope of averting a collision altogether had prevented Sir H. Hardinge* from bringing up to the frontier such a mass of troops as the occasion demanded; and Sir Hugh Gough's army at Lahore now numbered less than 20,000 of all arms, of whom only 3500 were Europeans. For the sieges, he would have required 70 or 80 siege-guns, with 1000 rounds for each; he had only thirty guns with 300 rounds for each. Even with reinforcements from Scinde, where Sir Charles Napier had 16,000 men and 60 guns, it is evident that the army at disposal would have been insufficient to undertake the real subjugation of the country.

The second method was one which had been very extensively employed in the past—that of a "subsidiary alliance." The meaning of this term has been explained in a previous chapter. The plan was to maintain the existing native Government with troops levied by the Company, but paid for by the allied State. When the British were surrounded by hostile or potentially hostile Powers, the military advantages of this method had been very marked; but by producing an ambiguous authority it was by no means conducive to good government within the allied State itself, and the British Government in India had steadily declared against such a policy in the Punjab.

There remained then the third policy: of attempting to establish a strong and friendly Government which should be independent of British support, and yet should not be a menace to the British Power in India; which should in fact stand to the British in much the same relation as the Lahore state had done when ruled by Ranjit Singh.

* Sir Henry Hardinge and Sir Hugh Gough were both rewarded at this time with peerages for their services. This intelligence, however, did not arrive till later.

Lord Hardinge then resolved to make the attempt at establishing in the Punjab a government strong enough to take care of itself, but with its military resources sufficiently curtailed to prevent it from being a standing source of possible danger. To this end certain preliminary conditions were necessary. The rehabilitation of the Khalsa army must be precluded; the British would have to be indemnified for the war; and, further, a substantial penalty must be exacted. Accordingly, the Jalandhar Doab was annexed to the British dominion (*i.e.* the south-eastern tract of the Punjab, lying between the rivers Beas and Sutlej); and a crore and a half of rupees, equivalent to one and a half millions sterling, was demanded. But only half a million was forthcoming from the exhausted Lahore treasury, so the cession of Kashmir was accepted in lieu of the other million. Then Gholab Singh of Jammu obtained his desire. As a reward for his consistently friendly attitude, he was confirmed in the independent sovereignty of Jammu, to which the newly ceded Kashmir was added in exchange for a crore of rupees—a transaction to which we shall presently revert.

From what may be termed the confiscatory provisions of the treaty proposed by Lord Hardinge, we turn to the arrangements made for the better government of the Lahore State, now curtailed to the Punjab proper and the trans-Indus provinces of Peshawur and the "Derajat."

The first condition of regular government was the permanent reduction of the Sikh army to manageable dimensions. To this end, the numbers were limited to 20,000 infantry and 12,000 cavalry; while the whole of the artillery which had been used against the British was required to be delivered up to the victors.

Next, the conduct of the administration was placed in the hands of a Council of Regency, comprising a few of the leading Sirdars, at whose head was Lall Singh, the Rani's favourite. A British Agent was appointed to exercise effective control over this Council, and to act as the mouthpiece of the British Government; this part being entrusted to Major Henry Lawrence.

At the direct request of the Sikh chiefs, who declared their total inability to control the Khalsa unsupported, it was agreed that the British troops should remain in occupation of Lahore until the end of the year; this limit of time being expressly insisted on by Lord Hardinge.

Such were the terms of the Treaty of Lahore, concluded on March 11th, 1846; the signatories being, besides the Maharajah, Lall Singh, Tej Singh, the Sirdar Ram Singh, and the astute finance minister Dina Nath. The Governor-General's parting words to the Council contained a note of warning: "Success or failure is in your own hands; my co-operation shall not be wanting; but if you neglect this opportunity, no aid on the part of the British Government can save the State."

When the Sikhs had thrown down their challenge to the British, they had produced a widespread effect among the peoples of India. Happily they had fought us single-handed, since the one army which might have lent them efficient help—that of Gwalior—had already brought about its own premature destruction. But every State, more especially every Hindu State, disaffected towards British rule, had looked to the Sikh rising with the hope that at last a Hindu army had appeared which might drive back the English; that the chances of Hindu supremacy were reviving. The wildest rumours prevailed as to the results of the campaign itself, due in part to the severe straits in which the British found themselves during the earlier stages of the war. It was not to be believed that the contest could have been brought to a decisive conclusion within a couple of months of its commencement; the British reports of success being thus discredited, it was questioned whether the Sikhs had been defeated at all. These questionings Lord Hardinge resolved to set at rest conclusively; and he made his march down from Lahore to Calcutta a visible and tangible proof of a decisive triumph, displaying at every station and every city on the way 250 guns, the spoils of the routed armies. The doubters required no further conviction.

The task which Henry Lawrence found before him at Lahore was no easy one. The Governor-General had impressed on him his own views on the difficulties with great clearness, while placing entire confidence in the judgment, ability, and sympathetic tact of the Agent between whom and himself there was a very warm friendship. The Rani was a born intriguer, and was certain to play for her own hand. The Council of Regency was small; the Sirdars excluded from it were sure to be jealous. The chiefs were likely to be perpetually suspicious of the intentions of the British; they must be induced to understand that we had no desire to interfere with internal administration, still less to annex, or to adopt the subsidiary system. Lastly, the army could not but remain an object of intrigue and a source of suspicion: an army which was notably brave; which had not fully lost the belief that it was a match for the British, and owed its own defeat to treachery; which had already tasted the sweets of political predominance, and learned to make its would-be chiefs pay for their support; which was loyal to itself and to "Govind," but to no living ruler.

The Governor-General therefore had written to Lawrence in these terms:—

> "The Sikh chiefs, excluded from power, will probably intrigue against the present Government, and may attempt to excite the soldiery against those who were parties to the Treaty of Peace. . . . It will be necessary at all times to be in a state of military vigilance. . . . You will [do] everything in your power to ensure the success of this trial of re-establishing a Sikh Government, which may eventually carry on its functions without British aid or British interference. Whilst we do not desire the annexation of the Punjab . . . the Government is determined not to lend itself to any subsidiary system, and as soon as its troops are withdrawn will decline to interfere in the internal affairs of the Sikh State."

The nature of the difficulties was promptly illustrated by a "Cow Row," when a European sentry in Lahore, being pressed upon by some cattle, slashed at them with his sword; whereupon the Hindu population became violently excited, and the British officers were mobbed. By dint of combined firmness and good humour the disturbance was quickly allayed; but the affair served as an example of the miscellaneous causes of friction which the casual misconduct of an unthinking soldier might set in motion. Nor was it long before the political disorganisation was illustrated by the open refusal of the Governor of Kangra to recognise the new regime. The fort of Kangra was strong, the Governor's words were bold, and it was very obvious that he was receiving encouragement from high quarters. Discretion, however, proved to be the better part of valour, when Lawrence's troops arrived before the fort; and no sooner were the siege-guns in position than the garrison surrendered.

These were small affairs, though symptomatic; but they were followed by a more serious disturbance.

A good deal has already been written about Gholab Singh, of Jammu, who had been converted by the recent treaty into the independent sovereign of Kashmir and Jammu. Comments on this transaction had been by no means uniformly favourable. There was no doubt whatever that Gholab Singh was a very able man, as his brother Dhian Singh had been likewise. It is no less clear that he was a cold-blooded, self-seeking ruler; a man who would cheerfully pocket a peasant's last farthing, and contrive the "removal" of an enemy without any sort of compunction; a man whose fidelity could be counted upon precisely so long as he considered it in his interest to be faithful. These evil qualities, however, were shared by the majority of native chiefs, and, in his case, they were tempered—as in most cases they were not—by a sagacity which restrained him from a wanton indulgence in them. That is to say, he was quite prepared to be merciful, even beneficent, if he thought his interest lay that way; and his fidelity to the British could be relied on, because he had wit enough to know that his interest *must* lie that way. He might play at disloyalty if hard pressed, but no man in the Punjab was so little likely as he to become actively disloyal. In short, it might be said of him that his policy would almost certainly be sagacious; of others, that their policy would be cunning. Therefore he could be depended upon to aim at some comparative decency of government, and to use his influence—covertly, even if he was professedly acting against them—on behalf of the British; which is more than could be said for the Sikh leaders.

Such was the man to whom Kashmir had been sold; and it must also be remembered that the province itself was not naturally a part of the Lahore State, but had been conquered by the Khalsa. When, however, Gholab Singh desired to take possession of his kingdom, the governor, Sheikh Imam-ud-Din, refused to give it up. Gholab Singh could not himself drive the recalcitrant Sheikh out by force of arms, and Henry Lawrence called upon the Lahore Durbar to carry out their Treaty engagement, and deliver over the province of Kashmir to its new owner.

And then was seen the very remarkable spectacle of the British Agent marching at the head of Sikh troops to wrest Sikh territory from Imam-ud-Din, in order to hand it over to the last of those Rajput brothers, who had always inspired the Sikhs themselves with intense jealousy. Supported by British troops from Jalandhar, Lawrence, in October, led 10,000 Sikhs, unwilling yet obedient, into Kashmir, under the command of Sirdar Shere Singh, compelled the submission of Imam-ud-Din without striking a single blow, and established Gholab Singh in his dominion. Nothing could have shown more conclusively the immense personal influence and prestige acquired by Lawrence than the way in which this paradoxical task was carried out.

The event proved at the same time that the Lahore Durbar was a hotbed of intrigue, for the deserted and disgusted Sheikh handed over to the British Agent documents signed by the Vizier, Lall Singh, which proved conclusively that he had countenanced and encouraged the rebellion. Armed with these documents, Lawrence required that Lall Singh should be brought to trial. In the presence of all the chief Sirdars the enquiry was held before a Commission of five British officers; Lall Singh's guilt was proved beyond question; the Sirdars acquiesced without hesitation in the verdict; and the Vizier was deposed from his office, and removed from public life and from the Punjab without any sort of opposition. The Viziership was placed in commission, which was composed of Tej Singh, Shere Singh, Dewan Dina Nath, and Fakir Nur-ud-Din. The truth was that Lall Singh had been the Rani's favourite, and owed his position to that and nothing else; consequently his colleagues had no sort of objection to his disappearance.

But the time was now at hand when, according to the Treaty stipulations, the British troops were to be withdrawn, and the Punjab Government was to take care of itself; whereas the Punjab Government was in no wise ready to take care of itself, being, indeed, aware that the immediate effect would be sheer anarchy. The ambitious Rani made great efforts to win over the Sirdars to her own point of view, which was that she should herself be made regent, while the chiefs pledged themselves to obey her. The Dewan Dina Nath, however, was alone in supporting her; and Shere Singh communicated to Lawrence, as his own desire and that of the leading Sirdars, the wish that the British should virtually constitute themselves guardians of the State until the young Maharajah came of age.

A Durbar was then held to make a definite settlement, the chiefs being offered their choice of two alternatives. Either they must be left entirely alone to manage their own affairs, without British interference, or, with the reluctant assent of Lord Hardinge, the entire civil and military administration of the Punjab must be placed absolutely under British control, though conducted through the Durbar, during the Maharajah's minority, on the termination of which the British would withdraw entirely.

CHAPTER II.

THE RULE OF HENRY LAWRENCE: 1847

Terms of the new arrangement—Lord Hardinge's military arrangements—Lawrence's men and methods—Bunnoo and Herbert Edwardes—Influence of British officers—The Rani's plots—State of the Punjab—Lord Dalhousie becomes Governor-General—Sir F. Currie takes Lawrence's place—Multan.

THE Sikh chiefs decided unanimously in favour of the British Protectorate. Every one of the fifty-two Sirdars who were accounted important enough to express an opinion voted in its support.

The formal arrangements of the "Treaty of Bhyrowal," * in which the new settlement was embodied, were as follows:—

There was to be a Council of Regency, consisting of eight members. Five of these are already known to the reader, namely, Tej Singh, Shere Singh (who was the Maharajah's brother-in-law), Runjoor Singh, the Dewan Dina Nath, and Fakir Nur-ud-Din. The other three—Utter Singh, Shumser Singh, and Bhaee Nidhan Singh—were all men of note.

The Council was to act "under the control and guidance of the British Resident," Lieutenant-Colonel Henry Lawrence. "The power of the Resident extends over every department, and to any extent."

* The earlier treaty was signed and ratified at Lahore. This treaty was signed at Lahore, but ratified by the Governor-General at Bhyrowal. In the "Life of Sir Herbert Edwardes," the *earlier* treaty is, by an apparent misapprehension, referred to as the "Treaty of Bhyrowal."

A fixed sum—twenty-two lakhs of rupees—was to be paid annually during the protectorate.

"A military force may be placed in such forts and posts, and of such strength, within the Lahore territory, as the Governor-General may determine. These terms give the British Resident unlimited authority in all matters of internal administration and external relation during the Maharajah's minority, which would terminate on the 4th September, 1854."

Alive to the military necessities of the new Resident's position, Lord Hardinge—having had personal experience of the dangers involved by an insufficient frontier force—enlarged the armies of the north-west, at and beyond Meerut, to 50,000 men, with 60 guns. Three brigades, organised as movable columns ready to take the field at once, were placed at Lahore, Jalandhar, and Ferozepore. It was the Governor-General's belief, however, that there would be no more fighting for several years; recent expenditure had been very heavy; and so, while the troops of the Company's army were redistributed, so as to increase the forces immediately available in the north-west, a very large reduction was made in the general military establishment, the sepoy army being cut down by the amount of 50,000 men. Since this was precisely the force whose services would be most required in case of troubles arising during the hot months of the year, it did unfortunately happen that the Commander-in-Chief's plan of operations in 1848 had to be adapted to the conditions produced by this reduction. At the same time, the expectation of peace on which Lord Hardinge acted had strong justification, since there was every appearance that Lawrence's administration of the Punjab was rapidly removing the danger of disaffection. Nevertheless, the event showed that now, as before the Sutlej campaign, Lord Hardinge acted on a too sanguine forecast.

Thoroughly trusted by the Governor-General, and

endowed with unlimited powers by the Bhyrowal Treaty, Henry Lawrence was now virtually director in the Punjab; with subordinates who were the men of his own choice, and to whom he in turn allowed a freedom of action and a weight of personal responsibility which were exactly suited to the conditions under which the work had to be done, but were practicable only where the subordinates were picked men, and in thorough sympathy with their chief. Among these were his brothers John and Major George Lawrence, M'Gregor and Abbott; Nicholson, Herbert Edwardes, Lake, John Beecher, Harry Lumsden, Reynell Taylor, Pollock, and Hodson; Cocks, Browning, Coxe, and Melville; men who rendered brilliant service, not only in the Punjab, but elsewhere. Many of these names are recorded on the undying roll of heroes; some are household words even to this day, though fifty years have passed.

Lawrence's men were distributed over the districts of the Punjab, with their guiding principle briefly summed up in the words, "Settle the country, make the people happy, and take care there are no rows." How the work was done, one of them, Herbert Edwardes, told the English public in his book, "A Year on the Punjab Frontier," where he detailed his own experiences. The pacification of Bunnoo is worth a brief reference here, because Edwardes's work there was typical, not exceptional, illustrating the methods and practice of Henry Lawrence's school.

Bunnoo is a district beyond the Indus, lying between the province of Peshawur on the north, and the provinces known collectively as the Derajat southwards. The inhabitants were an exceedingly mixed race, whose relations to the Sikhs were simple. Every village in the country was virtually a fort, and of them there were from four to five hundred. The Sikhs, therefore, had made no attempt to occupy, much less to govern, the country, but had periodically collected the tribute, or part of the tribute, considered due by sending an army, which raided the country and brought back what it could. The tribute was now considerably in arrear, and Edwardes went with a Sikh contingent to collect it. The Sikh soldiery had been in the habit of plundering right and left; but their British commander, after a hard struggle, brought them into order and discipline, amazed the Bunnoochees by marching through the country without laying it waste, and for the first time brought the troops and the population into something like friendly intercourse. The arrival of the hot weather made it necessary to retire before much had been accomplished, but later in the year Edwardes returned. Matters, of course, did not work with perfect smoothness—Edwardes, for instance, had to shoot a would-be assassin in his own tent—but the inhabitants were so impressed with the novel idea of a Government which set the example of orderly conduct, and of a Governor who worked, not by intriguing amongst the chiefs, but by proving in free discussion in which direction the general interest obviously lay, that the tribute was paid; and, more remarkable still, the fort-villages were dismantled, and one Government fort, practically impregnable, was established.

Such methods as these, accompanied as they were by a general lightening of the revenue burdens, could not fail to have an excellent effect on the popular mind, more especially in the subordinate provinces. The influence acquired by the British officers over the rude native tribes was immense, and the personal devotion to them was in some cases more than remarkable. Abbott, in the Hazara district, was the object of enthusiastic adoration; Nicholson, in later days, found it difficult to keep the tribesmen from deifying him. In judging, however, of the problem before the British Resident, it must not be forgotten (as it too often is in parallel cases) that immense portions of the Sikh dominion were not Sikh, properly speaking, but in subjection to the Sikhs; and the inhabitants might often be fairly described as victims of the Sikhs, and quite ready in turn to make victims of their rulers if opportunity offered. It by no means followed, therefore, that the introduction of good government, or the approbation of tribesmen, was agreeable to the dominant race, since it meant a diminution of their opportunities for plunder. Undoubtedly the capacity for command displayed by the "Feringhis" did greatly increase their personal prestige, even among the Sikhs themselves. But it did not remove, it only held in check, the two great factors which told against a peaceful settlement—the intrigues of the Rani and the temper of the Khalsa.

It was manifest from the beginning that the Rani would intrigue to recover her position. For that she had first sought the support of the soldiery; for that, when the soldiery declared themselves her masters, she had fomented their resolve to attack the British; for that she had done her best to get the British withdrawn in December; whereas now, while the British Resident was at Lahore, it was perfectly certain that she could take no ostensible part in public affairs. A conspiracy known as the Preyma plot was discovered. The primary aims were the assassination of Tej Singh, for whom the Rani had a violent hatred, and of the Resident; schemes for the corruption of the sepoy troops formed a part of it; and a correspondence between the Rani and Mulraj, the Governor of Multan, of which the full significance did not become apparent till later, was discovered in connection with it. The association of the Rani with the plot was indisputable. To have pressed the matter in such a way as to necessitate the publication of details would have been impolitic; but the facts being laid before the Council, it was agreed without question that the young Maharajah must be separated from his mother. The Rani was removed to Sheikapore, some twenty miles from the capital—Lawrence would have preferred her removal from the Punjab—and a proclamation was issued declaring that her presence at Lahore had prevented the proper education of her son, while it rendered the palace a focus of intrigue and treason.

It was not, however, until May of the following year, when she was proved to be deeply implicated in a plot for seducing the sepoys at Lahore, that the Rani's intrigues were finally ended by her removal to Ferozepore, and from thence to the home of dethroned monarchs at Benares.

The removal to Sheikapore took place in August, 1847; and in September it was found that Henry Lawrence's health had suffered so severely that he must leave for England at the close of the year. Much had been done during the months in which he was Resident, and it is matter of mere speculation whether his continued presence at Lahore, and the exercise of his unique influence, might have prevented the outbreak of the following year. However that may be, he left the Punjab believing that there was a good prospect of a healthy settlement; but he certainly did not suppose that there was no cause for anxiety. His own expectations had indeed been exceeded; the Khalsa had shown no signs of restlessness or insubordination; the Sirdars appeared loyal; the population generally was becoming acquainted with the benefits of orderly government. Still, to use his own words, "the people had not lost their spirit; and so fickle were they, so easily led by their party, so filled with pride of race and of their old triumphs, that it would be the extreme of infatuation to believe in their satisfaction with their present state, or in their not chafing at our victory and their own loss of power." And again, "no great conquest has ever been followed by complete peace and security, or by the universal goodwill of the people who have been beaten in the field." And just before he left India, "The Sikhs have come to terms, and have settled down because they have been well treated by us, and protected from their own army and chiefs; because scarcely a single jagheer has been resumed, and because the rights and even the prejudices of all classes have been respected." It is obvious, from this sentence, that "their own army and chiefs," could not be expected to view British administration in quite the same favourable light as the people.

During a brief interval, John Lawrence acted for his brother until the arrival of the new Resident, Sir Frederick Currie. On January 18th, 1848, Henry Lawrence sailed from India with the retiring Governor-General. The next day arrived the new Governor-General, Lord Dalhousie. It is impossible not to recognise that the simultaneous withdrawal of the Governor-General, and of the most experienced officer in the Punjab, was singularly unfortunate at so early a stage of the settlement. The result was that the head of the State was now a man of undoubted ability, but one who had as yet no first-hand knowledge of the peoples over whom he was to rule, or of the men through whom he was to rule them. At Lahore, a place where an experiment was being tried under conditions for which there was no precedent, where the chief and his subordinates had worked together with a success dependent on the strongest personal sympathy and mutual reliance, a new chief took over the control; who had been trained in the regulation school of Bengal officialdom, had no special knowledge of the Punjab, no special intimacy with the officers there, and no special personal touch with the natives. Whatever Sir F. Currie's abilities had been, it was literally impossible for him to carry on the administration on that principle of unlimited personal responsibility which had been the essence of Lawrence's method, and the grand factor in its success.

When Lord Dalhousie took up the Governor-Generalship of India, and Sir F. Currie became British Resident at Lahore, one of the two main disturbing factors had been only partially removed from the Punjab by the ejection of the Maharajah's mother from Lahore. The other remained. The whole population indeed needed watching. The hill-men of the north, or the trans-Indus Pathans, might give trouble. But the great danger lay in the Khalsa, with its traditions of dominion, its corporate loyalty, its religious sentiment, and its capacity for independent action and consorted insubordination. That danger had by no means been removed by the unexpected display of obedience and discipline during 1846 and 1847.

Yet if the Khalsa had been the only source of fear, it may be that the prophets of tranquillity would have been justified. For, contrary to all expectation, it was not in the Sikh army or the Sikh community, or even on account of Sikh interests, that the disturbance arose which led to the final Sikh war; but from a comparatively insignificant trouble on an outlying Mohammedan frontier.

CHAPTER III.

THE OUTBREAK AT MULTAN: MARCH–MAY, 1848

Apparent tranquillity—Dewan Mulraj—Attack on British officers at Multan—Revolt of Mulraj—The Derajat and Multan district—Action of Herbert Edwardes—Van Cortlandt and Foujdar Khan—Lord Gough's objections to a force for Multan—Endorsed by Lord Dalhousie—Position of Edwardes—Movements of Mulraj—Sir F. Currie's plan of operations—The Derajat operations—Capture of Dera Ghazi Khan—Advance of Bhawal Khan.

At this period, in the early months of 1848, when the Multan disturbance was about to break out, there appeared to be tranquillity everywhere. The districts were all quiet, and especially the great Sikh district of the Manjha, in which lay both Lahore and Amritsir, and which had been wisely controlled and influenced by a fine old Sirdar, Lehna Singh, of Majeetea. Such anxiety as there was seemed to be respecting the conduct of two men of note in the north, *i.e.* in the Hazara and Peshawur direction; one that noted Afghan intriguer Sultan Mohammed, the other Shere Singh's father, the Sirdar Chutter Singh, whose daughter was to marry the Maharajah Dhulip Singh. Both of these men were being carefully watched. The British representatives in that neighbourhood were Major George Lawrence, at Peshawur, and Major James Abbott, in Hazara. South of Peshawur, Lieutenant Edwardes, having settled Bunnoo, as we have seen, was now engaged in similar work in the still more southerly Derajat district, stretching from Dera Ishmael Khan to Dera Ghazi Khan, a town on the banks of the Indus, just opposite Multan, the Indus and the Chenab flowing between.

Multan itself, lying east of the Chenab, below its junction with the Ravi, and above its junction with the Sutlej, was a place of considerable importance, with a great reputation for strength. An outpost of the Afghan monarchy, it had long defied Ranjit Singh, and had been added to his dominions only after a stubborn contest. The present Governor was the Dewan Mulraj, the son of a very distinguished father, Sawan Mull. Mulraj, however, was no great ruler; he had, in fact, declared himself anxious to retire into private life, since the difficulty of raising the revenue demanded by Lahore was more than he was capable of coping with. It must be understood that this offer of resignation was purely voluntary, and was only accepted on his own urgent representations.

Finally, however, after much discussion and intrigue, he was informed that his resignation would be accepted, and he was requested to prepare the accounts of the last years of his office for the inspection of his successor. To this office, the Sirdar Khan Singh was appointed, in co-operation with two English officers, Mr. Vans Agnew, of the Civil Service, and Lieutenant Anderson; both men who were making a reputation for winning the confidence and friendship of the natives.

These officers received full instructions for their guidance on March 31st, and moving from Lahore partly by road and partly by river, arrived at Multan by degrees, from the 13th to the 17th April; having with them, as escort, about 1400 Sikh soldiers, a Goorkha regiment, some 700 cavalry, and 6 guns. On the 18th, they encamped at the Eedgah, about half a mile from the fort. Next morning, the British officers and Khan Singh, with some of their escort, accompanied Mulraj into the fort, went over it, and after discussing the arrangements to be made, were on their way back to the Eedgah; when one of Mulraj's soldiers, at the bridge over the ditch of the fort, struck and then wounded Vans Agnew—the signal, evidently, for an attack on the party. Mulraj rode off to his own residence, while his sowars attacked Anderson; but the Goorkhas rescued Anderson, and Khan Singh rescued Agnew, putting him on his own elephant. Both officers were brought into their encampment, where their wounds were dressed.

Agnew immediately wrote and despatched a report of what had occurred to the Resident at Lahore, and also sent off a messenger with a note asking for aid, addressed to either General Van Cortlandt (an officer of the Sikh army), or Lieutenant Edwardes, in the Derajat.

The results of these communications will be dealt with presently. Meanwhile, at Multan itself, Mulraj sent his emissaries over to the Eedgah to inform Agnew that his own people would not allow him to resign, and he could give the Englishmen no help. At the same time he invited the escort to desert and come over, and placed himself at the head of the revolt. In the evening, some of the soldiery and town rabble mobbed the Eedgah, took Khan Singh prisoner, and murdered the two English officers. The die was now cast; all the troops joined Mulraj, who forthwith proceeded to strengthen the fort, enlist troops, and send the fiery cross of revolt through the surrounding districts, calling on all to rise against the English, "who were treating the Maharajah and their proper rulers as prisoners." So far Mulraj.

Before attempting to follow the operations which will now be described, the reader will do well to impress the geography of the south-western Punjab on his mind; taking Multan as the central point of interest. The Indus and Sutlej form the sides of a triangle, the Chenab lying between them. A little above Multan, the Ravi flows into the Chenab on the east side; higher up, again, the Jhelum joins the Chenab on the west side. The land lying between two rivers is called a Doab; and thus in the district with which we are dealing we have (1) between the Indus and the Chenab, the Sindh Sagur Doab, (2) between the Ravi and the Chenab, the Rechna Doab; (3) between the Ravi and the Sutlej, the Bari Doab; (4) west of the Indus, the Derajat; (5) on the south of Multan, outside the Punjab, close to the Sutlej, the state of Bhawalpore, friendly to the British. Certain positions should at the same time be noted: in the Derajat, Dera Ishmael Khan at the north; Dera Ghazi Khan at the south; Dera Futteh Khan and Mangrota between the two: in the Sindh Sagur Doab, Leia, opposite Dera Futteh Khan, with the Indus between, and Munkhera: in the Bari Doab, Tolumba on the Ravi, and Mylsee near the Sutlej, as well as Shujabad, lying between Multan and Bhawalpore.

We now turn to the communications sent by Agnew to Edwardes or Van Cortlandt. The messenger found Edwardes in his court at Dera Futteh Khan, on the trans-Indus bank, halfway between Dera Ishmael Khan and Dera Ghazi Khan, and facing the town of Leia (which lies cis-Indus, but separated by the width of the Sindh Sagur Doab from the Chenab river). Edwardes's immediate action, after at once replying to Agnew, was to raise the neighbouring mountain tribes, and discipline the raw levies; gallantly and effectively aided by Van Cortlandt, at Dera Ishmael Khan, and by his own staunch *attachés*, Foujdar Khan and Futteh Khan. At the same time he wrote to Bhawal Khan, the chief of Bhawalpore, urging him to move with all his army against Multan, and to the Resident at Lahore, begging him to support this measure, and to send an English officer to the help of Bhawalpore.

Van Cortlandt and Foujdar Khan claim a few special words of notice. The former was a shrewd soldier, thoroughly versed in the Sikh character, and skilled in the Sikh methods, to whose guidance Edwardes owes not a little of his success. Foujdar Khan was a Pathan, loyal to the core, and with a consummate knowledge of the people, the country, and the local resources of every description. Edwardes had the most thorough and well-deserved reliance both on his fidelity and his intelligence, and confided his plans to him freely. Foujdar Khan's Eastern suavity cloaked a large capacity for acute criticism. He invariably accepted Edwardes's proposals with admiration; "they were all that could be desired; were, in fact, exactly the right thing—*But*"—and then he would proceed to point out that there was just one small defect, and another slight improvement to be made, until, as often as not, the plan as originally propounded was in shreds, and something quite new and a good deal more judicious had taken its place. And the new plan was the one adopted. Moreover, his conduct in the field was worthy of his conduct in council. Of Futteh Khan, it should be mentioned that he rendered excellent service in Bunnoo, subsequently when he was left in charge, though he was unable to prevent the troops there from ultimately joining the revolt.

At Lahore, the Resident on first hearing of the attack on Mr. Agnew, resolved to send towards Multan the British movable column stationed at Lahore, in order to support the Sikh Sirdars and the Durbar troops against Mulraj.

The view taken at this moment was that since the lives of British officers were in peril, an immediate expedition must be made at any cost. But when the news of the murder followed, the question became one of policy, and Sir F. Currie wrote to the Commander-in-Chief, asking his opinion from the purely military point of view. Lord Gough declared emphatically against any present action. He believed that Multan was exceedingly strong; that a very large expedition would be required to produce any decisive results, larger than there were present means for providing;* and that during the hot season the mortality of the troops would be tremendous. Also, he held that the rebellion was against the Durbar; that it was the Durbar's business to put it down; and that the employment of the

* See Appendix II., A and B.

Bengal troops would be more likely to precipitate than to check a general Sikh rising. On the other hand, by the time the weather became practicable, preparations could be made for an expedition on a comparatively irresistible scale; while in the meantime the risk of allowing small bodies of British troops to co-operate with large bodies of Sikh troops, who might betray them at any moment, was not to be thought of.

The views laid down by Lord Gough were endorsed by the two principal persons concerned, Sir Frederick Currie and Lord Dalhousie; it may be remarked that Sir Charles Napier subsequently declared that in his opinion they were right. Their decision was thus laid down in Lord Dalhousie's minute of 11th May:—

"We are fully sensible how important it is that this rebellion against the State of Lahore should forthwith be repressed, and that the insult offered, and foul treachery shown to the British power, should be followed by early and signal punishment. But, however imminent may be the risk, that, if the British troops do not now move, insurrection, apparently successful for a time at Multan, may extend its influence over the Punjab, and may cause disturbance and revolt throughout its bounds, we yet think that the dangers which would thence arise to British interests in India, are far less than those which would be created by our being compelled to discontinue operations once begun, before they had been brought to a satisfactory termination; and by the fearful loss among the troops which is anticipated as the consequence of entering on military operations on the scale required in such a district as Multan, at such a season of the year as this.

"We have determined, therefore, not to make any such movement at present, but we shall proceed to make the necessary preparations for enabling us, as soon as the season will permit, to enter on operations which we consider imperatively necessary for punishing the causeless rebellion of Mulraj, and for exacting ample reparation from the State of Lahore for the insult offered, and the deep injury inflicted on your Government in the base murder of your faithful servants, through the treachery, desertion, and crime of the servants of the Maharajah of Lahore."

This was the decision of Government three weeks after the murder of the English officers, during which period Mulraj had been strengthening his position and spreading revolt unchecked.

But with regard to Edwardes in the Derajat, it has to be observed that he was directly threatened by the Multan insurrection. Mulraj, unless some check was brought to bear on him, would be able to advance into the Derajat; and then the whole trans-Indus from Dera Ghazi Khan to Peshawur would be in a flame, since the Sikhs throughout the districts would be certain to join the rebels. Of the temper of the Sikh soldiery, Edwardes had a disagreeably intimate personal knowledge, since he had ascertained that the regiment with him was in active correspondence with the Sikh rebels in Multan; that an incendiary proclamation, signed "in the name of Govind," had been issued by the Khalsa leaders in Multan, and circulated among his own men; that there was a handsome reward offered for his own capture; and, in short, that his own prospects depended entirely on the loyalty of the Pathan tribesmen whom he had called to his standard. The presence of the Sikh regiment was a standing source of danger and weakness. From these considerations, Edwardes was convinced of the necessity, first, for at least confining Mulraj to the neighbourhood of Multan, if a sufficient force could not be provided to capture it; secondly, for doing this by the help of Bhawalpore, in the absence of British troops; thirdly, for keeping the Durbar troops out of the whole affair; inasmuch as the Derajat force was not sufficient by itself, and Sikh regiments might be confidently expected to join forces with the enemy.

Meantime, then, he had been raising levies and collecting a force on the right bank of the river opposite Leia, where Mulraj had been concentrating his own troops. On the 5th May, the Indus had risen so much that Edwardes would have to move somewhat to the rear to avoid the inundations, and was anxious about the effect that such a movement might have, when, fortunately, a much more marked movement was made by the enemy. Mulraj, having heard rumours of an advance of troops from Lahore, ordered back all the force from Leia to Multan on the 7th May, and sent an emissary, Mustapha Khan, to Edwardes, to sound him about terms of surrender. Of course, all terms were refused, though, in reply to a direct question, Edwardes said that certainly Mulraj could depend upon receiving a fair trial; a remark afterwards censured by Lord Dalhousie, as being an offer of terms to Mulraj.

And now Edwards was on the point of crossing to Leia, and there threatening Multan, when he received peremptory instructions from Lahore not to cross the Indus; but to operate on its right bank, with a distinct part to play as one of five converging columns. The scheme of operation was as follows:—

1. A force of 5000 men under Rajah Shere Singh, Shumser Singh, and Uttur Singh, was to move down the Bari Doab, along the Ravi from Lahore, towards Multan, as far as Tolumba. These generals were on the Durbar Council.

2. A column from the north was to move down the Sindh Sagur Doab to Munkhera, under Dewan Jawahir Mull.

3. A force under Sheikh Imam-ud-Din was to move down the Bari Doab, on the right bank of the Sutlej, to Lodhan or Mylsee. The Sheikh was the same who had held Kashmir against Gholab Singh, but had now quite made up his mind that the British was the winning side.

4. The Bhawalpore troops were to cross the Sutlej, come up the Doab, and get into touch with the third column at Mylsee; and—

5. Edwardes and Van Cortlandt were to occupy the whole Derajat along the banks of the Indus.

These columns would hem in the Multan revolt in a triangle, of which the north-east side would be a cordon from Dera Ishmael Khan, by Munkhera and Tolumba, to

Mylsee; the south and south-east, the Sutlej and the Bhawalpore force; and the west, the Indus.

But this scheme collapsed, owing to the failure of four out of the five columns to carry out the part assigned them. The three northern columns simply loitered on their way in consequence of the distrust of the commanders in their men, and Bhawal Khan had to wait until he could co-operate with the others, as he was not meant, and did not mean, to face Multan singlehanded.

The result was that the Derajat force took action prominently, by itself first, and then in conjunction with the Bhawalpore troops.

The *rôle* assigned to Edwardes and Van Cortlandt was the occupation of the Lower Derajat, the northern part of which, called Sungurh, has as its key the Fort of Mangrota; the southern part being the well-known district of Dera Ghazi Khan, opposite Multan. The first step to be taken was to secure the Fort of Mangrota. This was held by Mulraj's troops, under his officer, Cheytun Mull, but it was surrounded by the Khusrani tribes, with whom he was unpopular. Their chief, Mitka Khan, under Edwardes's influence, got Cheytun Mull to quit Mangrota, which thus fell into Edwardes's hands. At the same time, Cheytun Mull was held to have acted advisedly, as, though he evacuated Mangrota, he concentrated with his men on Dera Ghazi Khan, joining his nephew Louza Mull, who was its Governor, and to whose garrison his force was a valuable addition.

But with Mangrota in their possession, Edwardes and Van Cortlandt were much more free to act. Edwardes's first impulse was to cross the Indus on the 12th May, to Leia, where he had left a picket of 100 men. But on the 11th he heard that Mulraj, being advised of the ill-feeling in the troops advancing southwards on Multan, had taken heart, and was about to reoccupy Leia in force. The picket left there had orders to retire before any superior force, and recross to the right bank of the Indus; but, meanwhile, a brilliant skirmish had raised their spirits to a great pitch of eagerness. On the 15th, they had been reinforced by 200 men to help them in the withdrawal; and they were then attacked by an advanced detachment of some 400 of Mulraj's men, whom they defeated and routed utterly, killing many, and taking many prisoners, as well as all their guns, without the loss of a man.

But, in consequence of his being unmolested, Mulraj was becoming active and threatening the Lower Derajat seriously; the movement on Leia proving to have been only a feint. Van Cortlandt had 6 guns, one disaffected regiment, and only one regiment that could be depended on; Edwardes had under 2000 men and 4 guns; while Mulraj had 6000 men and 15 guns, with a fleet of boats available for the passage of the Indus. Edwardes, therefore, wrote urgently for the advance of the Bhawalpore men to create a diversion; and, after a false alarm of the enemy having already crossed the river, he concentrated on Van Cortlandt's force in the district of Mangrota, opposite Dera Deen Punnah, on the 18th; and there faced the whole of Mulraj's force on the left bank of the Indus.

Here, again, on the 20th, he wrote apprising the Resident that his force was unequal to coping alone with Mulraj, but that if Bhawal Khan could co-operate with him, Mulraj could be driven into Multan, and that fort invested; and this view was confirmed by the intelligence he was able to send forward next day of the complete victory of his partisans in the south, and the triumphant capture of Dera Ghazi Khan. The Khosuh clan, a Beloochee tribe, were friendly to the English, and at bitter feud with the Lugharees, who held Dera Ghazi Khan under Louza Mull and his uncle Cheytun Mull. Gholan Hyder Khan, a chief of the Khosuhs, offered to seize Dera Ghazi Khan; being permitted, he surrounded the camp of the Lugharees with his clan on the night of the 20th, and attacked and defeated them in the morning, killing Cheytun Mull, taking Louza Mull prisoner, and capturing the fort. This feat, with that at Leia on the 15th, caused much depression in the enemy's camp, and the clan, elated with their success, sent 400 cavalry to join Edwardes permanently for the rest of the campaign. The Khosuhs had captured all the enemy's fleets of boats, and now, under Edwardes's advice, they brought them close under their own bank of the Indus; just in time, as a large force of the enemy appeared a day too late, with the object of securing those boats and recapturing Dera Ghazi Khan.

South of the Derajat, however, within the trans-Indus territory, the strong fort of Hurrund, garrisoned by Sikhs and Pathans, was holding out for Mulraj under Mokhum Chund, one of his officers. But the surrounding Beloochee tribes were favourable to the British; hopes were entertained and soon fulfilled that the Pathans of the garrison might be won over; and for the present, at any rate, the fort was powerless for mischief.

The successful efforts of the English lieutenant and his supporters were soon rewarded by the news that Bhawal Khan was going to wait no longer for others, but was about to cross the Sutlej and move up towards Multan; in the hope that Edwardes would cross the Indus and the Chenab from the south of the Derajat, and co-operate with him. Though it soon transpired that the offer to cross the Sutlej was not so unconditional as it had at first appeared, still the inclination was clear; and so on the 30th, Edwardes wrote asking permission for the proposed movement, pointing out that Bhawal Khan's advance up the east bank of the Chenab would facilitate his own passage of that river, as well as of the Indus, and nothing would then be left intervening between him and Multan. Bahawal Khan's specific proposal now was that, after crossing the Sutlej, he should advance as far as Shujabad, and there await Edwardes.

CHAPTER IV.

ADVANCE OF HERBERT EDWARDES: JUNE AND JULY

Edwardes crosses the Indus—Prepares for junction with the Daoodpootras—Crosses the Chenab—Victory of Kineyree—Edwardes's plans—Battle of Suddoosam—Edwardes's wish to attack Multan—Lord Gough's view—Approach of the Durbar troops—Junction with them—Attitude of the Sikh soldiery.

On the 31st May, having received an appeal from Bhawal Khan direct, the Resident sanctioned Edwardes crossing the Indus, and co-operating with the Bhawalpore men—the Daoodpootras, as they were also called. A week afterwards, he posted Lieutenant Lake as the British officer with the Bhawalpore force, virtually its commander—and at length, on the 10th June, he sent instructions to Edwardes giving *carte blanche* for his co-operation with the Daoodpootras.

On receiving permission to advance, Edwardes directed Van Cortlandt to join him; and leaving Hurrund invested by a strong force of friendly Beloochees, besides 300 men under his own Kardar, he turned his whole strength towards co-operation with the Bhawalpore army, *viâ* Dera Ghazi Khan. On the 10th June, he learnt that the army was not all collected on the east side of the Chenab, and advancing towards Shujabad, as he had assumed; but that part of it was moving up separately on the west of the Chenab, between it and the Indus. He further found that the enemy on his front had broken up their camp, and were withdrawing towards the Chenab.

On the night of the 10th, Edwardes took 2500 men and

10 guns across the Indus, and then ascertained that his enemy had withdrawn to Khangurh, on the west bank of the Chenab—the convenient point for crossing that river on the way to Shujabad, where it was intended that reinforcements from Multan should join them. In fact, Mulraj was concentrating on Shujabad to meet the advance of the Bhawalpore force. Edwardes's first measure then was to send directions to those Bhawalpore troops that were like himself on the west bank of the Chenab, but lower down, to cross that river, and to join and reinforce their own main body on its east side. Edwardes was presently joined by Van Cortlandt, but he delayed moving till he was sure of the actual position of the enemy, and of the Bhawalpore army. On the 14th, he learnt that the enemy, after hesitating, had evacuated Khangurh. On the 15th, accordingly, he moved over to Khangurh and occupied it, with the object of crossing the Chenab and joining the Daoodpootras, having with him 3000 men and 20 small guns. Then he learnt that Mulraj was sending his whole force under his brother-in-law, Lalla Rung Ram, to meet and fight the Bhawalpore army before it should reach Shujabad.

Finding that the Western Division of the Bhawalpore force had not yet crossed over, Edwardes again wrote to its commander (Moozood deen Khan) to join the main body. At the same time, he wrote to Futteh Mohammed Khan, in command of the Bhawalpore main body, to throw up entrenchments and remain on the defensive until he Edwardes, should join.

These injunctions were carried out. Futteh Mohammed threw up entrenchments, Moozood deen Khan joined him; and his force was raised by this and other reinforcements to 9000 men and 11 guns. Ten miles still separated the Daoodpootras at Goweyn from Rung Ram, who halted two miles below Shujabad instead of attacking the Bhawalpore army, before the force from the Derajat arrived.

On June 17th, Edwardes made his arrangements for crossing the Chenab to Kineyree; and here, accordingly, Futteh Mohammed took up his position in order to cover the crossing. Meantime, the enemy, under Rung Ram, moved down eight miles towards it; and next morning, the 18th June, they attacked the Daoodpootra army.

Mulraj's troops numbered from 8000 to 10,000 men, with 10 guns. The Bhawalpore force was 8500 men, with 11 guns and 30 sumbooruks (camel-pieces). Edwardes's consisted of 1500 Sikhs and 15 guns, under Van Cortlandt; and some 5000 Irregulars, with 30 sumbooruks, under Foujdar Khan.

The river was three miles across, while there were only a few boats with which to effect its passage. On the night of the 17th, 3000 men under Foujdar Khan crossed over and joined the Daoodpootra army. In the early morning of the 18th, Edwardes, going over in a small boat, heard the firing begin, of the battle of Kineyree. The anniversary of Waterloo was not a day on which gloomy anticipations were permissible; but the omen was more encouraging than the crude material circumstances. When he reached the field, he found that the fight had started inauspiciously; the Daoodpootras, brave but undisciplined, taking the firing as a challenge, rushed wildly towards the enemy, well posted on commanding ground, and were checked by their superior artillery. Happily, Edwardes arrived in time to bring them into order, for the incompetent Futteh Mohammed considered that a general's principal function was to sit under a tree and do nothing. The Englishman, vigorously supported by Foujdar Khan, succeeded with difficulty in persuading officers and men that they must remain on the defensive until the arrival of Van Cortlandt should give the necessary superiority. This plan of operations was anything but to the taste either of the allies or of Edwardes's Pathans, who were ready to charge against any odds, but could not understand sitting still to be shot at. For six hours the enemy kept up their fire; the strain was becoming ominously severe; already the Bhawalpore men were beginning to be forced back slowly towards the river. The advance of the Multanis, however, called out all the best qualities of the Pathan soldiery on the left, and the enemy were checked, first by the hot fire with which they were received, and then by a brilliant cavalry charge headed by Foujdar Khan. The fight had lasted about seven hours, when the whole Multan line advanced to the attack; but, just in time, Van Cortlandt's troops completed the crossing, joined the Bhawalpore force, turned the tables on the enemy, overwhelmed their artillery fire, and drove back their whole line until they turned in precipitate flight.

Thus, in the battle of Kineyree, was Mulraj's army routed by the undisciplined troops of our Bhawalpore ally, and by Edwardes's levies, with the small body of artillery and the staunch regiments under Van Cortlandt.

After a halt of three days, the force moved on to Shujabad, where it was learnt that Mulraj, distrusting his Pathan adherents, was pinning his faith on the support of the Sikh troops, and was strenuously improving the defences of the Multan Fort. Having a total strength of 18,000 men and 30 guns, and expecting to be able to force Mulraj to withdraw from the open country and concentrate on Multan, Edwardes now suggested to the Resident that he should be allowed to commence the siege at once, that guns and mortars should be sent down the river to him from Ferozepore, and that Major Napier (afterwards Lord Napier of Magdala) should plan the operations. This proposal, dispensing with the employment of any except native soldiery, may have been a rash one; but Edwardes knew that Lord Gough was opposed to any present movement of British troops towards Multan, while he held it to be an imperative necessity to keep the area of Mulraj's insurrection and operations within the narrowest possible limits;

for, however successful he had been in his own proceedings, all was not smooth elsewhere. The Sikh temper was the chief danger. A fanatic, Bhaee Maharaj Singh, calling himself a Guru, had raised a band of followers, and, after having been supposed to have been destroyed, had reappeared at Multan; and the Sikh soldiery of the three columns from the north were said to be advancing, without or contrary to orders, on Multan, where it was doubtful whether they might not desert to Mulraj.

There was no doubt that the central one of these three columns, which should have been halted at Chichawatni, was within some 30 miles of Multan, and this could not now be helped. But Jawahir Mull's Sikhs (of the Sindh Sagur column) had partly deserted and partly returned to Lahore, and Sheikh Imam-ud-Din, of the Sutlej column, now sent back its Sikhs to Lahore and joined Edwardes with only his Mussulmans.

From Shujabad, Edwardes moved on the 26th to Secunderabad, halfway to Multan, and seized the fort there without further fighting. At the same time he learnt that Mulraj meant to oppose his approach to Multan, at the passage, at Sooruj Khoond, of a large canal which there crosses the road. On June 28th he advanced up to Sooruj Khoond, and was joined by Lieutenant Lake, who forthwith took command of the Bhawalpore troops, but, having a wise appreciation of the danger of divided councils, voluntarily assumed the position of Edwardes's subordinate. The position held by Mulraj was very strong, advantage having been taken with considerable skill of the banks and nullahs of the canal and its branches, while its bridge had been destroyed. Edwardes planned, therefore, not to force the passage at that point, but to march up his side of the canal till he should meet its passage by the road from Multan to the Rajghat ferry on the Chenab, and there turn and advance on Multan.

On July 1st he carried out this plan. Mulraj's troops

confronted him gallantly; but Edwardes had 22 guns to the enemy's 10; and as his artillery fire gradually subdued that of Mulraj's army, his line advanced, driving the enemy back at all points, and winning the day decisively with a brilliant charge of Van Cortlandt's Sooruj Mukhie regiment, which forced the defeated rebels within the walls of Multan.

Such was the Battle of Suddoosam, fought on July 1st, nominally in support of the Sikh Durbar against the rebel Mulraj. The whole struggle had been conducted under the pressure and guidance of Lieutenant Edwardes. At the outset, on April 25th, he had suggested the moving of a British (*not* a Sikh) force against Multan; but on learning Lord Gough's judgment, he deferred to it with entire loyalty, and refrained from repeating any such proposals. Now, however, he did suggest that some heavy ordnance should forthwith be sent him from Ferozepore down the Sutlej *viâ* Bhawalpore, which *at that time, early in July*, would, he thought, enable him, with the force he had, to capture Multan while its defences were comparatively weak. Besides, he was especially nervous at the threatened approach of Shere Singh and Shumser Singh's Durbar troops, and anxious that they should be held back by the Durbar at a distance from Multan. But the answer he received was that ordnance would be useless without artillerymen, and that that meant a British force, to which, as he knew, there was strong objection.

That special feature or reason in Edwardes's suggestion above referred to must not be forgotten, viz. that the fort of Multan was still unprepared for defence, although Mulraj had been taking steps to improve it; but that it would now grow stronger every day, and prove much more difficult to besiege and capture three or four months later. And Major Napier, at Lahore, concurred in this view.

Lord Gough, however, seems to have paid little regard to this theory, believing that Multan was already so strong that delay could not be utilised to make it effectively stronger. Moreover, heartily as he admired Edwardes's pluck and vigour, he had no great confidence in the young man's judgment, suspecting that he overrated his own capacity, and might be led into indiscretions in consequence. To supply him with guns but not troops he regarded as futile; his objection to sending either a small or a large detachment of British troops remained unchanged; while he judged from Edwardes's own reports that that officer was already strong enough to keep Mulraj in Multan, and to do more before a cold-weather campaign be held to be impracticable. Lastly, he did not believe that delay increased the danger of Sikh disaffection or treachery; not from trust in the Sikhs, but from the expectation that their disloyalty was more likely to be precipitated by premature action.

Under the Lahore plan of operations, three columns of Durbar troops had been despatched, under command respectively of Jawahir Mull, Shere Singh, and Imam-ud-Din—not a little to the perturbation of Edwardes. Of the troops under their command, some reliance could be placed on the Mussulmans, but none on the true Sikhs. None of the commanders had been in any hurry. Imam-ud-Din, however, had quite made up his mind not to go against the British; and he succeeded in bringing hardly any but Mussulmans to swell the forces, just before the Battle of Suddoosam. Jawahir Mull, also, by the time he did arrive, had shed his Sikh followers. But Shere Singh, a Sikh himself, with a large body of Sikhs behind him, was now nearing Multan. As far as can be judged, he himself at this time intended to remain loyal; but his men's sympathies were certainly on the other side, and the chances that they would desert on the first convenient opportunity were enormous. Shumser Singh, the second in command, and a personal friend of Edwardes, declared to him that but for the victory of Suddoosam, they would have gone straight over to Mulraj on arrival.

Naturally, when this column reached Gogran, five miles from Multan, on July 5th, four days after Suddoosam, Edwardes was nervous. Placed there, they could communicate with Mulraj. Accordingly, he arranged with Shere Singh that they should advance further, and take up their position in the rear of his own force at Sooruj Khoond, he himself being at Tibbee, three miles south-west of Multan. By this means he hoped to check communication with the rebels, while—somewhat rashly, perhaps—he rather looked forward to the Sikhs declaring themselves while he lay between them and Mulraj, hoping thereby to obtain a chance of getting rid of the Sikh contingent altogether. The actual effect, however, was to keep the Khalsa troops for the time being loyal.

Mulraj did his best to detach them. On July 20th, he made a sortie. The besiegers drew up in line, offering battle; and when he found that the Sikh troops were co-operating with them, and, crossing from Sooruj Khoond, were threatening Multan on the south-east, instead of deserting, he thought better of it, and withdrew. A similar attempt was made on the 26th, with a similar result; though it was believed that some of the Sikh cavalry would on this occasion have gone over, had they not been disconcerted by Shere Singh drawing up his whole force in line of battle.

About this time two *émeutes* had taken place across the Indus; one at Hurrund, the other at Bunnoo. Both, however, had been repressed by the Mussulman chiefs left by Edwardes in control of those districts.

Also two conspiracies were discovered, both instigated by Mulraj. One was a treacherous intrigue with Louza Mull, formerly Governor of Dera Ghazi Khan, now a prisoner in the camp, which resulted in his execution. The other was a plot, having at its head a trooper named Shujan Singh, to poison Shere Singh. The trooper was blown from a gun; but the incident showed forcibly the

N

secret leanings of the Sikh soldiery, and was evidence that so far they were under the impression that Shere Singh meant to be loyal, and were disgusted with him accordingly.

To which it may be added that all this time Mulraj's forces were freely augmented by Sikh deserters, while he was steadily and vigorously strengthening the defences of Multan.

CHAPTER V.

THE FIRST SIEGE OF MULTAN : JULY–SEPTEMBER

The Resident decides to send a force to Multan—Lord Gough increases the force—Chutter Singh—Arrival of Whish's force—Proclamation—Plan of attack—Difficulties of the situation—Fighting from Sept. 9 to Sept. 12—Shere Singh joins the rebellion—Story of his plot on Sept. 13—Change in the situation—Shere Singh prepares to summon the Khalsa—Making the war a national rising.

BEFORE the occurrence of the events last narrated, the report of Suddoosam had caused Sir Frederick Currie to change his mind, and decide to follow Edwardes's advice. The precise point of that advice, however, he had not grasped. At the time of Suddoosam, Edwardes had announced that Mulraj was shut up in Multan, and that he could capture the place if only he were slightly strengthened at once. "Major Napier, with a company of sappers and a few large guns" was the reinforcement he actually suggested. What he meant was that Mulraj could not leave Multan, and that the place might be taken if siege materials and some additional troops could be supplied at once—before the fortifications could be strengthened, or the situation complicated by the arrival of a quantity of disaffected Sikhs. But it was not till July 10th that Currie adopted his new resolution; and after consultation with General Whish, in command of the movable column at Lahore, decided to use the special powers allowed him for acting in emergency, and order a British force to move on Multan, partly from Lahore by the Ravi, partly from Ferozepore by the Sutlej.

A force which would not reach Multan till the middle of August scarcely answered to what Edwardes meant as one which would enable him to capture Multan. Moreover, that officer's report had conveyed to military head-quarters the misconception that he had Mulraj closely invested, whereas there was nothing to stop his egress on the north and west, though he could not venture to move any number of troops to any distance. There is no doubt, however, that Lord Gough, Sir John Littler, and others, interpreted the report to mean that Mulraj could not move outside the walls; in short, it was supposed that Edwardes's own position before Multan was much more dominant than was actually the case.

Lord Gough objected to the expedition altogether, having found no reason to change his view. But, since Sir Frederick had used his powers, the Commander-in-Chief, while expressing dissent from the policy followed, did not oppose the Resident, but said that since the thing was to be done, the force must be considerably augmented; the Governor-General endorsing both his views and his action under the circumstances.

The force despatched, as organised by Lord Gough's orders, was thus composed:—

Two brigades of infantry, each containing a British regiment;

One native cavalry brigade, and two troops of horse artillery;

A siege train with foot artillery.

This was constituted a division, and placed under the command of General Whish, with Major Napier as his Chief Engineer.

The British troops were to move down the two rivers by boat, while the native troops marched by night down the left bank of the Ravi and the right bank of the Sutlej respectively. The season was hot, but not otherwise unhealthy.

On July 22nd the Resident issued a proclamation of the British advance against Multan, and the two columns started on July 24th and 26th, a fortnight after Sir F. Currie had given orders for the move; but took about twenty-five days over it, not reaching Multan till the 18th and 19th August.

While the columns from Ferozepore and Lahore were advancing, no change took place before Multan. Mulraj went on with his defences; Shere Singh still professed loyalty, nor had his troops yet openly gone over to the enemy. But, in the meantime, the Sikhs in the north were breaking into open revolt, of which the history will be given later. Here, however, it may be remarked that the rebellion was as yet local, being confined to the Hazara district, where the leader was Chutter Singh, the father of Shere Singh. The importance of this, as far as concerned Multan, lay in the fact that the son was in constant receipt of urgent and sarcastic messages from the father, pressing him to throw off his allegiance; whereby his loyalty was put to a very severe strain, while his troops were hardly awaiting the word from him to join Mulraj.

When the Ravi force was still a march off, Edwardes arranged to interchange camping-grounds with Shere Singh, in order to facilitate his own junction with the new arrivals. The Sikhs, on entering their new camp, fired a series of salutes, thereby causing much uncertainty in the minds of the approaching forces, who, not knowing the meaning of the firing, were kept very much on the alert. Consequently they gave an unexpectedly warm reception to a body of Mulraj's troops which he sent out in the early morning to attack the advanced guard. This happened on August 17th, and on the 18th the Ravi column proceeded to Seetul-ki-Mari, three miles east of the fort, where it was joined next day by the Sutlej column.

The disembarkation of the siege-train and its transport to Multan was not effected till the 4th September, and on that day, General Whish issued a proclamation calling on Multan to surrender unconditionally. The wording of this proclamation clearly conveyed that the authority to be yielded to was not the Durbar, but the Queen of England. This receiving no attention, operations began. To improve the position, Edwardes's force was moved from Sooruj Khoond to Mosum Khan's Well, some three miles to the right and front, nearer Multan. This move was not made without some sharp fighting, during which General Whish and his staff reconnoitred the position.

The force was composed of—

2 troops horse artillery
4 companies fort artillery
5 companies of sappers
3 regiments of cavalry
2 regiments British infantry
4 regiments native infantry
13,400 native infantry } under Edwardes
5000 „ cavalry }
900 „ infantry } under Shere Singh,
3400 „ cavalry }

with 32 siege-guns and 61 light guns.

On September 6th, alternative plans which had been drawn up were discussed. Two proposals—(1) to capture the city at once by a *coup de main*, and (2) to attack the fort on its north by regular approaches—were negatived; while the third, to run a trench to a point called Ram Teerut, and there establish batteries, was approved. The trench works were accordingly begun the next day September 7th.

Many of the senior officers, however, and notably Major Napier (afterwards Lord Napier of Magdala), the chief engineer, very soon formed an adverse view of the prospects of the siege. The Bhawalpore men and the Pathan Irregulars were loyal and brave enough when it came to fighting; but they neither could nor would take their share in the essential trench and battery work, the whole of which consequently devolved upon the British Division alone. The known temper of Shere Singh's troops made them a source of anxiety instead of a real addition to the strength of the besiegers. Hence, without considering that the siege ought to be raised, Napier was clearly of opinion that the besieging force was inadequate for the reduction of the stronghold. This view was communicated to Whish on the 9th, but the General by no means acceded to it.

On the night of the 9th, then, in consequence of a mischievous fire from some buildings in front, an attack was made on them; but not with success, owing to the preparations not having been made in daylight.

On the 12th, Mulraj, having greatly strengthened his works between Multan and Seetul-ki-Mari, made a counter-attack on the besiegers in force. Edwardes's troops on the left drove back the enemy in their front, and held the village of Jummoondar-ke-kirree, half a mile from the Khoonee Boorj, at the southern angle of the city walls, which they could now see fully and breach. On the right, two columns of Whish's army cleared the ground in front of the projected batteries, storming and capturing the positions held by the enemy, especially a very strong one called the Dhurmsala; where the fighting was very fierce, and hardly any of the defenders returned to Multan to tell the tale. The enemy left 500 dead on the ground. This victory advanced the British position by half a mile.

A change, however, was close at hand. Hitherto it had appeared, on the whole, probable that Shere Singh himself meant to stand by the British. To this day it is uncertain when he made up his mind to join the revolt. According to Imam-ud-Din, his resolution had remained firm up till the failure of the besiegers' attack on the 9th; then for three days he remained irresolute, still acting loyally, but with an uncertain mind, while Chutter Singh's letters exercised an increasing influence on him. Despite the successes of the 12th, on the 13th he made up his mind, and on the

14th he went over bag and baggage to the rebels, taking his Sikh followers with him.

If this account is incorrect, it is undoubtedly curious that he took no earlier opportunity to desert. On the whole, it seems to tally with such evidence as there is. It was rumoured that his plan of action, formed on the 13th, was to support the advance of the besiegers against Multan, help them to force their way into the town, and then fall on their rear while Mulraj met them in front; but that the risk of detection made him afraid to wait. The rumour has some confirmation from an occurrence which did not become generally known, but is vouched for by a distinguished officer then present as a subaltern.

The officers attached to Edwardes's force used to dine together, and it was Shere Singh's custom to visit them when the meal was over. On the night of the 13th, Edwardes being at the head of the table, and Van Cortlandt at the foot nearest the entrance, Shere Singh came in as usual, but with more attendants than was his wont, and took his seat by Edwardes. Van Cortlandt, a very shrewd man, who knew the Sikhs thoroughly, at once had his suspicions aroused, slipped out, drew a guard of loyal Pathans round the tent, and returned quietly. But he succeeded in conveying to Shere Singh a hint of what he had done, and the Rajah withdrew unusually early. From the information subsequently obtained by Van Cortlandt, there seems little doubt that the Sikh chief had told off his followers to mark their men, and had intended to seize and secure the person of every officer present. Van Cortlandt had spoilt the plot, but Shere Singh felt that after that the tables might be turned upon him at any moment; that at any rate the others would now be on their guard; and that, consequently, the sooner he betook himself to Mulraj the better.

On the 14th, then, the besieging army was shocked, though not altogether astonished, to learn that Shere Singh with his army had marched from their camp to join the rebels.

Up to this date the capture of Multan had seemed a task which the besiegers might possibly succeed in accomplishing, despite the great strength of the defences; though Napier and others had already declared it to be beyond their powers. But after Shere Singh's defection, no such chance remained. The transfer of so large a body of troops from the besiegers to the defenders put it out of the question. Now, therefore, General Whish decided that the siege operations must be suspended, and the troops must fall back to the original positions at Tibbee, Sooruj Khoond, and Ram Teerut.

For the moment, the raising of the siege appeared to be the only effect of Shere Singh's desertion, for Mulraj gave him anything but a cordial reception, having, indeed, grave doubts as to the genuineness of the movement. He refused the Sikh General admission into Multan, directing him to encamp in the Huzuree Bagh under the guns of the fort, while his suspicions were actively fomented by the introduction of letters into Multan addressed to Shere Singh, as though the latter were a secret friend of the besiegers. But it was not Shere Singh's intention to confine himself to the Multan operations; his avowed purpose now was to raise and organise the Khalsa against "the oppression of the Feringhis," and though, under stress of Mulraj's taunts, he led out his army to attack Edwardes, he withdrew it again on finding the enemy fully prepared to meet him. From the latter part of September his preparations were all directed to a march on Lahore or to Gujerat (in the Jetch Doab), where Chutter Singh was urging him to gather the Khalsa; and on October 9th he marched from Multan to raise the Sikh nation in arms.

The movement of leaving Multan for a march northwards, whereby Shere Singh transferred the struggle to the Sikh districts, where he recruited the old Sikh soldiery as he advanced, and raised the Khalsa cry, commenced a new epoch, and was the beginning of the real Punjab campaign. The move was strategically a good one, throwing the whole weight of the Sikh force to the north-west front of the disaffected Manjha country, with the Multan thorn on the British flank, the great Punjab rivers to aid Shere Singh in his own warfare, and his rear supported by the Afghan Power, of which Chutter Singh was securing the alliance, by the cession of the much-coveted Peshawur districts.

Lord Dalhousie was perfectly alive to the character of the impending war, and left Calcutta for the front on October 10th, the day after Shere Singh left Multan. Before leaving Calcutta, he had, at a public banquet, announced the situation in these words, "Unwarned by precedents, uninfluenced by example, the Sikh nation has called for war, and on my word, sirs, they shall have it with a vengeance."

BOOK V.

THE CONQUEST OF THE SIKHS

BOOK V.

THE CONQUEST OF THE SIKHS: 1848-9

CHAPTER I.

THE SIKH RISING: AUG., 1848-JAN., 1849

Lord Gough's reasons for a winter campaign—General and specific—Suspension of Multan operations—Peshawur and Hazara in August—Chutter Singh and Abbott—George Lawrence—Refusal of a brigade for Hazara—Herbert at Attok—Lahore and the Jalandhar Doab—Govindguhr—Spread of the revolt.

The defection of Shere Singh may be regarded as opening the Sikh War proper. At this point the insurrection became a national revolt against British control; a rising for that final trial of strength, the expectation of which had been the fundamental justification of Lord Gough's military policy. He had, indeed, maintained that, so long as the rebellion was one against the Durbar Government, the Durbar itself was bound to put it down without British help. But beyond this, being convinced that the great war was inevitable, he considered it imperative to have at control, when it came, an army strong enough to bring matters to a final and decisive conclusion; to conquer the Sikhs thoroughly, not merely to scotch their power for a time; to ensure that there should be no moments such as had been experienced at Ferozeshah, when annihilation had to be faced as a grim possibility. If detachments intended to be effective were despatched to Hazara, to Peshawur, to

Bunnoo, and to Multan, his main army would be seriously weakened, and the detachments themselves might still prove insufficient. For, while the frontier force had been greatly strengthened by Lord Hardinge, a part of it only was really available for acting on the offensive, owing to the contemporaneous reduction of the military establishment generally. Lord Gough formed the plans, which were adopted by Lord Dalhousie, on the theory that the movement was one which could not be nipped in the bud by local successes; and that consequently the army should not move until it could do so in sufficient force to meet the Sikh nation in arms. Incidentally there was this additional objection to early action—that it would be dangerous for European troops to move in the hot weather, while sepoy regiments, without European support, could not be relied on to fight their best.

These were the general grounds on which Lord Gough based his objection to sending a force to Multan, or isolated columns to other parts of the country. Here, however, it will be well to enter into further details.

In the first place, as to the strength of Multan itself. At the beginning of July Edwardes believed that a small immediate reinforcement, accompanied by siege-guns, would enable him to carry Multan at once. Lord Gough believed that this theory was the result of a complete miscalculation of the strength of the defence. The one definitely ascertained fact is that, two months later, Napier, when he appeared before Multan, came to the immediate conclusion that Whish's Division was not strong enough for the purpose. Mulraj had, no doubt, in the interval, concentrated his energies on strengthening the defences, so that their condition in September is not conclusive as to their condition in July; still, the manifest inference is that a *small* reinforcement, sent earlier, would have been insufficient, as Lord Gough held. The presumption, then, is that a small force would have been merely wasted; and that view was strongly supported by past experience of the ability of the natives to hold a strong fort. Thus, for instance, twenty years earlier, Bhurtpore had held out for a month against an army of 25,000 men with 112 pieces of heavy artillery and 50 field-guns; and was then only taken by storm. The enthusiastic hopes of a young officer like Edwardes could hardly be expected to weigh against the practical lessons of experience.

The despatch of an overwhelming force, on the other hand, might have effected the immediate object of capturing Multan; but it would also have the effect of rousing the whole Sikh nation to arms, and the force immediately available could not crush the whole Sikh nation.

The obvious conclusion was that neither a small nor a large force should be sent at once to Multan; but that a force competent to crush the whole Sikh nation in arms should be collected; and such operations as the circumstances demanded should be then undertaken. But to collect such an army would take months. The required force, according to the Commander-in-Chief's calculations, would include some 24,000 of all arms, with 78 field-guns and 50 siege-guns. For this purpose, carriage must be supplied, in which Government had caused a serious deficiency; and troops would have to be brought up even from Calcutta; the sepoy army, greatly cut down by Lord Hardinge, having been further reduced by the large proportion of men absent on furlough.

These, then, were the views and designs which Lord Gough submitted to Lord Dalhousie. Whether they should be adopted or not was a matter for the most autocratic and independent of Governors-General to decide; and he decided absolutely and unreservedly in favour of the Commander-in-Chief.

Lord Gough had been prevented from acting on his own views in their entirety by Currie's action in despatching Whish to Multan; but in the main he was able to carry them out. The influence of the siege on the winter campaign was, however, confined to the fact that it detained Whish's troops until the fall of Multan in January.

From the time, then, of Shere Singh's defection, which translates the rising from a local outbreak into a national war, the siege of Multan became of secondary importance; the real centre of interest lying in the coming contest in the more northern districts. The principal object of hastening it was to release the troops engaged. Preparations were already on foot for the despatch of a column from Bombay; and orders were now sent that the actual siege should be suspended until the arrival of this contingent, since it was now abundantly evident that Mulraj was strong enough to hold out against the troops actually present.

Before continuing the Multan narrative, we now turn to the events which may be briefly termed the Rising of the Sikhs.

It has already been observed that during the month of August, while Shere Singh was still supporting Edwardes before Multan, his father, Chutter Singh, raised the standard of rebellion in the north.

In the northern district, the principal position was Peshawur, over the possession of which Sikhs and Afghans had waged a long contest in the days of Ranjit Singh. Here there was a large body of Sikh troops, under a loyal but aged governor, Gholab Singh,* distinguished by the class-name "Povindia" from the Rajah of Kashmir. Here the British representative was Major George Lawrence.

South-west of Peshawur lies Kohat, where Sultan Mohammed was governor; of whom mention has previously been made in the account of the Afghan troubles. He was one of the Barukzai brothers, of whom the most notable

* It should be mentioned that there was also at Lahore a third Gholab Singh, "Attariwalla," another son of Chutter Singh, of whom mention is made with some frequency in official correspondence at this period.

was Dost Mohammed, Amir of Kabul; who had been displaced to enthrone Shah Shujah, and restored in 1843. Sultan Mohammed was, of course, a Mussulman; he was under personal obligations to Henry Lawrence, and had always expressed the strongest personal attachment to George Lawrence also. But he had already shown an exceptional capacity for treachery. There was no British officer at Kohat.

Across the Indus, in the Hazara district, Chutter Singh was Nazim or governor. But among the true native population—Mussulmans—the British officer, Major James Abbott, had obtained an extraordinary personal influence.

Abbott long suspected the loyalty of the Sikh troops in the Hazara district, and believed that Chutter Singh was engaged in sowing disaffection among them. At last, in the beginning of August, some of the Sikhs prepared to quit their cantonments, obviously with intent to revolt; though their actual destination was uncertain. Chutter Singh, on the pretext that Abbott's influence had made the local population hostile, ordered out the troops at Hurripore. An officer, Colonel Canora (an American), refused to move without instructions from Abbott, and was shot dead. Abbott, however, forthwith called out the local peasantry, whose appearance in arms checked the movements of the Sikh soldiery. News of the disturbance being sent to Peshawur, Major Lawrence promptly sent down John Nicholson to secure Attok, close to the confluence of the Kabul river and the Indus. By these means the revolting troops were prevented from attempting immediate action.

Chutter Singh, however, while affirming that he was loyal, and declaring that his proceedings had been forced on him by the distrust and disregard of him which Abbott displayed, was engaged in active intrigues; as was afterwards proved. Not only was he sending messages to Multan inciting Shere Singh to revolt; but he opened communications with Gholab Singh of Kashmir, who, as usual, followed a policy of masterly inactivity; and also with the troops in Peshawur, with the Amir at Kabul, and with Sultan Mohammed. These latter intrigues proved more successful. The special object of drawing in Dost Mohammed was to obtain Mussulman support, which was not readily given to Sikhs; and for this purpose Chutter Singh counted it worth while to offer Peshawur itself as a bribe.

Yet within Peshawur, George Lawrence's influence was sufficiently strong to keep a force composed of Sikhs loyal for a surprisingly long time. It was not till near the end of October that their loyalty at length gave way, with the assurance that Sultan Mohammed meant to play the traitor. The British officers were obliged to evacuate Peshawur, withdrawing under an Afghan escort to Kohat; when it became rapidly clear that they were in effect prisoners; and they were shortly afterwards handed over to Chutter Singh.

Throughout September and October, Lawrence as well as Nicholson had been pressing on the Resident, at Lahore, the advisability of sending a British Brigade to the north-west. Lord Gough, however, adhered firmly to his determination not to allow small bodies of troops to be dispersed among distant districts, for the reasons already given. In the north, moreover, he considered that there was a special objection, owing to the doubts as to the possible action of the Maharajah of Kashmir. It was felt that if that monarch came to the conclusion that revolt would pay him, he certainly would revolt; and his forces joined to Chutter Singh's might bring disaster on any possibly available British detachment.

Thus, by the beginning of November, Multan was still holding out in the south; in the western Punjab proper, the old Khalsa soldiers were flocking to Shere Singh; while Peshawur and the northern part of the Sindh Sagur Doab had declared for the revolt; the only check on them being Lieutenant Herbert, who had taken Nicholson's place at

Attok, with a Mussulman garrison, and Major Abbott, with the Hazara tribesmen. Attok was stubbornly held against great odds; and it was not till Dost Mohammed's Afghans began to appear that the garrison declared to Herbert that they had done all that could be demanded of their loyalty, their wives and families were in the Dost's hands, and they must surrender the place. Herbert himself was captured while attempting to escape, and was sent to join the other prisoners in Chutter Singh's hands at Peshawur. The fall of Attok, however, did not take place till January 3rd.

While the advance of the great expedition was still being awaited, the Sikhs were displaying restlessness not only in the north, and in the districts where Shere Singh was at work, but also in the east. Ram Singh, son of the Vizier of Nurpur, one of the small hill states, rose in arms and proclaimed the end of British rule. By the energetic action of John Lawrence, who was commissioner in the Jalandhar Doab, the insurgents were suppressed; Sikh troops, unwillingly obedient, following the British leader against the party with whom their real sympathies lay.

At Lahore, Sir Frederick Currie long strove with a certain obstinacy to retain his confidence in the loyalty of the Sikh Sirdars. It was not till all possibility of doubt was destroyed that he would credit Abbott's reiterated warnings against Chutter Singh. Before September was over, the proofs of plotting on the part of leading members of the Durbar led to important arrests, including Runjoor Singh and Shere Singh's brother. Grave suspicions attached to the Sikh garrison of the strong fort of Govindguhr, dominatıng the sacred city of Amritsir. It was resolved to anticipate any hostile declaration by a stratagem; a small party of Guides was sent down to the fort nominally to escort some treasure. Matters not being yet ripe in Govindguhr, they were admitted; and early the next morning opened the gates to two sepoy regiments from Lahore, who had marched thirty-six miles by night, and now quietly and without resistance took the place of the Sikh garrison. It is noteworthy that in lieu of the two guns which, according to the Durbar authorities, constituted the Govindguhr artillery, eighteen were found ready mounted, and a quantity more—bringing up the whole number to fifty-two—buried, with the obvious intention that they should be unearthed and put in order when the critical moment arrived.

The capture of Govindguhr removed a very serious source of danger. The presence of the sepoy regiments at Lahore, and Amritsir, and in the Jalandhar Doab, coupled with the vigilant activity of the British officers and the influence of a very fine Sikh Sirdar, Lehna Singh, sufficed to prevent any organised rising in the Manjha district, but did not suffice to give any adequate feeling of security; and the knowledge that Lord Gough's army was now collecting on the border, and would soon be in motion, was exceedingly welcome. For before it was ready to start, Peshawur had already fallen; Attok was being besieged; the siege of Multan was at a standstill, awaiting the arrival of the Bombay contingent; the Bunnoo regiments had revolted, killed Futteh Khan, and were on the march to join Shere Singh; the disbanded members of the old Khalsa army were flocking to his standard; and the whole Sikh population north and west of the Chenab was virtually in insurrection.

Shere Singh himself had started from Multan on October 9th, at such speed that pursuit by a detachment of the slower-moving British troops before that city was out of the question. Moving rapidly up the Chenab he allowed it to be reported that he intended to attack Lahore, where the situation was felt to be somewhat critical. A troop of his cavalry even advanced so near the capital as to burn some boats on the Ravi not two miles away, at the end of the month.

It was known, however, that the grand army was

collecting at Ferozepore; and the arrival of an advance cavalry brigade, under Cureton, relieved the strain; this being soon followed by two brigades, under Godby and Eckford; Colin Campbell being in command at Lahore. It was supposed that the enemy would make a stand at Gujeranwalla, but they preferred falling back across the Chenab, Shere Singh's real object being to effect a junction with the Bunnoo troops. He now concentrated upon the fords at Ramnuggur, leaving only outposts on the eastern bank; and Cureton, who had been joined by Campbell with two regiments of native infantry, awaited the arrival of the main army.

Early in November that army was complete; on the 9th Lord Gough crossed the Sutlej, reaching Lahore on the 13th, and on the 16th the troops crossed the Ravi.

CHAPTER II.

SECOND SIEGE OF MULTAN: SEPT.-JAN., 1849

Order of the narrative—Period of inactivity—Renewal of active measures—Arrival of the Bombay column—Plan of attack—The enemy driven into the city—Bombardment—Capture of the city—Operations against the fort—Surrender of Mulraj, Jan. 22—Release of the Multan army.

THE bulk of the events narrated in the last chapter were contemporaneous with the two months of almost complete inaction forced on the Multan Division after Shere Singh joined the rebels—a term, by the way, of which the use is strictly accurate, since the official Government of the State continued to profess loyalty to the treaty with the British, and the whole revolt originated in the refusal of a local "Dewan" to obey the orders of the Durbar.

Active preparations for the second siege commenced in November, and the citadel surrendered on January 22nd. During this period Lord Gough commenced his advance, crossed the Chenab, and fought the actions of Sadulapore and Chillianwalla on December 3rd and January 13th.

For the sake of continuity, therefore, we shall now relate the whole of the Multan operations from September 16th, 1848, to January 31st, 1849, in this chapter, and then proceed consecutively with Lord Gough's campaign, with the last stage of which alone—Gujerat—the Multan force was associated.

On September 14th Shere Singh went over to Mulraj, and it became at once evident that active operations must be suspended until reinforcements arrived, to which end the Bombay Government were already making arrangements.

On September 16th Whish shifted his camp across the canal; and nine days later moved a mile and a half to the rear, so as to command the two roads leading respectively from Multan westward to the Rajghat ferry, and southward towards Bhawalpore. During the ensuing six weeks the enemy were engaged in occupying advanced positions, and throwing up works in front of the British lines. Mulraj, meantime, despatched emissaries to various points; to Peshawur, where, the place not having yet fallen, the messenger was hanged; to Bunnoo; to the Afghans and Pathans beyond the Indus. The design was shrewd enough; since by urging them into the Derajat, he might not only get material assistance for himself at Multan, but might seriously hamper the British forces, should they advance from the Manjha towards Peshawur, by threatening their flank. The response to his overtures was, however, by no means enthusiastic, Dost Mohammed finding employment for as many troops as he cared to send at Peshawur and in Hazara; while the Pathans generally were anything but devoted to the Khalsa.

The Bombay Column tarried, and Whish found the enemy's works among the canal excavations acting as a serious check on the British batteries. It was therefore resolved to make an attack in force on November 7th (about the time when Lord Gough's army was getting into motion from Ferozepore). The state of affairs was illustrated on the 6th by the desertion *en masse* of a Hindostani regiment in the service of the Durbar, known as the Katar Mukhi, which was occupying an advanced post under Van Cortlandt's command. They did not, however, attack their officers.

On the 7th, then, when the proposed attack was about to begin, it was found that the foe had already taken the initiative, and were advancing to attack Edwardes's position. Here, however, they were driven back, with heavy loss. Meantime Whish, on the right, advanced, and turned the left flank of the Sikh position; and then, sweeping down its whole length, captured all but three of their guns. This success served to keep the enemy quiet for the time.

On November 30th Colonel Cheape, the chief engineer of the army, arrived to take control of the engineering operations, Multan being the place where the activity of that branch of the service was most in demand. On December 6th, 13th, and 16th he made special reconnaissances. Major Napier had previously drawn up a project of attack, which was directed against the north-east angle of the fort, and this project had gone up to the Commander-in-Chief. On December 12th Colonel Cheape recorded objections to it, and proposed instead that the attack should be similar to that in the first siege—against and through the city, beginning at its southern bastion, the Khoonee Boorj. This was approved by General Whish, and preparations were made to start it on the arrival of the Bombay Column.

At last, after long delay, the Bombay Column actually arrived; delay caused, in part at least, by a curious piece of bungling. The Bombay authorities appointed General Auchmuty to the command; but, since he was senior to Whish, he would have superseded the latter, who had his appointment from the Supreme Government. Whereupon the Government required some one junior to Whish to be appointed in place of Auchmuty, who in the mean time issued orders to the troops not to move until he arrived to take command. Ultimately, Brigadier Dundas was sent. The first detachment arrived on the 10th; but it was not till the 21st that the whole column was assembled.

Two regiments of British and five of native infantry, with three regiments of cavalry, were thus added to the besieging force, while the artillery was brought up to 67 siege and 30 field-guns.

On the plan of attack being laid before Brigadier Dundas and his engineer, Major Scott, they agreed to support by preference a plan on the same lines as Major Napier's. But General Whish continued to adhere to Colonel Cheape's project, and the movements and positions adopted were in conformity to it, till the 26th; when, in deference to the officers who had to lead the column, he agreed, instead, to the plans of Majors Napier and Scott, in which the chief point of attack was the north-east angle of the fort. As the first step of the operation, the whole force was next day, the 27th, to drive the enemy back at all points in the semicircle from the south-west to the north-east.

The British position was in three parts—the Bengal Column on the right, with their camp at Seetul-ki-Mari; on its left, the Bombay Column, reaching to the Wullee Mahomed Canal; and, on the left of that canal, Edwardes's Force, with the Bhawalpore men.

The British force was to drive back the enemy, and Edwardes's troops were to cross the canal and support its left flank. The advance was in three columns; the right was to sieze the brick-kilns about a mile to the east of the fort, and work its way forward from that point; the centre was to operate against the eastern face of the city, through the suburbs there; and the left against the Khoonee Boorj, the southern bastion of the city.

The operations were thoroughly successful. The right column moved as far as the Amkhas, 500 yards from the south-east angle of the fort; the centre column drove the rebels into the city at the Delhi Gate; and it and the left column planted batteries on heights called respectively Mundee Awa and Seedee Lal-ka-Behr, a site also being seized for a breaching-battery 120 yards from the Khoonee Boorj.

During the following night and next day (the 28th) breaching-batteries were begun; on the 29th a battery of the right attack opened out, and on the 30th the battery against the Khoonee Boorj. Next day the centre battery was completed, and began breaching the Delhi Gate. Other batteries also were started, and, as they were completed, joined in the circle of attack.

During these days a determined sally was made against Edwardes's Division by a large body of Sikhs, but they were thoroughly repulsed. In this fight Henry Lawrence again appears on the scene; he having returned from leave in England, and joined the camp on the 28th.

On the 30th, the enemy's large magazine on the south face was blown up, and the minor defences near it destroyed. On January 2nd, the breaches in the city walls being thought to be practicable, the assault was delivered on them. The breach at the Delhi Gate was found insufficient, and the attacking column was accordingly halted; but the Khoonee Boorj was successfully stormed by the Bombay Fusiliers, and the two columns, acting together, then cleared the whole of the south side of the city, and opened all its gates. Thus the city was taken, but the fort remained in the hands of Mulraj, who, seeing the besiegers' success, closed the gates, so shutting out the troops that had been holding the city, and leaving them to their own devices for safety or flight, whilst he kept with him only about 4000 picked men. Next day both the Delhi Gate and the Dowlut Gate at the extreme north-east of the city were seized, the whole of the city wall thus being held by the besiegers, who were consequently enabled to survey and examine thoroughly the fort or citadel defences.

A brigade was at the same time moved to the Dewan Bagh, on the north of the fort, to complete the investment, and the saps or regular trenches of approaches were vigorously advanced. On the night of the 12th a sortie was made from the fort against the advanced saps, but was driven back, after doing some slight damage, and next day a fresh breaching-battery was begun. These took place on the right attack.

Meanwhile, however, work had also been in progress at the esplanade on the city side of the fort, and two breaching batteries had been constructed.

The full knowledge now procured of the several lines of defence made it certain that the best point for the attack lay, as originally thought, at the north-east angle, near the point called Bahawal Huk. Here, therefore, the saps, batteries, and mines against the outer defences were being vigorously carried forward; but meanwhile other batteries attacked the interior lines, and succeeded in breaching the upper wall on the 20th. On the 21st, the successive lines had all been breached, and the passage of the ditch made practicable; so the route was settled for the assault.

But the assault was unnecessary. Ever since the capture of the town, a terrific and increasing cannonade on the fort had been maintained; the buildings had been knocked to pieces, and before preparations for the final attack were completed, the besieged had peremptorily demanded that Mulraj should adopt one of two courses—cut his way out at their head, or yield. He chose the latter alternative. On January 22nd the siege was terminated by Mulraj surrendering at discretion to the victors; the entire garrison laying down their arms and becoming prisoners of war.

No terms had been granted, since all negotiation had been steadily refused. Mulraj got the one thing which Edwardes had told his emissary he might count on—a fair trial. He was taken to Lahore, charged with complicity in the murder of Agnew and Anderson, and found guilty, but with extenuating circumstances. He spent in confinement the remainder of a life which was prolonged only for a short time.

No great demand was made on the forces to hold the captured fort in security; and the two British columns made immediate arrangements to march north, to join Lord Gough; the Bengal troops starting on January 27th, followed by the Bombay column four days later.

CHAPTER III.

THE CROSSING OF THE CHENAB: NOV.–DEC. 4TH, 1848

Lord Gough's force—Shere Singh on the Chenab—British advance to Ramnuggur—Cavalry skirmish—Col. W. Havelock's charge and death—Preparations for crossing the Chenab—Necessity of the operation—Thackwell's march to Wazirabad—Passage and descent to Sadulapore—Engagement at Sadulapore—Defeat of Shere Singh—Retreat of the Sikhs to Russool—Comments on the operations.

WHILE General Whish's Division was still posted before Multan, awaiting the tardy arrival of the Bombay Column, and more than two months before the fall of the citadel, the grand army under Lord Gough's personal command entered Manjha territory, and advanced to wage the decisive struggle with Shere Singh.

The army of the Punjab was constituted as follows:—

CAVALRY DIVISION, under Brigadier Cureton—

1*st Brigade*, Brigadier White: British, 3rd and 14th Light Dragoons; Native, 5th and 8th Light Cavalry.

2*nd Brigade*, Brigadier Pope: British, 9th Lancers; Native, 1st and 6th Light Cavalry.

INFANTRY—

1*st Division*, before Multan.

2*nd Division*, Major-General Sir Walter Gilbert.

1*st Brigade*, Brigadier Mountain: British, 29th Foot; Native, 30th and 56th Native Infantry.

2*nd Brigade*, Brigadier Godby: British, 2nd European Light Infantry; Native, 31st and 70th Native Infantry.

3rd Division, Sir Joseph Thackwell.

1st Brigade, Brigadier Pennycuick: British, 24th Foot; Native, 25th and 45th Native Infantry.

2nd Brigade, Brigadier Hoggan: British, 61st Foot; Native, 36th and 6th Native Infantry.

3rd Brigade, Brigadier Penny; 15th, 20th, and 69th Native Infantry.

[It will thus be seen that Lord Gough's command contained three British and four Native cavalry regiments, besides Hearsey's Irregulars; with four British and eleven Native infantry regiments.]

ARTILLERY, Brigadier Tennant.

Horse Artillery, Lieut.-Colonel Huthwaite; 6 troops, or batteries, commanded respectively by Lieut.-Colonel Lane, and Majors Christie, Huish, Warner, Duncan, and Fordyce.

3 *Field Batteries*, Major Dawes, and Captains Kinleside and Austin.

2 *Heavy Batteries*, Major Horsford: commanding Majors Shakespear and Ludlow.

These were exclusive of the troops established at various points in the Manjha district, and the Jalandhar Doab, as well as those before Multan.

General Cureton, with the greater part of the cavalry division, had preceded the rest of the army by about a fortnight, having been despatched to cover Lahore, in case Shere Singh should contemplate an advance on the capital. The Sikh chief was now lying with his army on the western bank of the Chenab, opposite Ramnuggur. Cureton, who was joined, on November 16th, by Brigadier Colin Campbell (afterwards Lord Clyde), in command at Lahore, and Godby, took up his position about eight miles from Ramnuggur, on the east side of the river, from whence the cavalry were employed in daily reconnaissances, but avoided any engagement.

The Chenab at this point is very wide from bank to

bank. The river-bed being extremely sandy, sand-banks are constantly forming and changing in its course, splitting it up into channels, sometimes wet and sometimes dry. At Ramnuggur there was a fairly good ford; and the Sikhs had consequently thrown an outpost across the river, with which communication from the main body was easy, so that the troops there could be reinforced or withdrawn at pleasure; while to force a passage from the east was practically impossible. Before they could be effectively dislodged, therefore, it would become necessary for the opposing army to find a way across the Chenab.

On November 21st, Lord Gough, with the main army, came up to the advanced brigades, the heavy artillery being still behind, and resolved at once to make a reconnaissance in force, so as to ascertain the real position and strength of the enemy, and to drive their outposts across the river.

Accordingly, early in the morning on the 22nd, an advance was made on Ramnuggur. The Sikhs, aware of the approach of the British, could be seen drawing up on the opposite bank, in manifest excitement over the prospect of again meeting the British face to face. Their artillery, always, until the battle of Gujerat, stronger than our own, opened a heavy fire; while numbers of their cavalry crossed over to reinforce the cis-Chenab outpost, by fords somewhat on their left.

The Commander-in-Chief, however, had no intention of indulging in a general engagement. His object was simply to drive the outposts over and obtain information. Accordingly, while some of the light artillery advanced and opened fire, the 1st Light Dragoons were moved forward alone. At first Ouvry's squadron was pushed on to reconnoitre; but the Sikh cavalry coming to the east bank of the river in increasing numbers, Brigadier White ordered the regiment to drive them back, which was done successfully. White, however, perceiving that the river-bed and its immediate neighbourhood were not at all fitted for a cavalry attack, halted the regiment, which was now joined by the 8th Light Cavalry, and began to withdraw. On seeing this movement, the Sikhs became greatly excited, and began to come on. On the cavalry fronting round, they again fell back, but once more advanced as the withdrawal was renewed. On reaching better ground, however, White again halted, turned, and now charged, driving the enemy back helter-skelter, but again halting when the broken and sandy ground was reached.

So far, matters had progressed favourably enough. The immediate object in view was accomplished with few casualties, and the cavalry continued to fall back unmolested. But, at this stage, an unlucky accident occurred, one of the guns, which had been sent forward to cover the cavalry, and a couple of waggons, sticking hard and fast in the sand. The most strenuous efforts could not move them, and the Sikhs, seeing that some contretemps had befallen, directed a hot fire on the spot, and were evidently making preparations to come on once more.

It was evident that the gun itself could not be withdrawn, and that sheer waste of life was the only alternative to its abandonment.

There was, however, another ford on the Sikh right, near the site where Lord Gough—having accomplished what he wanted—intended to pitch his camp; and some of the Sikh "Gorchurras," or irregular cavalry, had crossed over, and were appearing on the ground at this point. Lieut.-Colonel Havelock, with the 14th Light Dragoons, was accordingly ordered by Lord Gough to charge them, simply for the purpose of clearing the ground, and with express instructions not to advance into the heavy ground by the river-bed.

The conduct of this charge was the grave mishap of the day. Havelock rushed down on the Sikhs with the 14th Light Dragoons, supported by the 5th Light Cavalry, and drove the Gorchurras before him; but, when the broken ground was reached, he became aware that the dry channel close at hand was full of Sikh infantry, hitherto concealed. To his headlong valour, the opportunity seemed irresistible. He was seen to be forming up his men for another charge. Cureton, realising the danger, dashed from the Commander-in-Chief's side to stop Havelock, but almost immediately a bullet struck him in the chest. Before any fresh order could be dispatched, Havelock had made the second fatal charge, and the horses began to flounder in the sandy river-bed. The Sikhs swarmed down on them; and though the brigade succeeded in cutting its way back, Havelock was slain. The lives of Cureton, of Havelock himself, and fifty soldiers, were a heavy price to pay for that last charge, which—perhaps naturally, certainly most unjustly—was popularly imputed to the recklessness of the Commander-in-Chief, who was at once too chivalrous and too heedless of popular censure to refute the accusation.

The 14th lost, besides their Colonel, Captains Fitzgerald and M'Mahon and Cornet Chetwynd; and Captain Gall was severely wounded. The 5th also suffered considerable loss. But it is to be noted that the casualties of the day, from Cureton's death down, were nearly all due to that last unfortunate charge in the river-bed.

Such was the cavalry affair of Ramnuggur. The foremost purpose, however, had been effected, and the Commander-in-Chief encamped near the village, opposite the Sikh army; devoting the ensuing days to the further examination of the enemy's position, and of the Chenab fords, and to preparations for accomplishing the crossing.

It was ascertained that there was a ford at Ghurriki, seven miles above Ramnuggur, held by a detachment of 4000 Sikhs; another higher up at Runniki, also guarded; and a third, higher still, at Ali-Sher-ke-Chuk, which was unguarded, but dangerous, owing to the strength of the stream. Failing all these, the passage would have to be effected at Wazirabad, 22 miles above Ramnuggur; for it is obvious that to cross a broad Indian river, with a shifting sandy bottom, in the face of a battery of artillery, is practically impossible, and is certainly not to be thought of when the ford is commanded by an entrenched position as at Ramnuggur. On the other hand, it is no less clear that a force which had to march 20 miles up one bank of the river, and 20 miles down the other bank, would have the greatest difficulty in maintaining touch with the troops which would have to remain at Ramnuggur to prevent the Sikh main body from moving; while the entire evacuation of Ramnuggur would leave the way open to Lahore. Yet the ejection of Shere Singh from his present quarters was necessary; since, while he continued there, he could accumulate both supplies and recruits with ease, and his proximity to Lahore encouraged the hopes of the disaffected Sirdars and others behind the British army; whereas, if our troops had the Chenab at their backs, with the Sikhs driven up to the Jhelum, they might be held more easily in check until Multan should fall and release the division detained there, even if they were not caught and crushed where they were.

Therefore the conclusion arrived at was that the extended operation must be undertaken of throwing a division across the Chenab, above Runniki at any rate; and that the division must be a strong one.

Sir Joseph Thackwell was placed in command, with White's Cavalry Brigade (in which, however, two regiments of Irregulars took the place of the 14th), and the 24th and 61st (British) Foot, and five regiments of Native Infantry, under Colin Campbell; besides 30 field-guns and 2 heavy guns. The artillery had come up with the main body since the Ramnuggur affair, and the force was ordered to assemble at midnight of November 30th.

The night happened to be extremely dark, and the start was delayed for a couple of hours in consequence, some of the infantry having mistaken their route for the point of assembly. Hence Runniki was not reached till 11 o'clock. A halt of three hours to examine the fords here and at Ali-Sher-ke-Chuk resulted in the decision that to attempt a crossing at either would be too risky, and the whole force moved on to Wazirabad. John Nicholson, mentioned before in connection with Attok, who fell gloriously not nine years later at the siege of Delhi, was with Thackwell's army. The moment the decision was arrived at, he proceeded at full speed to Wazirabad, where with extraordinary energy and promptitude he had already collected every boat on the river, and staked out the fords by the time the division arrived, about sunset. For, although the troops had been on the move since an hour before midnight, it was imperative that the passage should be made and a strong force established on the opposite side forthwith; lest the enemy should come up during the night, and the whole movement be rendered futile.

Accordingly, three regiments, one British, and two native, were at once ferried over in boats; and another detachment (Native Infantry) marched over the ford without a halt, bivouacking on an island; throughout the night the artillery were being conveyed across, while the cavalry and the remainder of the infantry bivouacked on the left bank, crossing early on the following morning (December 2nd).

By noon the whole force was established on the west of the Chenab, and messages were despatched to the Commander-in-Chief to report the successful completion of the passage. At two o'clock Sir Joseph commenced his march down the right bank of the river; advancing until, in the evening, a point was reached about nine miles from the Sikh position, where the British force encamped. By this movement the Sikh outposts at the fords and elsewhere were driven in, Ghurriki (the ford below Runniki) being now no longer guarded, and communication with Lord Gough at Ramnuggur being thus established.

During these two days, December 1st and 2nd, Lord

Gough had successfully concentrated Shere Singh's attention on Ramnuggur, by keeping up a constant cannonade and making demonstrations as though with a view to forcing the fords at that point.

On the following morning, December 3rd, Sir Joseph moved forward with the intention of attacking the Sikh flank, while Lord Gough should engage them from Ramnuggur. But he was still some way from his destination when a message reached him to the effect that reinforcements were on their way to join him by way of the Ghurriki ford. Sir Joseph certainly believed that his instructions were to secure the ford, and on no account to attack until the reinforcements arrived, which they did not do till the following morning, Godby having failed to effect a passage. Accordingly, Thackwell occupied ground at Sadulapore, and sent a native regiment to guard Ghurriki. On the other hand, it seems equally clear that Lord Gough intended him to act on his own discretion, according to circumstances.

The consequences of the misunderstanding were somewhat unfortunate. Shere Singh, finding Thackwell so near, marched against him from Ramnuggur with great part of his troops, and the British were startled at about two o'clock by the sudden commencement of a cannonade. The British fell back some 200 yards, to avoid some fields of sugarcane serving as cover for the enemy, who at first rushed forward in excitement; but then, perceiving that the movement had been made merely for security, and that its object was already attained, they showed no further disposition to come to close quarters. Shere Singh, in fact, had shown the customary skill of the Sikhs in choosing a strong defensive position which his men might be relied on to hold with their wonted stubbornness. But also, as usual, neither leaders nor followers understood how to attack; and they now contented themselves with maintaining a hot cannonade, to which the British replied with vigour. Colin Campbell was now anxious to attack, and it seems probable that if he had been given his way, a very severe blow might have been dealt. But Thackwell, believing that he had the most positive orders not to attack till the expected reinforcement should arrive, would not give permission. A further message from Lord Gough, with express instructions to the General to use his own judgment about waiting, did not arrive till the day was drawing to its close. With the experience of Ferozeshah behind, the risk of advancing and storming Sikh entrenchments as the darkness fell seemed too serious, and the enemy were allowed to retire. Under cover of night, Shere Singh withdrew from his entrenchments with his entire army, falling back to a very strong position northwards on the Jhelum; and he had already gone too far for effective pursuit when the morning broke.

It would seem, therefore, that, owing to a misunderstanding, Thackwell lost an opportunity of inflicting a very damaging blow on the Sikhs. But the immediate purpose of the extremely difficult and complicated movement had been successfully effected. Shere Singh was driven back from the Chenab to the Jhelum; from a rich country, where supplies were readily obtainable, to jungle; his opportunities of intriguing with the Durbar were cut off by the increased stretch of territory lying between him and Lahore; and the whole invading army had passed the Chenab with only the slight losses caused by the cannonade at Sadulapore.

This movement of the troops across the Chenab had been a source of the gravest anxiety to Lord Gough, since it had compelled him to divide his army in the face of the enemy, under circumstances which made steady communication difficult; yet the Sikhs had to be driven from their position, and there was no other way of doing it. Its successful accomplishment was therefore an intense relief to him, and to those who understood its importance—a feeling by no means extravagantly expressed in the terms of his despatch.

Still, the position now occupied by Shere Singh was exceedingly strong, and covered to a great extent by jungle. His troops greatly outnumbered Lord Gough's, while he was decidedly superior in artillery. The Commander-in-Chief therefore resolved to be content with holding him in check, until the fall of Multan should enable Whish to come up, and so give the force the strength both in men and artillery requisite for striking a decisive blow. It was unfortunate for Lord Gough's plans that the siege was so long protracted as to make an advance necessary before the desired reinforcement from Multan could move.

Just a month after the retreat from Ramnuggur, Attok fell into the hands of Chutter Singh and his allies. The insurgents were now free to give their exclusive attention to strengthening the army on the Jhelum. Thus the risks of continued delay seemed to outweigh those of an engagement; and on January 12th the advance began.

CHAPTER IV.

CHILLIANWALLA: DEC. 4–JAN. 13, 1849

After Sadulapore—Advance by Dinghi—Composition of army—Chillianwalla occupied—Action forced by the Sikhs—Order of battle—*On the left:* Movement of guns on the left—Robertson—Mowatt—Campbell's Division: he takes the left brigade—Pennycuick's Brigade—Campbell leads Hoggan's Brigade—Supported by Mowatt—Successful advance—His losses—White's Cavalry Brigade—Losses—*On the right:* Pope's Cavalry Brigade—Disastrous movement—Gilbert's Division—Godby's and Mountain's Brigades—Joined by Campbell—Penny's Brigade—Rout of Sikhs—Lane's detachment—Losses of Gilbert's Division.

A DEGREE of uncertainty appears to attach to the grounds for Lord Gough's forward movement. For a month after Sadulapore he had remained in the same neighbourhood, at Heylah, resolved not to give battle to Shere Singh till the arrival of Whish's reinforcements should give him the strength to make the fight conclusive. The policy of delay was emphatically Lord Gough's own, and was of a piece with the principle which he had throughout maintained of concentrating the whole available force for one crushing blow. Lord Dalhousie appears to have given the Chief instructions in the same sense; but so far his interference in a purely military question was of little consequence, since Lord Gough's view of what ought to be done coincided with his own. But during December the Governor-General's ideas appear to have changed, and before Christmas he had written to Lord Gough expressing his desire that Lord Gough should attack if he thought it safe to do so. Whether Lord Dalhousie himself ever went further in the way of pressing an immediate advance is not certain, owing to apparent breaks in the correspondence. But Major Mackeson, the political Agent, was urgent with the Commander-in-Chief for an advance, and the latter seems to have regarded the pressure from him as inspired by the Governor-General.* It appears that Lord Gough would have preferred waiting for his reinforcements; but that believing himself—quite accurately—to be in fact strong enough, at any rate, to strike an effective blow, and knowing that the enemy would be very shortly reinforced by Chutter Singh, after the fall of Attok, he allowed the Governor-General's known desire and the Agent's urgency to turn the somewhat nicely adjusted scale. The result was the advance on Chillianwalla, and a victory; but one which was both indecisive and expensive. Why it was so we shall presently see.

On January 12th the army advanced to Dinghi, lying nearly due east of Shere Singh's position beyond Chillianwalla.

Sir Joseph Thackwell had now been placed in command of the cavalry division in lieu of Cureton, the command of his infantry division being transferred to Colin Campbell. The whole force, therefore, was now made up as follows, amounting in all to about 14,000 men and 66 guns:—

CAVALRY DIVISION, Sir Joseph Thackwell commanding.

1*st Brigade*, under Brigadier M. White: 3rd Light Dragoons; 5th and 8th Light Cavalry.

2*nd Brigade*, under Brigadier Pope: 9th Lancers; 14th Light Dragoons; 1st and 6th Regiments Light Cavalry.

The European cavalry regiments numbered about 400 men each, the native cavalry 300, effective in the field.

* There is a note in Lord Gough's private diary: "Jan. 9. Heard from G.G. that he would be glad if I gained a victory."

INFANTRY (2nd Division),* under Major-General Sir Walter Gilbert.

1st Brigade, Brigadier Mountain: H.M.'s 29th Foot; the 30th and 56th Regiments Native Infantry.

2nd Brigade, Brigadier Godby: 2nd European Regiment; the 31st and 70th Regiments Native Infantry.

3RD DIVISION, Brigadier-General Colin Campbell, commanding.

1st Brigade, Brigadier Pennycuick: H.M.'s 24th Foot; the 25th and 45th Regiments Native Infantry.

2nd Brigade, Brigadier Hoggan: H.M.'s 61st Foot; the 36th and 46th Regiments Native Infantry.

3rd Brigade, Brigadier Penny: the 15th, 20th, and 69th Regiments Native Infantry.

ARTILLERY DIVISION, under Brigadier Tennant.

Six troops of Horse Artillery under Brigadier Brooke, with Colonels Brind and C. Grant; the troops respectively under Lieut.-Col. Lane, Majors Christie, Huish, Warner, Duncan, and Fordyce.

Two batteries of four 18-pounders and two 8-inch howitzers each; under Majors R. Shakespear and Ludlow; Major Horsford commanding.

Three field batteries: No. 5, commanded by Lieutenant Walker, in the absence of Captain Kinleside, sick; No. 10, commanded by Lieutenant Robertson, in the absence of Austin, wounded; and No. 17, commanded by Major Dawes.

The Foot Artillery under Brigadier Huthwaite.

The European infantry numbered about 900 each, and the native infantry about 700. H.M.'s 24th, an exceptionally strong regiment, turned out 1000 men in the field.

The Sikhs were lying with the Jhelum behind them,

* The 1st Division of the army of the Punjab was employed in the siege of Multan.

on the west, occupying a group of villages protected by jungle, with their left reaching to Russool, where there was a belt of hills. Chillianwalla, in advance of the line, was held only by outposts. Lord Gough's intention, therefore, was to march from Dinghi to Chillianwalla, drive in the outposts, and defer the attack till next day, when more accurate information as to the details of the position should be obtainable; unless circumstances should point to the advisability of an immediate engagement.

At 7 a.m., on the 13th January, the army advanced from Dinghi, formed in line of contiguous columns.

About twelve o'clock Chillianwalla was reached, and the enemy's outpost promptly driven in. From a high mound in front the Sikh entrenched position, stretching from Russool on their left to Moong on the right, was clearly visible; and Lord Gough had two alternatives before him: one to attack at once while there was plenty of daylight, and force the jungle without obtaining more complete knowledge of the ground; the other to encamp, and employ the interval in reconnoitring before giving battle on the morrow. This was the course which Lord Gough selected, and preparations were in progress for laying out the camp, when the Sikh guns opened fire, in doing so revealing the position of their batteries; whereupon Lord Gough, perceiving that the Sikh army had advanced beyond their entrenchments, gave orders to prepare for immediate action.

Historians and others have committed themselves to a total misconception of Lord Gough's action in giving battle when he did, and have talked as if the sound of the Sikh cannon proved too much for his self-control. But the simple fact of the matter is, that until the Sikh guns by opening fire betrayed the position of their batteries, all that could be seen or learnt about them gave the impression that encamping would be safe, and delay could be turned to advantage. But the action of the Sikh guns revealed that they had moved forward from the line of villages,* and so disposed their forces that encamping was for us a sheer impossibility. There was no alternative but an immediate engagement. On the other hand, the very conditions which enabled the Sikhs to force an engagement—their advance beyond the line of villages—removed the principal reason which had before made delay seem desirable. An attack on them was now the less formidable, since they no longer had the shelter of their entrenched position. And it may here be added that if Lord Gough's plan of action had been carried out, the engagement would have been decisive; as will become apparent from the course of the narrative, and the subsequent examination of its leading features.

For an hour the battle was an artillery duel, in which the enemy had the advantage both of position and of guns. At three o'clock the advance commenced.

The course of the battle is not easy to follow, and it is of no little importance to master at first the position of the different brigades.

On the flanks were the cavalry: White's on the left, Pope's on the right. Hoggan's Brigade was on the left of the line, with Pennycuick's next, both under Colin Campbell; then came Mountain's, and then Godby's, both under Gilbert; with Penny's Brigade (the 3rd of Campbell's Division) in reserve. The artillery were ranged: in the centre the heavy batteries; attached to Campbell's Division, three troops Horse Artillery (Brind), and Walker and Robertson's field-batteries, both under Major Mowatt; attached to Gilbert's Division, three troops Horse Artillery (Grant), and Dawes's field-battery.

On the other side the Sikh line extended for about six miles, covered by thick jungle, and with their right considerably overlapping the British left.

According to the plan of action, Campbell, with the brigades of Hoggan and Pennycuick, was to advance,

* See Appendix III., A.

supported by the guns attached to his division. Consequently the Horse Artillery on the extreme left moved forward, and came into action at effective range against a powerful battery of Sikh guns. Mowatt and Robertson at the same time moved forward with the lines of skirmishers thrown out by Pennycuick's and Hoggan's Brigades respectively; but almost immediately a staff officer, who —happily for his own reputation—has never been identified, rode up to Robertson, and ordered him to "take his three guns to the left, and assist the Horse Artillery to silence those guns." There appears to have been no authority whatever for the order, which was given in entire disregard of Campbell's movement; but Robertson was, of course, bound to act upon it, and did so, being thereby prevented from performing the specific function he was really intended to serve. Trotting out to the left for about 500 yards, he discovered a considerable body of Sikh horse on his front, on whom he opened fire, quickly dispersing them. Advancing again in the direction pointed out to him, the position of the enemy's guns was made known to him by a shot or two crossing his front, aimed apparently at the advancing infantry. Thereupon he brought up his right, and came into action against them, they being now engaged with Brind and the Horse Artillery. Placed where he was, his fire completely enfiladed the Sikh guns, and after about half an hour the latter were completely silenced. Having thus carried out his orders, and rendered signal service to the Horse Artillery, he proposed to rejoin his division, an exceedingly risky process, since it was out of sight, and he was without an escort. He succeeded, however, by the designed deliberation of his movements, in deceiving the Sikhs into the belief that he was supported, until, coming in sight of Hoggan's Brigade, he was able to trot on rapidly and join it, passing on the way four deserted Sikh guns and numbers of dead, marking the track along which the infantry had in the mean time advanced.

While Robertson's battery was thus diverted from the purpose for which it was intended, Mowatt advanced in line with Pennycuick's skirmishers on Hoggan's right; but, as he afterwards told Patrick Grant, the Adjutant-General, Pennycuick's Brigade advanced so rapidly that they were carried in front of the battery at the very commencement of the action, so that he could not render them the desired assistance; although, as will be seen, he was able to render most material service to Hoggan.

Thus, with regard to the artillery attached to Campbell's division, Robertson, owing to the unauthorised orders he received, did excellent service to the Horse Artillery, instead of to Hoggan's Brigade: Mowatt, for a different reason, rendered equally good service, but to Hoggan instead of to Pennycuick. To Mowatt's action we shall revert presently, but clearness in an extremely confusing narrative will best be attained by first turning to the movements of the infantry division itself.

According to generally recognised principles, it was Campbell's primary function, as divisional commander, to control the action of both his brigades, so that they should act in concert. But before the advance commenced he formed the opinion that the nature of the jungle made it impossible to control the co-operation of the two brigades; and accordingly he informed Pennycuick that he would leave to him the sole direction of the right brigade, taking himself the lead of the left brigade; judging that, of the two, it occupied the more responsible position, because of the overlapping of the Sikh right. By so doing he abrogated the duties of a divisional commander to discharge with splendid success those of a brigadier. He himself, and others who were present, maintained that the nature of the ground made any other course impracticable; but in the result, the want of co-operation between the brigades proved most disastrous to that of Pennycuick: and on the other hand, Gilbert, with difficulties to face of precisely the same kind, manipulated his division with marked success.

Pennycuick's rapid advance rendered the intended support of the field-batteries nugatory at a very early stage. The ground for some distance, being comparatively open, soon became interspersed with trees and thick, thorny bushes, impeding the regularity of the advance and screening from observation whatever might be in front. So serious was the obstruction that the line became disordered, and the companies were reduced to columns of sections. After moving forward a few hundred yards, the right brigade came under a fire of round shot, which was converted, as it advanced, to an incessant fire of grape, directed principally upon H.M.'s 24th, the centre regiment. This was the more formidable as the enemy were still completely screened from view. Officers and men began to fall in increasing numbers; nevertheless, the brigade continued to advance most steadily, although the difficulties of the jungle increased as it approached the enemy; until finally, about fifty yards in front of the Sikh guns which at last came into full view, the 24th came upon an impassable swamp, or pond, partially filled with water, and surrounded by scraggy trees and stumps, the ground being much broken. Thus two companies were obliged to file in rear, and so it happened that the centre of the regiment, and several of the companies on the left, were brought up nearly to the muzzles of the guns in masses and in much disorder, and were received by a tremendous discharge of grape and musketry. Brigadier Pennycuick and many officers and men fell as they closed on the enemy. Colonel Brookes was distinctly seen in front of the colours of the 24th, showing a splendid example, and cheering his men on. The 24th never for a moment hesitated, but pressed forward and captured the guns at the point of the bayonet without firing a shot; but only for a moment. The Grenadier company on the right, having experienced less difficulty in the advance, carried the position in front of them before the rest of the regiment, and Lieutenant Lutman assisted Private Marfield in spiking one of the guns. The enemy's fire was, however, so heavy, that the Grenadiers were forced back; but, led by Captain Travers, again advanced to the charge, again carried the guns, and more were spiked. Captain Travers here fell, cut down by a tulwar. The whole regiment was now hotly engaged and numbers fell on both sides. Colonel Brookes was seen to fall close to the guns; Major Harris was mortally wounded and carried to the rear; Lieutenant Collis and Ensign Phillips, carrying the colours, both fell, struck by grape, close to the guns; Lieutenants George Phillips, Woodgate, and Payne fell at the guns. Thus in the short time that elapsed between the advance and this struggle on the part of the regiment to hold the position it had so nobly won, all their leaders and many officers, thirteen in all, were killed; ten more officers were wounded, and an immense number of non-commissioned officers and men had fallen. Exhausted by their exertions, and the rapid advance for so long a distance; wholly unsupported, for no support was available at the critical moment; was it to be wondered at that the regiment which had made so splendid a fight, and suffered so fearful a loss, at length gave way? For some time the few officers who remained were unable to restore order, nor was the regiment re-formed till it had got clear of the jungle. Its loss, in addition to the officers, amounted to 231 killed and 266 wounded. With the 24th advanced the 25th regiment Native Infantry on the right and the 45th on the left, meeting with the same obstacles, and advancing also under a heavy fire of all arms; they also suffered severe loss, and on the retreat of the 24th they also were compelled to give way.

Several parties of both regiments were, however, quickly rallied. Captain Clarke kept his whole company, the rifle company of the 25th, together, and about 100 of the 45th

Native Infantry rallied round the colours of the regiment under Lieutenants Oakes and Tozer, Ensigns Trotter and Evans. These parties by their fire drove off the Sikh horsemen who attempted to follow up the brigade. They advanced again and moved with White's Cavalry Brigade when taking ground to the right, and subsequently joined Hoggan's Brigade. The 25th regiment lost 1 European officer, 6 native officers, and 105 men killed; 2 European officers, 3 native officers, and 87 men wounded. The 45th lost 20 non-commissioned officers and men killed, 4 European officers, 1 native officer, and 54 men wounded.

Pennycuick's Brigade behaved with gallantry and exemplary devotion, but its advance was too precipitate, and unfortunately he had no support from artillery.

Hoggan's Brigade on the left advanced under the personal command of Colin Campbell; the jungle soon causing it to lose touch with Pennycuick. Unlike Pennycuick's, it received considerable help from the guns; the artillery duel already narrated serving to check, and then silence, the fire of a powerful battery, by which it would have been otherwise enfiladed, on the left, while Mowatt's battery also covered it on the right.

That officer had advanced as related with No. 5 Battery. He had found considerable difficulty in forcing his guns through the thickets of stunted trees, and for some time could get no sight of the enemy, a distant sound of guns to his right being all he heard. After going half a mile or more he caught sight, on a sudden, over the tops of the trees and through an opening in the jungle, of a crowd of the enemy straight in front of him, about 700 or 800 yards distant. The position being unsuitable, he urged his men forward another 300 yards, during which time two or three Sikh guns opened on his left flank, the shots passing in rear of him. He then came to clearer ground, beyond which he saw on a crest a crowd of Sikhs, distant about 450 yards, their guns and masses appearing through the smoke. These immediately opened a heavy fire of round shot, shell, and musketry upon him. Here he promptly came into action, bringing as heavy a fire as he could upon the Sikhs, their shots mostly going over the heads of his men and tearing through the trees to his right and left, but, fortunately, not doing him much harm. In about twenty minutes the Sikh fire began to slacken, and through the smoke he saw their numbers melting away.

All this time nothing had been seen, on the right, of Pennycuick's expected brigade; but now on the left he did see Hoggan's emerge from the jungle and go straight at the Sikhs, keeping up a heavy fire as they advanced.

In the interval Campbell, leading the brigade, had regulated the pace with great care, and so kept his troops well in hand during the advance, although the nature of the ground had caused frequent breaks in the line. Nor had he met with obstacles so serious as those encountered by Pennycuick. After half a mile of jungle, he came out on comparatively open ground, where he found a large body of Sikh cavalry and infantry with four guns which had been playing on the advancing troops. The 61st charged and dispersed the Sikh cavalry; the 36th Native Infantry attacked the infantry, but were thrown into some disorder by a body of Sikhs falling on their flank; Campbell, however, wheeling the two right companies of the 61st, charged and repulsed these, capturing two guns. Now it was that Mowatt saw the brigade "going straight at the Sikhs," and forthwith concentrated his fire upon the opposing infantry. Throughout this most difficult operation, nothing could have been better than Major Mowatt's action, nor more serviceable to Hoggan's Brigade. The Sikhs at this point were most gallantly led by a few chiefs, but found the attack too fierce, and fled back to the jungle.

The brigade now rapidly formed to the right, astride the enemy's line; in doing so the 46th Regiment, on the left, was attacked by the Sikh cavalry in considerable strength;

these they gallantly repulsed under their commander, Major Tudor. At the same time the Sikhs brought up two more guns and fresh infantry against the right, upon which those who had just been driven back again formed. This was, in the opinion of General Campbell, the most critical moment of the day; but so ably was the brigade led, and so steadily did it behave, that this difficult change of front, whilst actually engaged with the enemy, was effectually and successfully carried out. The whole brigade advanced to the attack, driving the Sikhs before it, and capturing, one after another, thirteen guns, all of which were obstinately and bravely defended by both Sikh infantry and gunners, and only taken after a sharp struggle. So close was the fighting that the Brigadier-General himself was severely wounded by a sword-cut on his right arm. The brigade continued to move swiftly on, rolling up the Sikh line as it advanced, and overcoming all opposition; being exposed all through the movement to repeated attacks of Sikh cavalry, who were following up, compelling General Campbell at intervals to halt, face his troops about, and drive them off. Thus Campbell completely defeated and dispersed that portion of the Sikhs which just before had inflicted so terrible a repulse and such severe loss on Pennycuick's Brigade. Seeing a battery of artillery on his right, and finding it to be Mowatt's, which had maintained its fire until now, he ordered it to join, and continued his movement till he fell in with Mountain's Brigade, when he again wheeled to the left, forming his line on the original front. It was during this flank movement that Campbell first heard from Colonel Brooke, commanding the Horse Artillery, of the disaster that had happened to his right brigade. About the same time the division was also rejoined by Robertson's battery, and Warner's troop of Brind's Horse Artillery, which, with an escort of a squadron of the 8th Light Cavalry, had been ordered up by Sir Joseph Thackwell to his support.

Campbell's loss in this attack and sharp hand-to-hand

fight, though considerable, was by no means excessive, seeing the difficulties of the country and the obstinate defence of the enemy. H.M.'s 61st Foot lost 11 men killed, 3 officers and 100 men wounded. 36th Regiment Native Infantry, 1 native officer, 27 men killed; 6 European officers, 2 native officers, 69 men wounded. 46th Regiment Native Infantry, 3 men killed; 3 native officers, 48 men wounded.

The loss of the artillery was comparatively small. Fordyce lost 5 men and 2 horses wounded; Duncan's troop, 1 officer and 6 horses killed, 2 men and 1 horse wounded; Warner's troop, 1 man and 1 horse killed, and 1 man and 1 horse wounded; No. 5 Light Field Battery, 5 men wounded, 11 horses killed and 2 wounded; No. 10 Battery, only 1 horse wounded. Although the Sikh gunners stood well to their guns, they had not learnt the art of shooting straight.

Away on the left, White's Cavalry Brigade had advanced at the same time as Campbell's Division. But the ground was quite impracticable for the action of cavalry; unable to see anything in their front, they came suddenly under a very heavy fire of round shot, which mostly struck the ground in front of the line and ricochetted over the heads of the men. The brigade formed in support of the guns. On the Sikh battery being silenced by the Horse Artillery, as already related, Sir Joseph Thackwell proposed to follow up the advantage by a cavalry attack, and accordingly ordered the Grey squadron of the 3rd Light Dragoons and the 5th Light Cavalry to charge. These two bodies, led respectively by Captain Unett and Captain Wheatley, advanced. The 5th Light Cavalry coming upon a mass of Sikhs, were received with a considerable musketry fire, and, being much broken by the thick and scrubby jungle, were unable to make any impression on the enemy, and were repulsed; they, however, rallied at once very steadily and in good order on the 8th, the centre regiment. Unett's squadron of the 3rd Light

Dragoons, coming on a smaller body, broke through and swept on right through to the Sikh rear; then, re-forming his men and wheeling about, he cut his way back, but did not rejoin the brigade till towards the close of the action, causing great anxiety to Thackwell, who feared he had been annihilated. This splendid charge was unfortunately attended with very severe loss, for the line being broken by the jungle, the Sikh horsemen followed up, and, falling upon those who were isolated and separated, cut down many gallant soldiers. The squadron lost 23 men killed, 2 officers and 15 men wounded, 15 horses killed and missing, 7 wounded. The want of success that attended this attack prevented Sir Joseph Thackwell attempting any further offensive movements, and he was obliged to content himself with affording such protection as he could to the left of Campbell's Division. He detached Warner's Horse Artillery troop and a squadron of the 8th Cavalry to join Hoggan's Brigade, and with the remainder of the brigade took ground to his right, following Campbell's movements. In doing so the cavalry crossed the line by which Pennycuick's Brigade had advanced, and the field, littered with the bodies of the fallen, attested the severity of the struggle. Here were picked up some parties of the 45th Regiment who came on, and the brigade formed up in rear of Hoggan's and Mountain's Brigades on about the centre of the position originally held by the Sikhs. Thus fared the left attack. The loss of the Cavalry Brigade was: 3rd Light Dragoons, 24 men killed, 2 officers and 15 men wounded; 5th Light Cavalry, 2 European sergeants and 4 men killed, 2 officers and 14 men wounded; 8th Light Cavalry, 1 man killed and 2 wounded.

From the stubbornly contested fight on the left and left centre, we now turn to that on the right and right centre.

When Sir Walter Gilbert prepared to advance, shortly after the beginning of Campbell's movement, the troops were thus drawn up. On the extreme right, Pope's Cavalry Brigade, with the three troops Horse Artillery under Colonel Grant; then Godby's (Infantry) Brigade, and Mountain's, with Dawes's battery between them.

On the left, as the narrative has shown, the cavalry manœuvres had comparatively little influence on the course of the battle; on the right it was far otherwise. The action of Pope's Brigade is a painful and unaccountable blot on the day, and may fairly be held responsible for the indecisive results of Chillianwalla.

The greater numbers of the Sikhs enabled them to threaten our right flank as well as our left; and accordingly, Pope, observing a considerable body of Sikh horsemen on the slopes towards Russool, detached a wing of the 1st and 6th Light Cavalry, and the 9th Lancers (retaining the other wing of each regiment, with the 14th Light Dragoons), with some guns, under command of Colonel Lane, to protect the flank.

Then, advancing in line with the infantry brigades, he found a body of Sikh horse immediately to his front. The guns were immediately pushed forward; but before they could come properly into action, Pope with the cavalry passed in front of them, thus masking their fire, and making it practically useless. He advanced with his nine squadrons in one line, with no supports or reserves. Proceeding in such order and at such speed as the ground permitted, they soon came upon the enemy; but a charge under such conditions could hardly deserve the name. It was delivered slowly and without momentum; and almost immediately Pope himself was disabled, and had to be conducted from the field. Then occurred an event happily rare in the annals of British cavalry. Somebody, it is said—who, no one knows—was heard to give the order, "Threes about." Some of the men turned; a movement to the rear was started, which speedily degenerated into a panic; and the whole brigade went galloping in a reckless stampede to the rear, in spite of the strenuous exertions of the officers, plunging through the guns and throwing them into wild confusion, and leaving the infantry flank wholly uncovered. A body of Sikhs followed on their heels, fell on the guns, cut down many of the men, severely wounded Major Christie in command, and carried off four guns and two waggons. As for the cavalry, they could not be stopped till they were clear of the field, and were at length with difficulty rallied by the exertions of the Adjutant-General, Colonel Patrick Grant, Major (now Field-Marshal Sir Frederick) Haines, and Colonel Gough, on the staff of the Commander-in-Chief.

Such sudden panics are among the most inexplicable phenomena of war. The bravest troops may succumb to them. The one thing certain is that they are wholly and utterly unreasoning and incalculable, quite unrelated to the degree of danger to which the men are exposed; though raw soldiers, however brave, are more liable to them than veterans.

This disaster, however, must in great measure be attributed to the astonishing disregard of all recognised rules displayed by the brigadier in the manner of his advance. It is essential that cavalry in attacking should form with due supports to follow up an advantage or retrieve a check. No arm of the service is so liable to be disorganised, even in a successful charge, and a point to rally on is a vital necessity. When the advance had to be made through jungle, which of itself broke up the lines, and inevitably caused confusion, the need of supports was all the more imperative. Yet Pope led the advance absolutely without supports, in one line. Bad handling produced disorganisation; with no point to rally on, disorganisation developed into panic; and the flight of some of the finest troops in the service left the right flank of the advancing infantry division open for the enemy to turn.

This melancholy episode was accompanied by little

enough loss to the culprits. Their punishment was different. The 14th had only 1 officer killed, 1 man killed, and 14 wounded; the 9th, 3 men killed, 4 wounded; the 1st, the same; the 6th, 1 European officer, 2 native officers, and 4 men killed, 2 officers and 8 men wounded. With the guns, 12 men were killed, and 5 wounded, and Major Christie died of his wounds. But the Sikhs carried off 53 horses and 4 guns, and rendered 6 more useless for the day.

This most serious disaster occurred as Gilbert was leading his division to the attack, Dawes and his battery being in line with the skirmishers in front. The flight of the cavalry, which took place before the infantry joined battle, compelled him to refuse his right (Godby's) brigade in order, to some extent, to protect his right flank; but his troops behaved magnificently. Continuing their advance with perfect steadiness, covered by the very effective fire of No. 17 Field Battery, Mountain's Brigade came upon a strong battery of the enemy in front of the village of Lullianee, and promptly charged, carrying the whole of the guns at the point of the bayonet; this attack being almost immediately followed by Godby's Brigade, who also charged and carried the Sikh guns in their front.

Godby now halted his brigade, re-formed his line, and was collecting the wounded, when suddenly a fire was opened on him from his rear. His flank, left unguarded by the movement of Pope's Brigade, had been completely turned by a large body of Sikhs; and, in fact, he was surrounded. The journal of a subaltern of Godby's Brigade records in stirring language the incidents of the day. Godby's order was coolly given, "Right about face." Major Dawes's battery, which seems to have been everywhere at the right moment, was splendidly handled, and, moving to the right flank, poured in a heavy fire and scattered the Sikh horsemen who attempted to charge, knocking over men and horses in heaps. Sir Walter

Gilbert at this moment rode up, and, seeing Major Steele, commanding the 2nd Europeans, addressed him coolly and cheerily, "Well, Major, how are you? Do you think you are near enough to give those fellows a charge?" "By all means," answered Steele. "Well, let us see how you can do it." Such conduct was equal to a reinforcement of 1000 men! In an instant the brigade, led by the 2nd Europeans, marched to the rear, and, with a cheer, rushed upon the Sikhs. These fought manfully sword in hand, and strove to break through the line; but after a short, sharp struggle, they were swept away, and the "2nd Europeans," now known as the Royal Dublin Fusiliers, again stood masters of the field.

Mountain's Brigade, equally well led, met with the same desperate resistance, and were compelled to face about to repulse the enemy; but about this time Colin Campbell, with Hoggan's Brigade and White's cavalry, and the whole of the artillery of the left, moved up and joined them.

Meantime, Penny's Brigade, which had been ordered up by Lord Gough from its position in reserve, on the report of Pennycuick's disaster, had followed a devious course. Losing its bearings in the intricacies of the jungle, it had moved diagonally from the centre to the right, and suddenly found itself on the front and right of Godby (whose brigade, it will be remembered, had faced about); and here Penny in turn was attacked in front and right and rear, until the ubiquitous and inevitable Dawes came to the rescue with his guns, and drove the enemy off.

By this time Campbell had joined on to Mountain's Brigade, the whole of the artillery were brought up, and a destructive fire was opened upon the Sikhs, who now, in great disorder, were in full retreat upon Tupai.

Colonel Lane, detached on the right as related, virtually took no part in the main engagement. His movement, ordered by Pope, was unknown beyond the brigade authorities; and in the confusion caused by Pope's wound, and the subsequent panic, no instructions were sent to him. In fact, he appears to have known nothing of what was going on; and having himself neglected the duty of keeping in touch with the proceedings on his left, omitted the necessary measures for retrieving the worst effect of the cavalry disaster and covering Gilbert's flank. The service for which he had been detached was a judicious precaution in itself; but the Sikhs whom he was engaged in watching, and on whom he fired with some effect, never gave a sign of being a serious danger, not even returning his fire; while the immediate duty of covering the flank of the infantry brigade was of paramount importance. When Godby and Mountain had already stemmed and turned the counter-attack of the enemy, Lane advanced and poured a heavy fire into the large bodies of Sikhs whom he now observed retiring. But by this time the approach of darkness made it impossible to follow up the retreat, and the engagement was over. The Sikhs had been driven in to Tupai, and the British fell back to Chillianwalla; the enemy during the night succeeding in recovering and carrying off such of their own guns as had been left on the deserted field of battle.

The detailed losses of Gilbert's Division were as follows:—Godby's Brigade: the 2nd Fusiliers, 2 European officers wounded, 6 men killed, and 60 wounded; 31st Regiment Native Infantry, 3 men killed, 1 European officer, 1 native officer, and 54 men wounded; 70th Regiment Native Infantry, 2 native officers and 3 men killed and 20 men wounded. Mountain's Brigade: 29th Foot, 31 men killed, 5 European officers and 203 men wounded, and 3 missing; 30th Regiment Native Infantry, 2 European officers, 1 native officer, and 64 men killed, 9 European officers, 9 native officers, and 200 men wounded; 56th Regiment Native Infantry, 2 European officers, 4 native officers, and 39 men killed, and 36 missing (who may be added to the killed), 6 European officers, 6 native officers, and 227 men wounded. Dawes's Battery No. 17, lost 2 officers wounded, and 3 men; 3 horses killed, 1 missing. The loss of Penny's Brigade amounted to 12 men killed, 5 European officers, 1 native officer, and 103 men wounded.

The total loss of the British force was 22 officers, 16 native officers, and 561 men killed, and 98 men missing, who may be added to the number; 67 officers, 27 native officers, and 1547 men wounded. Grand total, 2338 men.

CHAPTER V.

AFTER CHILLIANWALLA: JAN. 14–FEB. 21

Further movement stopped by rains—Popular impressions of the battle—Misjudgment on the Commander-in-Chief—Injustice of the charge of impetuosity—True explanation of the events—Anecdotes of Lord Gough—Of Sikh generosity—Subsequent movements of the Sikhs—Lord Gough's command of the situation—Sikhs move on Gujerat—Lord Gough's counter-moves—Final concentration.

The routed Sikhs had not been able to retire directly upon Russool, where the real strength of their position lay, but had been driven to Tupai on the Jhelum (see map). Had the defeat been completed with a little more time to spare, the mass of them would in all probability have been driven right into the river. This end might have been accomplished by an advance next day; but, as ill-luck would have it, for two days after the battle rain descended in such torrents as to render any further movement impossible for the time, the soil in the neighbourhood of Tupai being turned into a species of soft pudding. The Sikhs were thus enabled to regain their practically impregnable position at Russool. It would otherwise have become apparent that the blow struck at Chillianwalla was by no means so ineffective as it seemed. For, a few days later—on the 19th—Elahi Buksh, commandant of the Sikh artillery, came in; and reported that immediately after the action the troops had been in a state of utter demoralisation, although now, since Chutter Singh had arrived with large reinforcements, they were beginning to reckon the affair as a virtual victory.

Public opinion at home, hastily formed on insufficient data, endorsed the adverse view. The advantages gained were not obvious; the casualties had been exceedingly heavy; three regiments had lost their colours; four guns had been lost; and a British regiment had given way to unreasoning panic. In the shock of this knowledge, the fact that immense numbers of the enemy had fallen, thirteen of their guns been captured, and many more spiked (fifty out of sixty brought into action were said by Elahi Buksh to have been either taken or spiked) was forgotten. That the loss of the colours was due to the bearers being shot down unperceived in the confused jungle fighting was overlooked. Public opinion, as usual, demanded a scapegoat, found it in the person of the Commander-in-Chief, and his recall was decided upon; but happily, before it could take effect, he had already achieved the crowning triumph of Gujerat.

That the feeling against the Commander-in-Chief was altogether unreasonable and unwarranted, will be apparent on a calmer review of the facts than has usually been given. But it is to be recorded that, even while it misjudged him, the public did not forget those qualities of Lord Gough which had won him a place in popular affection, and the devotion of his men.* Indomitable resolution, fearless courage, a most chivalrous sense of honour, a very warm heart, were characteristics universally recognised. But from these, other qualities were inferred, quite incorrectly. Because he was personally daring almost to rashness—it has already been related how at Ferozeshah he exposed himself to draw the enemy's fire from his men—it was imagined that he was rash as a commander. Because he had much trust in cold steel, he was accused of being over-hasty in its employment. The current tales—fiction quite as often as fact—told of him would never have been fastened on to a chief who was not regarded with a species of fond enthusiasm.

* See Appendix IV.

But they also made it the easier to believe that he had a besetting tendency to rashness.

Now, in the first place, nothing can be clearer than this—that his plan of campaign could not be charged with want of caution. Month after month the political Agents had urged him to send a brigade here, and a brigade there; to run heavy risks; to take the chances of throwing away, as he held, an immense number of lives in a series of minor expeditions. He had held stoutly to the principle that no force was to be employed unless it was really adequate. He had refused to advance against Chillianwalla without his Multan reinforcements, until strong pressure was put upon him. When he did advance, it was only because the chances were in favour of his striking a thoroughly effective blow; and after Chillianwalla, when he was again subjected to perpetual pressure, and was constantly urged to advance again, he remained imperturbable, waiting and watching till he could crush the foe once and for all.

At one point only can it be argued that he attacked when in insufficient force—at Chillianwalla. The answer is that, as a matter of fact, he was in sufficient force; that but for circumstances and mischances for which it was not he that was to blame, his victory there would have been decisive; and that although a certain risk was run, it was worth running at that particular stage, for the sake of preventing the imminent junction between Shere Singh and his father.

Lord Gough was the last man to bring forward the failure of his subordinates in his own defence. But it is to be remarked that his method of attack was precisely the same which he adopted with such signal success at Gujerat, modified only by the fact that at the later battle he was *for the first time* stronger in artillery than the enemy. That of itself points to the soundness of his dispositions; and the view that if his plans had been properly carried out the victory would have been decisive, will be borne out by a review of the battle.

In the first place, according to his orders, the attack was to be made under cover of the artillery; but Robertson's battery was ordered out of its proper place by the unknown staff-officer, Pennycuick's Brigade advanced too rapidly for Mowatt, and Pope's went in front of the guns intended to support him.

In the second place, Campbell's two brigades should have acted together; but the Divisional Commander allowed Pennycuick to act independently, holding that the nature of the ground rendered co-operation impossible, and never making the attempt. The result was disaster to Pennycuick. Nor is it possible to avoid the remark that Gilbert, with the right division, with just the same difficulties in his way, performed his function of Divisional Commander, and kept his brigades working together, with entire success.

In the third place, the cavalry and guns on the right ought to have covered Gilbert's Division. Under proper handling, Christie's guns would have been allowed to remain in advance, would have cleared the ground in front of Pope, and have poured an overwhelming enfilading fire on the battalions opposed to Gilbert. Not only would his advance have been facilitated, but the turning of his flank would have been impossible; while the cavalry would have been available to strike at the right moment, and to fall with overwhelming effect upon the retreating foe, thereby rendering the victory complete and decisive. The whole plan was wrecked by Pope's total disregard of the first principles of cavalry action.* Pushing in front of the batteries, he masked their fire and made them useless. On ground where he could not charge effectively—where the jungle necessarily broke his line and disorganised it—he advanced in single line, with no supports whatever. Next, being wounded himself and forced to retire, he never notified the fact to the next senior officer. And so the men, badly as they had been handled, were seized with an unreasoning

* See Appendix III. B.

panic, rode over the guns to the rear, and left the infantry flank open for the foe to turn, unshielded by horse or artillery.

Lastly, Lane, with his cavalry and guns, might have retrieved this mishap; but he neglected to keep himself informed of the course of events, and remained watching a distant body of Sikhs—troops who never so much as fired a shot—while the mischief was done. Thus nothing but the magnificent behaviour of Godby's Brigade averted a most grave disaster.

It is a curious instance of irony that the Chief's silence with regard to Lane in his dispatches was translated into a deliberate slight on that officer's invaluable services. The theory appears to have been that, by staying where he did Lane triumphantly effected precisely what he failed to do. He was described * as having by his "firmness" prevented the masses of horse and foot on the enemy's left from bearing down upon our right and rear. As a matter of fact, by remaining isolated, he allowed the masses of the enemy to turn the right and rear, while he held in check a detachment which never showed any inclination to take a serious part in the engagement at all.

Thus the comparative ill-success of Chillianwalla was to be attributed to the failure of some of the guns to fulfil their proper functions, for which, on the left, the Divisional Commander in the main, and on the right, Pope, were responsible; to the separation of Hoggan's and Pennycuick's Brigades; to the cavalry disaster; and to the negligence of Colonel Lane. The disasters to Pennycuick and to Pope's Brigade were in great measure retrieved by the splendid conduct of Hoggan's Brigade and Gilbert's Division respectively. But the check delayed victory till the approach of night prevented its completion; while, in spite of all, the greatly superior force of the Sikhs was beaten fairly from the field.

* Sir H. Durand, in the *Calcutta Review*.

But for these circumstances, for no one of which could the Commander-in-Chief be held responsible, his plan of action would have been fully vindicated; the enemy would have been in full flight much earlier than they were, and their shattered regiments would have been driven into the Jhelum in total rout before the shades of night descended to shelter them.

As for the story that Lord Gough only commenced the action because he found the smell of powder too exciting, it is a fiction. His intention was to encamp if the Sikhs remained in their entrenchments, while he was equally prepared to fight and vanquish them if they did not. When the Sikh batteries opened fire, they forced the second alternative on the Commander-in-Chief; the immediate engagement had become a necessity, but, owing to the change in the Sikh position, not an unwelcome one. If Lord Gough then failed to achieve his purpose, this narrative has shown to whom the blame is to be rightly attributed.

Lord Dalhousie, better informed than the general public, addressed to the Chief an exceedingly sympathetic and gratifying letter. "God be thanked," the old soldier wrote in his diary; "he sees the case in its proper light."

A highly characteristic story, which had the further merit of truth, may be here repeated. When the fight was over, officers and men were worn out; and, more particularly, were suffering severely from thirst and want of water. One after another came petitions for leave to go back to water; and to one of these requests the Chief's answer was memorable and conclusive: "I'll be damned if I move till my wounded are all safe!"

Another of the current tales of the Chief's personal combativeness has a humorous aspect which makes it worth recording; though even as fiction it belongs not to Chillianwalla but to Gujerat. It was related that in order to prevent Lord Gough from plunging personally into the fray, Patrick Grant enticed him on to the roof of a house and then took away the ladder. That the Chief was reluctant to remain in a position of personal security was, in fact, no doubt true enough; but that he recognised the necessity and acted on it without any such extraneous compulsion, is equally certain. In the words of one who was there, "he came away when he chose; just exactly when he chose." Undoubtedly he did mount the roof of a house, but for the obvious reason that it was one which gave him a particularly complete view of the field.

The accounts of the battle make mention of the cruelty shown by the Sikhs when they returned to the deserted field under cover of darkness. They certainly mutilated the slain, but it does not seem likely that there were many wounded left for them to murder. On the other hand, it is remarkable, and not a little to their credit, that on the 18th Shere Singh sent back to the British camp two men belonging to the 9th Lancers, who had been caught straying in the jungle and taken captive. And Chutter Singh not only allowed George Lawrence to go to Lahore on parole, but likewise permitted Lieutenant Bowie—who had been taken in the Derajat, and was now a prisoner within the lines of Russool—to visit Lord Gough's camp on parole. It need hardly be said that both these officers observed their parole loyally. The remarkable fact is that the Sikh chiefs not only knew that they might be trusted, but were generous enough to give them the benefit of that confidence.

The three days of heavy rain made it impossible, as we have seen, to follow up the defeat of Chillianwalla; and during that time large reinforcements were received by the enemy, who had now been joined by Chutter Singh. Under these circumstances, it would have been manifestly unwise to engage further, the position at Russool being extremely strong and well entrenched; and Lord Gough reverted to his determination to wait for the fall of Multan, and the reinforcements from the south. The two armies lay at Russool and Chillianwalla, watching. On the 25th the joyful rumour reached the camp that Multan had fallen; next day the news was confirmed, and now it was certain that the final conflict would not be long deferred.

Some doubt prevailed as to the intentions of the Sikhs, who were known about this time to have removed part of their forces to Pooran, lying a little to the north, without resigning their hold on Russool.

There were rumours of an intended advance; and early in February, still without leaving Russool, Shere Singh brought part of his army down to Khoree, threatening Dinghi. As early as February 5th it was ascertained that part of the Russool entrenchments had been evacuated, though the Russool position was still held by a considerable force, and was far too strong to be attacked.

Mackeson, indeed, was urgent with Lord Gough that the attack should be renewed. The Chief, however, maintained that deliberate patience which is so curiously overlooked in the popular idea of his character. Shere Singh sought to entice him into a battle by demonstrations, approaching so near as Nur Jemal; but in vain. The Multan Division was on its way, though the Bombay column moved with irritating dilatoriness; but Lord Gough, holding the interior lines, could intercept any attempt Shere Singh might make to circumvent him. The fords of the Chenab were guarded, and could be secured before they were seriously threatened. The line of communications was held by way of Dinghi; and, in spite of the movement to Khoree and Nur Jemal, the Commander-in-Chief still refused to give battle, even when, on the 12th, Shere Singh made a strong demonstration of attack; contenting himself with holding the enemy in check by means of a few squadrons of cavalry. Shere Singh, in fact, was not prepared to attack him where he lay; nor could he venture to march by him southwards, since he would thus be caught between Whish's advancing division in front, and Lord Gough's army on his rear; while, if he attempted to cross the Chenab higher up, the latter could still intercept him.

On the 14th, the Sikh army left its encampments for Gujerat, and next day Lord Gough moved to Lassoorie. Learning that the enemy had now placed themselves precisely where he wanted them, Lord Gough, pushing forward a column to Wazirabad—whither Whish had already despatched a detachment, under Colonel Byrne, to secure the ford—moved on the 16th to Pukee Nuggar and Sadulapore. From the 17th to the 19th the forces from Multan were joining, the army being completed in its full strength on the 20th. During these days the Commander-in-Chief made a series of very short marches by Ishera and Tricca to Shadiwal, moving always in order of battle, so that the enemy were kept in uncertainty as to the moment when the blow would be struck.

Thus, throughout these weeks, Lord Gough had successfully resisted every inducement to give battle to the enemy prematurely; and, while holding their movements in check, had also so kept them in hand that he could concentrate his entire force to deliver the final blow, and utterly shatter the Khalsa army when he delivered it.

CHAPTER VI.

GUJERAT AND THE END OF THE CAMPAIGN: FEB. 21

Force before Gujerat—Sikh views on artillery—The Sikh position—British order of battle—Advance—Artillery to the front—Overwhelming effects—Advance of the line—The villages carried—The Scinde Horse—The Afghan Horse on our right—Rout of the Sikhs—Gilbert's pursuing column—Surrender of the Sikh army—Summary of Gujerat.

On February 20th the arrival of the Multan army gave Lord Gough the force—and especially the preponderance in artillery—which he desired, in order to deliver the final blow to the enemy who had held the British power at bay with a stubborn skill hitherto unparalleled in Indian warfare.

In the first place, there were the same regiments which had taken part at Chillianwalla. The divisional commanders were as before; but Brigadier Penny was now in command of what had been Godby's Brigade, in Gilbert's Division, while Penny's and Pennycuick's Brigades, in Campbell's Division, were commanded by Carnegie and M'Leod.

To these were added the 1st Infantry Division, under Whish, with Brigadier Markham in command of the 32nd Foot and the 49th and 51st Native Infantry, and Hervey in command of the 10th Foot and the 8th and 72nd Native Infantry; also Dundas's Bombay Column, 60th Rifles, 3rd Bombay Native Infantry, Bombay Fusiliers, and 19th Native Infantry.

The Scinde Horse and four regiments of Irregulars were added to the cavalry. The artillery, under Brigadier Tennant, now numbered 96 guns, 18 being of heavy calibre. The engineers and sappers were under command of General Cheape, who had conducted the engineering operations at Multan.

Major George Lawrence had been brought down by Chutter Singh when he joined his son. Lawrence had been very well treated, and had made friends with many of his captors. Being allowed to visit Lahore on parole, to see his brother Sir Henry, he communicated a remark which they had frequently made, to the effect that although the British artillery was what they most feared, it had never been fully brought into play against them. The same remark had been made by Elahi Buksh. With fuller information, they would have learnt that the reason for this hitherto had been the exceedingly simple one, that their own artillery was the stronger; though it was true that at Chillianwalla there was the further reason that both Pennycuick and Pope had advanced beyond the support of the guns. These things were to be very effectually remedied at Gujerat. A curious fiction, however, prevailed, that, because Lord Gough had not won his battles by artillery when it was not strong enough for the purpose, therefore he would not have used his artillery when it *was* strong enough, except under pressure from Lord Dalhousie. Whereas, if the Commander-in-Chief had been reinforced with the guns from Multan in early January, he would have fought Chillianwalla precisely as he fought Gujerat, without requiring advice either from the Governor-General or the enemy.

The morning of February 21st broke in splendour over the open fields of young corn which lay between the opposing armies; beyond in the distance the mountain ranges shot their snow-clad peaks into the blue, forming a glorious scene. The Sikhs lay in the form of a rough crescent, facing nearly due south. Their right flank lay across a deep dry nullah or watercourse; which curved round the city behind them, and covered part of their front, then took a sharp turn south, and passed through the centre of the British encampment. Their left reached to a smaller nullah full of water, which ran south into the Chenab. Their cavalry—Afghan horsemen for the most part—extended beyond the nullahs on right and left. Between the two nullahs they had occupied, fortified, and loopholed, with the skill for which they were remarkable, the villages of Burra Kalra and Chota Kalra (Great and Little).

The British faced them, looking north, their line divided by the great nullah.

Next to this nullah, on the right, was Gilbert's Division; beyond that, Whish's, with Hervey's Brigade in the front line, and Markham's in the second. On the flank were the cavalry brigades of Lockwood and Hearsey.

On Gilbert's left was the heavy battery of 18 guns; Whish was supported by three troops Horse Artillery, with Dawes's Battery and two troops Horse Artillery for the time in reserve. The cavalry were supported by Warner's troops of Horse Artillery.

On the left of the nullah was Campbell's Division, with Carnegie and M'Leod in the front line, and Hoggan in second line, supporting Dundas and the Bombay Column on the left. White's Cavalry Brigade, with Sir J. Thackwell, was on the left flank, supported by two troops of Horse Artillery. The Bombay Column was supported by Blood's Bombay Horse Artillery; Campbell, by the two light field-batteries of Ludlow and Robertson.

A reserve, consisting of the 5th and 6th Light Cavalry, the 45th and 69th Native Infantry, and the Bombay Field-Battery, was in charge of the rear.

Having broken their fast, the troops were in motion by half-past seven. Somewhat too soon for their own interests, the Sikhs opened fire, exposing the position and range of their guns; so that the advancing line was halted, out of their reach, and the whole force of artillery was moved to the front, covered by infantry skirmishers. At nine o'clock the long line of guns was in position, some 800 yards from the Sikhs, and then the storm began in earnest. For two hours and a half the hail of shot and shell poured in upon the enemy; the first shot being fired by the inevitable Dawes. By the end of that time it may be said that the defence had been pretty thoroughly knocked to pieces, although our artillery suffered very considerably in the duel.

At half-past eleven, a general advance of the line was ordered, the artillery still leading. But, in spite of all they had suffered, the gallant Sikhs were still determined to fight to the last. From the village of Burra Kalra, they poured so fierce a fire on our advance party, sent forward to occupy it under the impression that it was deserted, that the place had to be stormed in the teeth of desperate resistance by the 2nd European Light Infantry of Penny's Brigade, led by the Brigadier himself and Major Steele. Similarly, Chota Kalra was carried by the 10th (part of Hervey's Brigade), led by Colonel Franks. More than once the stubborn foe attempted to stem the advance, and even to advance themselves against the brigades of Markham and Hervey on our right; but each time the fire of the Horse Artillery overwhelmed them.

So completely effective was the action of the artillery, that on the left the nullah was cleared out by it, and Campbell's infantry needed not to fire a single shot.

Out on our left, the Afghan horsemen had shown an inclination to try and turn our flank; but Thackwell sent forward the Horse Artillery to open fire upon them, and cover a magnificent charge by the Scinde Horse, supported by the 9th Lancers; who shattered the opposing squadrons and drove them in headlong flight, thus enabling Thackwell to turn the enemy's flank. The ground prevented the cavalry from being brought further into play; but the guns were now brought up so that they could enfilade the Sikh position, and play a vigorous part in hastening the flight, which was now becoming general.

On our right, the movements of the Afghan horsemen kept attention very much alive, but no real conflict took place, the ground being ill adapted for cavalry action. A troop of these audacious warriors did, however, succeed in getting round; some thirty of them venturing even to dash along the British rear, and approaching the spot where Lord Gough stood with his staff. But they were charged and cut to pieces by the Chief's escort, a troop of the 5th Light Cavalry, led by Lieutenant Stannus.

By half-past twelve, the whole Sikh army was in full flight. By one o'clock, Gujerat itself, the Sikh camp, their baggage, and most of their guns, were in possession of the victors. On the left of the town, Dundas and Thackwell passed in pursuit; on the right, the other divisions. For twelve miles the cavalry pursued the fugitives, till darkness fell, compelling them to drop as they fled most of the few guns which they had succeeded in withdrawing from the field.

With the least possible delay, Sir Walter Gilbert—whose prowess as a horseman has already been alluded to—was despatched with some 12,000 men of all arms in pursuit across the Jhelum. George Lawrence, to the intense admiration of the enemy, fulfilled his pledge and returned to their camp, and passed frequently to and fro with proposals for terms from Shere Singh. But no terms were to be granted save unconditional surrender. So hotly were the Sikhs pressed, that they had no chance of obtaining rest or supplies; and worn out with the flight, their ammunition exhausted, with no means of obtaining food, they first, on March 6th, restored all their prisoners, and finally, on the 12th, surrendered at discretion.

Sir Colin Campbell, who had been sent with a column

to secure the subjection of the northern districts, overtook Gilbert about this time, and describes the bearing of the vanquished chiefs, who boldly affirmed their right to do as they had done, while frankly recognising the hopeless completeness of the disaster which had come upon them. In the hour of surrender as in the hour of battle, they approved themselves a worthy foe, as in days to come they were to prove themselves worthy comrades in arms.

A few days later, the last remnant of opposition was ended with the surrender of Peshawur, and the flight of the Afghans across the border.

Little in the way of comment needs to be added to this account of the triumph of Gujerat. From first to last, there was no flaw in the conduct of the fight. With his artillery at last brought up to the desired strength, Lord Gough had used it to the full; and for all the desperate valour of the Sikhs, the battle was won before the line advanced. Horse, foot, and artillery, every arm of the service did thoroughly and successfully what it was called upon to do. Throughout the campaign, the Sikh leaders had displayed higher qualities than in the Sutlej campaign; their followers had assuredly shown no falling off. Yet this great army was at Gujerat utterly shattered beyond conceivable hope of recuperation; and the achievement cost the victors a total loss of 5 officers and 91 men killed, 24 officers and 646 men wounded. The principle which Lord Gough had maintained from the beginning, that the whole available force must be concentrated to deal the decisive blow, was vindicated. On that he had rested his objection to the Multan expedition, or to a Hazara expedition; to the deviation from it (though on exceptional grounds, as already explained), and to exceptional accidents, was due the comparative failure of Chillianwalla; to the imperturbable maintenance of the same principle after Chillianwalla was due the final triumph. The one great Power left in India was prostrated after two wars which it had wilfully forced upon us. Lord Gough, recalled from his command because he had been misrepresented through ignorance, answered his detractors once for all by a victory ranking with the most brilliant achievements of our Indian armies.

CHAPTER VII.

SUMMARY AND CONCLUSIONS AS TO THE SIKH WARS

Reasons of the Sutlej campaign—Of the second war—And their result—Character of the wars—Lessons in criticism—Military policy of the Sutlej campaign—Of the Punjab campaign—Misconceptions as to loss of life—As to the Commander-in-Chief's "impetuosity"—Close of Lord Gough's Indian career—His farewell to the army of the Punjab.

THE war was ended. It was not four years since the Khalsa, full at once of religious fanaticism, military ardour, and arrogant self-confidence, had first launched itself against the tide of British power. Ranjit Singh, whose penetrating vision and cool brain had enabled him to direct his policy and control his ambition in a very precise relation to his strength, had gauged the possibilities of the situation with an astuteness denied to his successors. He knew that the native State which hurled itself against the British was doomed to shatter itself, sooner or later—probably sooner. But the disaster of Kabul dealt a crushing blow to British prestige, for which Meanee and Maharajpore failed to atone. If the Gwalior army had not then been too precipitate, and brought destruction on itself while still single-handed, it is hard to say what might not have resulted from a junction between Sikhs and Mahrattas. As it was, the Sikh army crossed the Sutlej with the confident expectation of a triumphant career, whatever the shrewder of the Sirdars may have thought. Once, at least, during the conflict they were within an ace of a victory which would have set all India in a blaze. They were beaten; but they half believed that they were not fairly beaten. The magnanimity of their conquerors obtained no recognition. The mother of their Maharajah fanned the smouldering flame of their resentment. The voices of their soothsayers prophesied an early restitution of the Khalsa. Once again they crossed swords with the foreigners; but this time, so overwhelmingly decisive was the arbitrament of war, that they accepted the inevitable. The respect for British fighting qualities then engendered, was so confirmed by the beneficent influences of our Government, that the Company's most stubborn foes have become the most loyal subjects of the Empress of India; and the race whom fifty years ago our "political" officers were wont to condemn as traitors, have shown their mettle as the staunchest comrades in arms of the British soldier in many a hard-fought field.

The termination of the second Sikh war is a fitting point at which to draw both some general conclusions, and others relating specifically to Lord Gough's conduct of the wars.

In the first place, it is to be noted that the enemy we had to deal with was neither a miscellaneous horde of mercenaries, nor troops of daring but undisciplined hill-men; but an army of soldiers trained on the European model, better provided with artillery than our own until Gujerat, far outnumbering the troops opposed to them, and full of religious enthusiasm and dogged courage.

Secondly, both were wars of pitched battles, some of them extremely sanguinary.

Thirdly, the first campaign was concluded in two months, and the second in three months, from the time when the Commander-in-Chief actually took the field.

But the British public has been accustomed, by the brilliant exploits of small armies in India from the days of Clive to those of Havelock, to expect British troops to face enormous odds, and achieve victory after victory with very small loss. If there is hard fighting, as must inevitably be the case where such an army as that of the Khalsa has to be met, there is a general inclination to believe that the British commander must be to blame. Anything in the shape of a reverse is magnified into a disaster; while there is a common disposition to believe that any force will do to overcome any resistance, without running any risks. Obviously no one would own to adopting the theory thus baldly stated, but virtually that is what a great deal of popular comment on our "little wars" amounts to.

And yet it would seem sufficiently manifest that a war in which the armies opposed to us are well trained, stubborn, superior in numbers, and equal in armament, are not picnic parties, but affairs in which many lives must be lost; not to be reckoned by scores, hardly even by hundreds.

Further, it should be borne in mind that there is a false economy in lives as well as in money.* It may very well be the case that a three months' campaign which involves a heavy expenditure of money and lives may be both in money and lives much less expensive than a series of campaigns which cost much less relatively to the time over which they are protracted.

The attitude of the public towards Lord Gough exemplifies forcibly the wrong way of looking at matters. When the news of the desperate fight at Ferozeshah reached England, there were plenty of voices raised to condemn the Commander-in-Chief's "rashness." They were well answered before the Board of Directors by the Chairman, Sir Archibald Galloway. "Complaints are made that Sir Hugh Gough at Ferozeshah took the bull by the horns. But, gentlemen, in this case *the bull was all horns*." As to the actual method of attack, the bull was indeed all horns in the sense that wherever an attack might be attempted, the Sikh entrenchments were equally strong. If the bull was attacked at all, he had to be taken by the horns. And the

* See Appendix III., C.

plain fact was that the crossing of the Sutlej made it absolutely imperative that the Sikhs should be met and fought at once with the available force. That the force available was far too small was no fault of the Commander-in-Chief's. We have seen the reason. A choice had to be made between trying to avert war and having an adequate force on the frontier. The former policy was followed, and the frontier force was inadequate. The result was that we narrowly escaped an overwhelming disaster.

In the case of the Punjab Campaign, the choice was a somewhat different one; but again it depended on a calculation of chances—to decide what course to follow, it must be assumed that the Sikhs were sure to rise *en masse*, or that they were sure *not* to rise *en masse*. On the latter assumption, the employment of small forces to nip the revolt in the bud would have been sound policy; on the former it could only have led to disaster. Lord Gough held that the risk was too great, particularly if the forces were scattered amongst untrustworthy allies, and therefore he resolved on the winter campaign.

In the first war, Sir Henry Hardinge resolved to run the greater risk in the hope of averting war altogether; in the second, Lord Dalhousie adopted Lord Gough's view, preferring the certainty of a big but successful war to the chance of a small war with the risk of a serious disaster thrown in. The event proved Sir Henry's calculation to be wrong in the first instance; there is certainly no proof that Sir Hugh's was not right in the second.

The loss of life at Sobraon and Chillianwalla was, of course, made a ground of reproach against the Commander-in-Chief. As to Sobraon, no defence is needed. As to Chillianwalla, a word may be added to what has already been said. That battle could not have been otherwise than sanguinary, even if none of the errors committed by Lord Gough's subordinates had taken place, for the simple reason that the Sikh position was far too strong to be carried without much loss. They were adepts in the art of preparing rapid entrenchments; the advance against them had to be made through jungle; and their artillery was powerful. But when at last, at Gujerat, the British troops were supplied with a force of guns which obviated what had always been a necessity before—the arbitrament of the bayonet and the tulwar—the loss of life was small out of all proportion to the magnitude of the victory. A table is given in an Appendix,* showing the loss of life and the forces engaged at Lord Gough's battles as compared with some others; and considering the character of the Sikh soldiery—the real odds against which Lord Gough was fighting—such a comparison is legitimate, and may fairly be held to exonerate the Commander-in-Chief from the charge of reckless disregard of life.

In fact, that the loss of life was excessive can be maintained only by overlooking the fighting capacities of the enemy. If, as has happened often enough in Oriental warfare, our opponents had taken to flight on the first approach of British bayonets, or if they had adopted the not uncommon practice of charging the British lines and being shot down before reaching them, the result would have been different. But, on the contrary, they met cannonade with cannonade, avoided miscellaneous rushes, and stood up against cold steel as stubbornly as a European foe would have done, standing their ground and selling their lives dearly.

But the common charge against Lord Gough is that of inpetuosity. First at Ferozeshah, where Sir Henry Hardinge overruled his plan of action. The facts, however, have been set forth. The conflict of opinion was simple. Both Sir Henry and Sir Hugh knew that a battle must be fought and a victory must be won. But Sir Henry considered that the risk of a reverse would be minimised by waiting for a junction with Sir John Littler. Sir Hugh held that to wait would increase the risk—that the additional

* Appendix III., C.

forces would not compensate for the lateness of the hour and the approach of darkness. He urged his plan, not because he was thirsting for the fray, but because he considered it the safer. In the result, Sir Henry's plan was followed; the additional forces gave no practical help, and all the unhappy consequences of delay foreseen by Sir Hugh occurred.

Nor is the case for rashness made out at Ramnuggur, where nearly the whole of the losses were incurred by a charge being carried beyond the point to which Lord Gough had limited it.

Lastly, at Chillianwalla, the accusation is based exclusively on the fact that Lord Gough gave up his intention of camping, and joined battle when the Sikhs opened fire. Yet, it is clear that he had no choice, while, to deprive him of choice, the enemy had, at the same time, deprived themselves of the shelter of their entrenchments. He attacked because encamping was impossible, only when the truth that it was impossible, hitherto concealed by the jungle, became evident by the unmasking of the Sikh batteries.

The truth appears to be that Lord Gough's personal daring gave colour to an expectation that he would be rash. What people expect, they are apt to discover justification for, and every act was labelled as rash which did not bear *primâ facie* marks of caution. It is probable that the popular accounts of the engagement at Maharajpore,* when the Gwalior army was crushed, stereotyped the idea that he was a sort of happy-go-lucky, reckless hard-fighter, and that the idea was consequently read into his subsequent campaigns. And since he consistently refused either to vindicate himself or to let his friends vindicate him from the aspersions of his critics, it is, perhaps, hardly surprising that he has been so erroneously judged.

With the victory of Gujerat, Lord Gough's services in

* See Appendix I.

India practically terminated. The last embers of the revolt were stamped out, as related, by Sir Walter Gilbert, and the Punjab was annexed, as will be told in the next Book. It was not till the middle of April that his successor, Sir Charles Napier, arrived, nearly two months after Gujerat had turned the vituperation of detractors into pæans of applause; and again, three months later, came the announcement, marking the rapid change of public opinion, that he had been made a Viscount. And so, at the age of seventy, Lord Gough departed from the scene of his services. This section of the narrative may well be closed by quoting the General Orders, in which he bade farewell to the army he loved.

31st March, 1849.

The Commander in Chief in India announces his farewell and adieu to the Army of the Punjaub.

The troops which, since October, have been in arms under his command, are dispersed to their respective cantonments, and on this, the last occasion of addressing them, Lord Gough desires to place on record his sense of the great services and exertions through which the sway of British India has been now extended over the broad plains and classic rivers and cities of this kingdom.

The tide of conquest which heretofore rolled on the Punjaub from the west, has at length reached and overcome it from the east; and that which Alexander attempted, the British Indian Army has accomplished. It is with no common pride that the Commander in Chief applauds the conduct and the valor which have led to so glorious a result.

The favor and approbation of the country and Government will, without doubt, mark enduringly the estimate entertained of its desert; and no time will efface from the memory of this army, and every true soldier in the field, the high sense of triumph and of the glory with which this campaign has terminated. Undismayed by stern opposition, untired by the procrastinations and delays which circumstances forcibly imposed, or by the great labors and exposure which have been borne so manfully, the army has emerged with a fame and a brightness, only the more marked by the trying nature of its previous toils and endurances.

The mere battle day, when every glowing feeling of the soldier and the Gentleman is called into action, will ever be encountered nobly where British armies are engaged; but it is in the privations, the difficulties, and endless toils of war, that the trial of an army consists; and it is these which denote its metal, and show of what material it is formed.

Since the day when at Ramnuggur the too hasty ardour and enthusiasm of the troops first gave signal of the determined character of the war, and of the fierceness with which a mistaken but brave enemy were bent to oppose the progress of our arms, till now, that a crushing and overwhelming victory has prostrated at the feet of our Ruler and his Government, an independent, a proud and a warlike people; Lord Gough, relying upon British courage and endurance, has never for one moment entertained a doubt of the result; nor yielded even to adverse chances and circumstances a lurking fear of the successful issue, which true constancy and firmness never fail to attain.

The rule which, despite the signal clemency and considerate mercy of the Government, it has nevertheless been found at length necessary to impose upon the Seikhs and their country, has not been thrust upon a defenceless or unresisting people; their valor, their numbers, their means and preparation, and the desperate energy with which, in error and deceived, the Khalsa and Seikh nation mustered and rallied for the struggle, have been conspicuously apparent; and the army which, in virtue of a most persistive constancy, has reduced such a race and such troops to submission and obedience, merits well the highest eulogium which Lord Gough can bestow.

The Commander in Chief lingers upon the severance of those ties which have bound him to that army: the last which in the field it was his duty and his pride to command. Long practice and experience of war, and its trying vicissitudes, have enabled him to form a just estimate of the conduct and merit of the troops now being dispersed; and the ardour, the vigilance, the endurance, the closing and triumphant bravery and discipline which have marked their path in the Punjaub, will often recur to him in that retirement he is about to seek; and in which the cares, the earnest exertions, and grave anxieties inseparable from the duties of high military command, will be richly recompensed and rewarded, by the sense of duty performed, and the consciousness of unwearied and uncompromising devotion to that Sovereign and country, which in common with the British Indian army, it will ever be his boast and his pride to have so successfully served.

To every General, to every individual Officer and soldier, European and Native, of the Army of the Punjaub, Lord Gough finally repeats his cordial and affectionate farewell. Their persons and services are engraved in his heart and affections, and to those among them who may hereafter, within the brief span of life yet before him, revisit their Native country, he tenders the unaffected renewal of that intercourse and friendship which mutual esteem and regard and mutual dangers and exertions have produced and established.

BOOK VI.

THE ANNEXATION

BOOK VI.

THE ANNEXATION

CHAPTER I.

THE NEW ADMINISTRATION

Annexation become necessary—Dalhousie's responsibility—Henry Lawrence's view—Antagonism between Sir Henry and Dalhousie—The proclamation draft—Formal annexation—Divergences of opinion—The Governing Board—Sir Charles Napier—Problems of annexation—Henry Lawrence—John Lawrence—The Punjab men.

We have seen how, before the Sikhs crossed the Sutlej in 1845, every effort had been made by Sir Henry Hardinge to avoid a collision with them. The maintenance of Lahore as an independent and friendly state had been held to be politically so desirable that a serious military risk was run for the sake of it. When the Khalsa was shattered at Sobraon, no critic would have questioned the justifiability of immediate annexation; yet, in place of it, the most strenuous endeavours were made to reinstate a healthy and independent native government. What might have resulted, if Henry Lawrence had remained to exercise his unique influence over the Sirdars, no one can say with certainty. But what did happen when he departed was, that the Sirdars got out of hand, revolt was allowed to spread, the Sikh nation challenged the British a second time; and after that, annexation was virtually the only course open.

The fact was that Lord Dalhousie's arrival initiated a change in the whole policy and methods of the supreme Government. Able, energetic, resolute, and entirely self-confident, he was a born autocrat; to whom it seemed obvious that the extension of British rule was necessarily for the benefit of the ruled; and that the use of officers was to take their orders from him. When the Multan crisis arose, Lord Gough was appealed to as the supreme military authority, and the Commander-in-Chief of necessity gave the military view of the policy to be followed. His reasons were sufficient; they were endorsed by Sir Charles Napier; Lord Dalhousie found them conclusive. It rested, then, with the Governor-General to decide whether the greater military risk should be run, in the hope of carrying through the policy of Lord Hardinge and Henry Lawrence; or the smaller risk taken, with the practical certainty of annexation in the end.

In adopting the second course, Lord Dalhousie acted directly on the principle—precisely the reverse of Lord Hardinge's—which avowedly guided his policy throughout his administration. In his own words, used on a subsequent occasion, it was his "strong and deliberate opinion that in the execution of a wise and sound policy, the British Government is bound not to put aside or neglect such rightful opportunities of acquiring territory or revenue as may from time to time present themselves." While the war was in progress, he wrote (February 1st, 1849) to Henry Lawrence, "I do not seek for a moment to conceal from you that I have seen no reason whatever to depart from the opinion that the peace and vital interests of the British Empire now require that the power of the Sikh Government should not only be defeated, but subverted, and their dynasty abolished."

In view of these explicit declarations, it is evident that Lord Dalhousie would at any time have inclined to prefer adopting towards a native state the line of policy which was likely to provide a "rightful opportunity" of acquiring territory and revenue. He was not therefore the less disposed to act upon Lord Gough's view of the military exigencies. Besides, it must be remembered that the Sirdars had consistently and invariably affirmed their own inability to control the Khalsa unsupported; and if there was no little force in their plea that they were driven to join the rebels because British support was not forthcoming, the plea itself showed their incompetence for rule, and the need for annexation.

Now, as we have already noted, before the war was over, Henry Lawrence had returned to the scene of his labours. No living Englishman understood the Sikhs as he did; no other was held in such regard as he throughout the Punjab. There could be no question at all that he was the man to whom the settlement of the conquered country must be entrusted; yet, from the outset the antagonism between his own views and those of Lord Dalhousie was apparent.

In the first place, Lord Dalhousie regarded annexation as a thing in itself desirable; Lawrence counted it at best an unfortunate necessity—a necessity which he would have risked much to avoid—whereas the Governor-General might be said to have courted it. In Lawrence's eyes, the Sirdars, at least, had the strongest excuse for their conduct; in Dalhousie's they had been deliberately, wantonly, the aggressors. Lawrence felt that the policy which he had been engaged in carrying out had been wrecked to a great extent by the action of the British themselves. The delicate handling which the situation demanded had not been recognised. The display of more tact and consideration in dealing with Mulraj might have averted the Multan outbreak altogether. When Mulraj rebelled, making resistance to the British his watchword, the Sikh troops had been allowed to enter the radius of the insurrectionary vortex without adequate check. The hostile feeling of the Khalsa had been permitted to grow unopposed till the pressure became too great for the Sirdars, from Shere Singh downwards. These facts, in Sir Henry's view, entitled the Sikhs to claim that though they were vanquished they deserved to have every consideration shown them in their fallen state. Lord Dalhousie seemed to him to hold that they deserved only to be chastised for their insolence.

Moreover, Lord Dalhousie was a man by no means prone to take advice. He wanted information, not opinions; instruments, not counsellors. But Sir Henry's knowledge was unrivalled, and obtained first-hand; his opinions were strong; and he was accustomed to acting on his own judgment with the full confidence of his chief. Dalhousie probably felt that he must from the outset show Lawrence, in the most unmistakable manner, that he was emphatically a subordinate, and that the Governor-General was master of the situation.

Lawrence arrived at Lahore on January 18th, and was invited by Lord Dalhousie, in anticipation of the final destruction of the Sikh army, to prepare a proclamation. Sir Henry did so, and submitted the draft to the Governor-General. The terms of the reply, addressed to a man in Sir Henry's position, could hardly be paralleled. It is evident that Sir Henry had been guided in the language he used by his own sense of the excuses which the Sirdars had for their conduct, their generosity to the prisoners who had fallen into their hands, and his own chivalrous and politic desire to deal generously with such a foe. Lord Dalhousie rated the proclamation as "objectionable both in matter and manner," as holding out hopes of leniency which he should not feel justified in showing, and as implying that Lawrence would himself be a "peacemaker for the Sikhs"; whereas, "I can allow nothing to be said or done which should raise the notion that the policy of the Government of India, or its intentions, depend on your presence as Resident of the Punjab." Such language, addressed to the man who had already been virtual dictator of the Punjab, and whose rule had been marked by astonishing success, was scarcely calculated to remove friction. From this, and from other communications subsequently received, Lawrence necessarily formed the belief that the utmost severity would be exercised, and that any annexation would be carried out in such a manner as to fill the conquered province from end to end with hate for the conquerors. If he had doubted the justice of annexation before, he doubted it the more now; and a measure which, at its best, he had come to regard as perhaps a political necessity, became in his eyes positively impolitic when carried out in the spirit proposed.

Gujerat decided the fate of the Punjab, and there was question only as to the way and the time of carrying it out. It was natural that Sir Henry preferred to avoid a personal interview with the Governor-General, who by his wish discussed the arrangements with John Lawrence instead. Immediate annexation was decided upon, and Sir Henry, feeling that his views had been simply set aside without consideration, and in a distinctly offensive manner, and that the prospect of his working harmoniously with Lord Dalhousie was painfully remote, sent in his resignation. Dalhousie, however, was alive to the serious result that would follow from the withdrawal of Sir Henry's unique influence, and conveyed to the latter his strong desire that he should reconsider the resignation—backed up by the argument that there was much more chance of giving effect to his more generous ideas if he remained than if he went. The implication that there would be an opportunity for softening the extreme harshness anticipated in carrying out the annexation had its effect, and Lawrence withdrew his resignation. On March 30th, in full Durbar, the proclamation was read which formally placed the Land of the Five Rivers under the British sovereignty; the young Maharajah receiving a pension of £50,000 per annum, with leave to reside where he chose, on condition of not entering the Punjab.

In taking this step, Lord Dalhousie was acting within his powers as Governor-General, though the circumstances and the decision were subject to review and revision by the authorities in England. One only of his council, Sir George Clerk, was opposed to the step, and when Dalhousie's dispatches reached England, the annexation was confirmed with the warmest approval, Lord Hardinge himself being of opinion that after the second war nothing else was possible.

The annexation was now an accomplished fact. But, in carrying it into effect, either of two strongly divergent principles might be adopted; one of which was represented by the opinions of Lord Dalhousie, the other by those of Sir Henry Lawrence.

This divergence related primarily to the treatment of the Sirdars and Jaghirdars—a term to be presently explained more fully. Broadly speaking, the Lawrence theory was: As a matter of justice, their chiefs ought not to be severely punished, since their will was to remain loyal, but they had been forced into rebellion by the pressure of the Khalsa, and the British delay in vindicating their own position. As a matter of policy, they ought to be conciliated, because they could then be relied on to be a powerful and friendly influence throughout the country; whereas their hostility, if they were given a grievance, would be a perpetual source of general disaffection. On the other side, Dalhousie held that, as a matter of justice, they had no claim whatever to consideration; while, as a matter of policy, the less influence they were allowed to retain, the better; since, stripped of their wealth, they would at any rate be powerless for harm; while the general diffusion of prosperity under British rule would produce a contented and therefore loyal people.

There was a second and hardly less important divergence on the subject of methods. In the Governor-General's idea, the subordinate officers should always wait for their orders from superiors. Lawrence's method had been to train subordinates to think and act for themselves within recognised but ample limits.

Yet Lord Dalhousie wanted his own policy to prevail, and at the same time could not afford to remove from the Punjab the man who was admittedly superior to all others in knowledge and in influence.

He solved his own difficulty by an expedient unique and inevitably temporary. Sir Henry, as Resident, would of necessity have greater independence than the Governor-General cared about. The way out was found in the institution of a Governing Board, consisting of Henry Lawrence as President, with his brother John, and Mr. Mansel. Henry, the trained "political," was to have the main control of political affairs; John, the trained civilian, of administration and primarily of the revenue department; Mansel, the judicial member, of the legal and judicial. But all three were to be jointly responsible. John's capacity was beyond question, and his leanings were towards Dalhousie's views on general grounds, strengthened by a respect for considerations of revenue in which his brother was somewhat lacking. The brothers were certain to pull different ways; and while, as the event proved, such an antagonism could not but have results personally painful in the highest degree, the event also proved that in policy each counteracted the extreme views of the other. The effect was a very excellent government, though partisans of either brother would maintain that one or the other, left free, would have produced results still more admirable.

The third member of the Board, Mansel, was eminently adapted for that position, having an abstract method of regarding all questions as rather subjects of philosophic disputation, than as demanding immediate practical solution. As a consequence, he would rarely side with either of his colleagues, so that the effect of his influence was usually either to check action altogether, or to favour the *via media* when action could not be deferred.

To this collection of remarkable personalities on whom the future of the Punjab depended, a fifth—most remarkable, perhaps, of all—was added by the arrival of Sir Charles Napier, the new Commander-in-Chief. Probably there never existed a man more firmly convinced that he was right, and everybody who differed from him wrong. He and the no less autocratic Governor-General began by telling each other home-truths in their first interview. He announced his opinion at an early stage that all boards are incapable, and this one more so than most. He called Dalhousie "the Laird of Cockpen," and described him as "a young Scotch lord, with no head for governing an empire." He wanted to transform the Punjab into a military province, ruled as he had ruled Scinde, and, as John Lawrence put it, "to introduce the blessings of courts-martial." The common antagonism probably led the Governor-General to modify the other antagonism between himself and Sir Henry. It was a serious misfortune for the army in India that the old warrior's extravagances and his vehement differences with Lord Dalhousie deprived the country of the services of, as some thought, the most brilliant British soldier then living except the aged Duke of Wellington, by leading to his resignation at the close of 1850.

However, the Board was constituted, and, in spite of Sir Charles, it was not superseded. The country was divided into seven districts, each with its commissioner and subordinate officers—Lahore being entrusted to Robert Montgomery, who subsequently took Mansel's place on the Board—and the work of organisation began.

Truly the task was a gigantic one. Here was a vast territory in which the highest form of government that had hitherto existed was of a most primitive type. The sway of a host of individual chiefs who were more than half bandits had been developed into the sway of a military despot, whose primary care had been to organise and maintain a mighty army, and extract from his subjects a revenue sufficient for that purpose. The despot died, and the army continued to rule on its own account, regarding the maintenance of the Khalsa as the be-all and end-all of the whole State. Everything available for taxation was taxed, the collectors handing over just so much as they thought would satisfy the authorities, and pocketing the rest. Of the method of treating the hill-tribes, we have had an example in the brief sketch of Bunnoo. For every sort of crime the punishment—if it happened to be inflicted—was fine or mutilation. Life and property found little protection. Infanticide, despite the beneficent injunctions of the pious Nanuk, was prevalent. Girl-children were too expensive. If they grew up, husbands had to be found for them, and weddings were appallingly costly. Brigandage—"dacoity"—was always rife, and the disbandment of the soldiery tended naturally to increase it.

Into this chaos, law and order had to be introduced; oppression and violence had to be put down; the arts of peace had to be encouraged; the dominant classes had to be deprived of their opportunities for misappropriation; respect for the Government had to be, we may say, invented; and all this had to be done by the conquerors to the conquered in such a fashion that the Sikhs should bless the very people who had crushed their proudest aspirations, and the sullen and bitter resignation of the vanquished should be transformed into honest content and hearty loyalty. That such a consummation should have been actually attained, and within so short a time, is one of the greatest achievements that any conquering nation has to show in the world's records.

The task, it may safely be said, would not have been accomplished for many a long year—would perhaps never have been accomplished at all—but for the exceptional character of the men to whom it was entrusted.

Admittedly foremost among them stands Henry Lawrence. There was no other man who had already so effectively and so widely won the personal admiration and confidence of the natives; so that his appointment to the highest office predisposed them to place a degree of trust in the new administration which nothing else could have secured. His large and generous sympathy, his immense capacity for understanding and respecting the native point of view, with its deviations from abstract conceptions of justice based upon misleading Western analogies, combined with his geniality of demeanour to give him a quite unique influence. Apart from variations on specific points of policy, it was also the spirit of Henry Lawrence, which was the inspiration of the younger men who were called in to aid his work.

Next to him stood his brother John; harder of head, less tender of heart; his theories perhaps more convincing to the Western mind, but less appreciated by the Oriental; and therefore probably less consummately adapted to the conditions of the work. With a boundless capacity for unremitting labour, and a genius for detail, with great administrative experience, he too, though not reverenced like his brother, had acquired a great degree of respect with the natives, while the Governor-General allowed his opinions a greater weight than he was wont to accord to those of others—perhaps because they were more often in accord with his own.

But besides the Lawrence brothers, the men in subordinate positions were picked men, not a few of whom had already learnt how to do the exceptional work before them in the Punjab itself under Sir Henry's own inspiration. Herbert Edwardes, James Abbott, John Nicholson—these were already names to conjure with; of them we have already heard, and the world was to hear more. Of Robert

Montgomery we shall again have occasion to speak. Robert Napier, Hodson, Alexander Taylor, Neville Chamberlain, were among those makers of the Punjab.

"In a new country" (wrote Sir Henry to one of them, when he had been some fourteen months in office)—"in a new country, especially a wild one, promptness, accessibility, brevity, and kindliness are the best engines of Government. Have as few forms as possible, and as are consistent with a brief record of proceedings. Be considerate and kind, not expecting too much from ignorant people. Make no change, unless certain of decided improvement in the substitute—light assessment, considering the claims and privileges, even when somewhat extravagant, of the privileged classes, especially where they affect Government and not Ryots" [*i.e.* the peasantry].

That piece of advice expresses, succinctly and accurately, the spirit which guided the Punjab administration from top to bottom; Sir Henry himself setting the example in a series of extended peregrinations of the entire province. These tours, indeed, offended Lord Dalhousie, partly, to do him justice, because they seemed to transfer an undue share of routine work to the other members of the Board; but they were invaluable, as enabling the President not only to maintain a first-hand knowledge of, and insight into, the condition of the country not otherwise procurable, but also to exercise the charm of his own personality with its singular influence, over a widely extended sphere; with most beneficial results.

CHAPTER II.

THE WORK OF THE GOVERNING BOARD

Disarmament—Dacoity—Police—Infanticide—Public works—The frontier force—Revenue arrangements—A paying province—General taxation—Land assessment—*Jaghirdars*—Opposition of Henry and John Lawrence—John's policy prevails; the consequence.

THE first duty of the Board—the condition of giving effect to all those other reforms which were at the same time promptly and rigorously initiated—was obviously the introduction of law and order; to which end the first step was the disbanding of the army, and the disarming of the population. The troops who surrendered to Sir Walter Gilbert had already yielded up their arms and their horses, and had been dispersed. The rest of the Khalsa soldiery were now discharged, though some of them were embodied in new corps raised in the British service. This being accomplished, a proclamation was issued for the disarming of the entire population—with an exception. The terms of the orders given to the officers who had to carry out the proclamation are instructive.

"Immediately on your arrival [at a village], call the head-men, and inform them that it is the order of the Durbar that they give up all arms and ammunition; and allow two hours for their doing so. Keep your men together and on the alert. Do not search, but give the head-men distinctly to understand that if arms are hereafter discovered to be in their villages, they will be individually held responsible, and will be liable to imprisonment; and to have all their property confiscated. Take a note of the names of the head-men who appear before you. Inform them that no man in their villages is henceforward permitted to carry arms unless he is in the service of the State."

The instruction as to not searching is peculiarly noteworthy, as introducing to the head-men the idea of their own direct responsibility and personal participation in enforcing the orders of the Government.

The exception referred to is in the case of the hill-tribes, where the disarmament of the peaceable would have meant simply their subjection to the violence of the freebooters and brigands in districts where the population themselves must serve as their own police.

Further, prompt measures were immediately taken for the suppression of dacoity. The bands of brigands who infested the jungle roads were hunted down and stamped out. The disappearance of dacoity brought to light the hitherto unsuspected existence of the barbarous institution of "Thuggee," that is of a secret murder society, whose members, however, less subtle and skilful than some of their *confrères* in other parts, were before long tracked out and put to death.

For these purposes a large body of police was raised—2700 mounted, and double that number on foot—their services being seconded by the regulation of bodies of city watchmen and local village constabulary, with the effect of a rapid and salutary diminution in crime of every kind. Infanticide was also, of course, brought within the pale of the law, the great inducement thereto being at the same time removed by the suppression of those hosts of beggars who attended every marriage, and devoured the substance of the unfortunate parents, who accounted their satisfaction a religious duty. The principal engine, however, employed in checking this particular type of crime was rather the active cultivation of a less barbarous public opinion than a resort to the terrors of an alien law, since the imposition of a law which is greatly in advance of the recognised ethical standard is always felt to be tyrannical; and in the pacification of a high-spirited race it is essential to avoid even the suspicion of tyranny.

Here, also, we may refer to other branches of public activity which were of the greatest service to the immediate prosperity and general sense of security—the simple codification of the law, undertaken by Robert Montgomery; and the rapid pushing forward of such public works as road- and canal-making. The great improvement in the means of transit, and the vast benefit obtained from the new irrigation by the agricultural population, can hardly be overrated.

Turning from the measures taken to secure internal peace, we have next to note the steps by which the military position was secured. By the careful cantonment of troops throughout the province, any serious temptation to fresh efforts at insurrection was averted. The posting of a large garrison at Peshawur, containing an unusually large proportion of European troops, checked all menace from the north-west; while the protection of the line of frontier was entrusted to bodies of locally raised irregulars. These troops, afterwards known to fame as the Punjab Frontier Force, included the renowned corps of Guides, and absorbed in support of Government a considerable proportion of the more turbulent spirits, who might otherwise have proved an eminently troublesome element in the situation. In the result, they showed themselves thoroughly capable of keeping border forays and disturbances within bounds; and the Amir at Kabul, having come to the final conclusion that the British power was not to be lightly subverted, entered in 1855 upon a treaty with Lord Dalhousie which bore invaluable fruit when, in 1857, every soldier who could be spared from the Punjab was imperatively needed at Delhi.

Of equal importance to the prosperity and contentment of the country was the question of revenue arrangements. Remarkable as was the success which attended the efforts of the Board in its arrangements for order, peace, and security, not the least striking of its achievements is the fact that from the beginning the newly acquired province paid its way. There were critics who denied this; but they arrived at their conclusions by charging the whole military expenditure of the frontier to the province itself; whereas, Lord Dalhousie pointed out unanswerably that the great bulk of that expenditure was essentially imperial, not provincial, and was merely transferred across the Sutlej by the extension of the Imperial boundary. The Punjab accounts, therefore, showed in the first three years surpluses of 52, 64, and 70 lakhs of rupees; and between 1849 and 1857, the revenue rose from 134 lakhs to 205.

The sources of revenue may be generally divided into taxes on goods and taxes on land; while the latter may again be subdivided as a subject of assessment into land in general, and *jaghirs*. It was on this last question that serious differences of opinion arose on the Board.

Hitherto the primitive financial principle had been applied to goods—tax everything possible, as heavily as possible, and as often as possible. An enlightened political economy has taught us that the method defeats its object. Light taxation means lower prices, followed by increased demand and increased supply, while high taxation is also a direct inducement to smuggling, and to the bribery of officials. The number of taxable articles was promptly cut down, and the taxes on the remainder greatly reduced, consequently the contribution to the treasury was very materially increased; while the consumers had all the benefit of increased production and lower prices.

On the general question of land-assessment, also, there was no material disagreement. The assessment continued to be based as it had been before on the value of the produce. But whereas in the days of Ranjit Singh the state had claimed one-half of the gross produce, this was now reduced to a quarter or even an eighth, with no diminution of the amount received, owing to the abolition of the middlemen, who heretofore had appropriated the difference. A further change was made, by the abolition of payment in kind, on which the old Maharajah had always insisted.

But the vital difficulty lay in the treatment of the jaghirs; *i.e.* grants of local land revenue free from any charge to the Government, except in the form of military service, made to various chiefs at various times.

Now the wealth, and in consequence the power, of all the Sikh leaders, had been in fact drawn from the jaghirs. The problem was, how far ought they now to be allowed to retain them.

Moreover, the problem was complicated by the fact that nearly every individual case required to be treated on its own merits, and looked at from the point of view both of justice and of policy, while further complications of legality could also be brought in; that is to say, in Western phraseology, it might constantly be affirmed that the jaghirdar had not really any vested interest in his jaghir, because it was always liable to resumption by the Crown at pleasure, whether as a punishment or merely to suit the Crown's convenience.

Here, then, were absolutely endless sources of dispute. Henry Lawrence considered that policy required the jaghirdars to be converted into friends with a maximum of prestige and influence; that justice demanded the most liberal view of their claims; that the Government, in short, should concede everything it reasonably could. John took the Dalhousie view, that the less power and influence they were left the better; and that in bare justice they were mostly entitled to nothing more than a subsistence. Between the extremes of complete rehabilitation and complete denudation, differences of opinion as to the loyalty, disloyalty, and general character of the various jaghirdars opened up endless subjects for dispute. John's views, being those of the Governor-General, prevailed in the main from the beginning; Montgomery, who succeeded Mansel on the Board at the end of 1850, inclined to the same side. Hence, although, after Henry left the Province, John considerably relaxed the severity of his attitude—which had, no doubt, been intensified by opposition—the practical outcome was that the Sirdars became so impoverished, that in 1857 there was hardly a man among them, except Tej Singh, who had the power, even if he had the will, to raise large bodies of troops in any force in support of the British. To this may be added that, at a very early stage after the annexation, it was ascertained that Chutter Singh and Shere Singh were engaged in correspondence of an exceedingly questionable character, and they were removed from the Punjab in consequence. The fact may be interpreted very much according to the reader's bias. In the view of one side, it points to the inevitable irritation and *new* disloyalty produced by the severity meted out to the Sikh chiefs; in that of the other, it points to the persistence of the *old* disloyal spirit, and the risk involved in leaving them any influence.

From the available evidence it is assuredly no easy matter to judge which policy was the right one, apart from the question who was to carry it out. If the Sirdars were inherently disloyal, conciliation would have been wasted; if they were prepared to be loyal, an opportunity for acquiring powerful support was thrown away. There was no one who knew the men so well as Henry Lawrence; yet his natural generosity may have led him to think better of them than they deserved. It may, therefore, be that his policy, carried out by a less sympathetic and attractive personality, would have failed. But it was an article of faith with those who knew him best, that if he had been allowed to carry it out himself in his own way he would have succeeded; and the Sikhs in 1857 would have poured down to our assistance at Delhi when Lawrence raised his hand, in force so much greater as to have crushed the rebellion at the outset. The

Sikh hatred of the Hindostani, coupled with the hope of loot in Delhi, would also no doubt have exercised a useful influence on the doubtful.

But, for good or ill, it was the policy of Dalhousie and John Lawrence that was enforced in this particular, though the evil results which Henry Lawrence foresaw were in a great degree counteracted by his personal influence on the manner of the enforcement. In other particulars, as we have observed, the brothers were in substantial agreement as to principles, though they might differ in details; and thus, while the chiefs and their belongings were humbled, an era of unprecedented prosperity and tranquillity opened for the Punjab population at large.

CHAPTER III.

EPILOGUE

Difficulties of the Lawrence brothers—Henry transferred to Rajputana—John Chief Commissioner—Conclusion.

FROM the outset it had been certain that government by the Board must be a temporary expedient. Its primary object was served when it had enabled Lord Dalhousie to carry out his own theories by the hand of Henry Lawrence.

But the demand made on both the Lawrences had been cruel, more especially on Sir Henry. He had been compelled to subordinate his own views, in a country which he understood better than any man living, to those of a man far less experienced than himself; he had been placed in a position involving perpetual antagonism with his own brother; to prevent a worse thing befalling, he had become the instrument in part of a policy which he regarded as neither wise nor just. The evil had been aggravated by the imperious tone adopted towards him by the Governor-General, and by Dalhousie's habit of openly showing more confidence in the younger of the brothers; though this was, perhaps, an inevitable result of those peregrinations already referred to, which forced an increase of communication between the stationary member of the Board and the Supreme Government. The trouble had hardly been lessened by the addition to the Board of Montgomery, who was an intimate friend of both

Henry and John, and on whom devolved the exceedingly trying task of receiving the complaints of each, and endeavouring to serve as a buffer between them. Matters gradually reached a point at which both brothers felt that it was impossible for them any longer to work together with tolerable harmony; and when, in 1852, the Residency of Hyderabad became vacant, each brother applied for it, as offering an honourable opportunity for one or other to withdraw from the Punjab. It was obvious that, so far as personal claims went, Henry's title to retain the Punjab was the stronger; it was equally obvious that Lord Dalhousie would prefer the man whose views agreed with his own.

If the Governor-General had simply taken the line that the policy he wished to carry out in the Punjab was so impossible to reconcile with Sir Henry's views, that his appointment must inevitably result in a perpetual collision of wills, he could hardly have been blamed. But in accepting the resignation of the President, he succeeded in making more bitter still the blow which must have been bitter enough, however kindly administered. In effect, he informed Sir Henry that he was not competent for the post, which required a trained civilian. It can hardly be wondered at that the manner of Sir Henry's removal was felt by him and by his friends to be little short of an insult, utterly unwarranted, however inevitable the removal itself might have been—as, indeed, it probably was, if the government was to be conducted on Lord Dalhousie's lines.

Sir Henry was given, not Hyderabad, but the Residency of Rajputana; where his sympathetic influence worked with its usual magic effect upon the chiefs and princes, who were dismayed and nervous spectators of Lord Dalhousie's attitude towards the native States. To the reassuring influence of Sir Henry's tenure of office, for four years after his departure from the Punjab, must be attributed the fact that Rajputana stood aside from the great conflict of the Mutiny.

When Sir Henry Lawrence left the Punjab, the British control was thoroughly established; the foundations of sound government were securely laid. John Lawrence was appointed Chief Commissioner; and the manner in which he did his work there has been painted with skill and enthusiasm by many an able pen.

On the further history of the Punjab we do not propose to enter. Our task has been to tell that part of its story which is less familiar to the British public—the story of a people who remained stubbornly loyal to their faith through centuries of Mussulman persecution; who, when the great Power at Delhi sank to decay, became in no small degree the bulwark of Hindostan against the marauding power beyond the passes; who, under the sway of Ranjit Singh, developed into a military State more efficient than any other in India; and who, when the guiding hand of the great Maharajah was removed, challenged the mightier Power from the West with a stubborn valour unparalleled in Eastern warfare; and who finally, when once they had acknowledged and accepted the sway of the conqueror, have approved themselves loyal with the most loyal, and trusty with the most trusted; not least notably in the great crisis of 1857.

We have told how the battle was fought out between Sikh and Briton; and have endeavoured to set forth in true colours the account of two great wars, as to which the popular impressions—if, indeed, popular impressions of them may be said to exist at all—are demonstrably erroneous in many particulars, especially with regard to the personal reputation of Lord Gough. Beyond telling that story clearly and truthfully to the best of our power, it is no part of ours to distribute praise or blame. In the Land of the Five Rivers, great men have wrought a great work and done great deeds. None will grudge the best that has been said of any one of them. From the days of Nanuk the Saint and Govind the Lion, to those of Hardinge and Gough, of Edwardes and Nicholson, of the Lawrence brothers and Dalhousie, all honour to the heroes of the Punjab!

APPENDICES

held the real control, and had also accumulated means sufficient to attract the army to support them. On the other hand, that a State in the position of Gwalior should be controlled by its army was intolerable to the British Government. Thus, on the one side, the British were pressing for the disbandment of the army, and on the other the leaders who had come to the top were dependent on that army. The prospect of getting the difficulty settled without a fight was small; and the Gwalior army was encouraged by two very strong considerations—the recent loss of British reputation over the Kabul disaster, and the growth of anti-British feeling in the other great Native army beyond the Sutlej, encouraged by Hira Singh.

It was thus imperative that the British should be prepared for a fight, and that if it came it should be short, sharp, and absolutely decisive. A prolonged or an indecisive contest would inevitably, under existing conditions, bring the Khalsa down to co-operate with Gwalior. The only alternative to a war was the disbandment of the Gwalior army; and the longer war was deferred, the more assured would Sikh co-operation become.

Therefore a great "Camp of Exercise" was formed at Agra, where Sir Hugh Gough, the Commander-in-Chief, was in command; and a considerable body of troops was massed at Jhansi. Every effort, however, was still made to induce the Maharani to surrender the person of the prime intriguer—the Dada—and to transfer the government to Anglophil chiefs. The Dada was at last given up, but the circle round the Maharani succeeded in frightening or persuading her after all into virtual defiance by not attending the meeting which had been arranged between her and the Governor-General on December 26th (1843); the British troops having in the meantime been brought down to Dholpore. The challenge was instantly accepted. On the 28th December, General Grey started from the South for Gwalior with the Jhansi forces; and on the 29th were fought the two decisive actions, on the north of Gwalior by Gough at Maharajpore, and on its south by Grey at Puniar, which annihilated all further chance of resistance.

In order to reasonably criticise this brief campaign, certain of the conditions must be kept in mind, viz. :—(1) The threatening attitude of the Sikhs, at this time actually advancing on the Sutlej. A challenge from them, though temporarily averted, was known to be possible at almost any moment. (2) Consequently it was quite out of the question to draw upon the British forces in the north-west from Meerut to Ferozepore. (3) Hence, also, it was of vital importance that the blow struck should be absolutely and immediately decisive. (4) Although the Gwalior army was numerous and well-trained, the British political officers affirmed that it could offer no serious resistance to us. There was talk of "horsewhips" being the only weapons required; and not only the Governor-General, Lord Ellenborough, himself, but even a party of ladies accompanied the advance.

On December 28th, then, Sir Hugh Gough was at Hingoni on the north bank of the Kohari River, with a force numbering 4820 infantry and 1340 horse. He had also 30 field-guns, and a battery of siege-guns.

The Gwalior army was established at Chonda, a mile and a half south of the village of Maharajpore, the position being very strongly entrenched. Maharajpore was known to be held as an outpost. Between the two, but

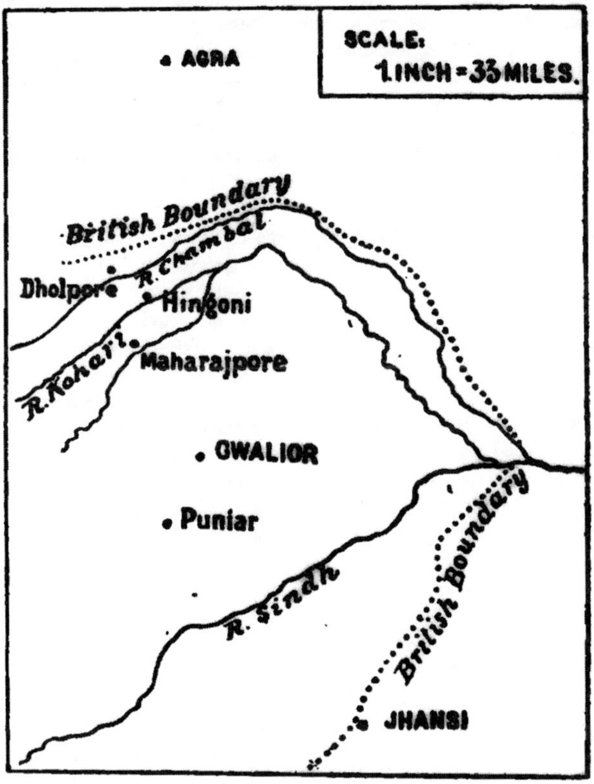

east of the direct route, lay the village of Shikarpore. Early on the morning of the 29th Sir Hugh commenced the advance, and the neighbourhood of Maharajpore was reached at about eight o'clock. During the night, however, the Mahrattas had advanced in force from their entrenched position at Chonda to Maharajpore, which was not entrenched. This fact they now notified by opening fire with their batteries at long range. The movement was exceedingly ill-advised, since the Maharajpore position was too far from the much stronger one at Chonda to receive adequate support, and the subsequent defeat was made the more complete; but it precipitated the general engagement.

The *whole* of the British guns were promptly brought into action, with the exception of the heavy batteries under command of Colonel Tennant. On this exception rests the popular charge that the guns were "unaccountably" left behind, and the use of artillery neglected by Sir Hugh. But the truth was that, according to Colonel Tennant's report, it would have taken four and a half hours to bring those guns into action, and, being quite unfit for field operations, they were left at Hingoni. Tennant, indeed, had with him three 8-inch howitzers, which ought to have been pushed forward and brought into action; but in spite of three messages from the Commander-in-Chief, and, notwithstanding the exertions of Colonel Tennant, the howitzers did not succeed in getting to the front until the enemy were already in retreat, owing to the difficulties of transit.

The British had advanced in three columns. The left, with which was the Commander-in-Chief, was commanded by Sir John Littler; it consisted of Wright's Brigade—H.M.'s 39th Foot and the 56th Native Infantry; Scott's Cavalry Brigade—the 4th and 10th Bengal Light Cavalry; two batteries Horse Artillery and one Field Artillery; in reserve, Stacey's Brigade—14th, 31st, and 45th Native Infantry.

The centre column, under Major-General Valiant, consisted of H.M.'s 40th Foot, and the 2nd and 16th (Native) Grenadiers, which had all recently rendered good service under General Nott in Afghanistan.

The right column, under Sir J. Thackwell, consisted of H.M.'s 16th Lancers, the 1st Native Light Cavalry, the Governor-General's Body-guard, and the 4th Irregulars, with Horse Artillery.

On finding Maharajpore held in force, the guns, as related, were at once brought into action against the enemy's batteries; and Littler was ordered to make a front attack while Valiant swept round on the Mahratta left and rear, with Thackwell's cavalry to cover and support, and to follow up any advantage.

Wright's Brigade then advanced and drove the enemy from their guns back into the village; meeting, however, with an unexpectedly determined resistance, which became more stubborn and desperate as the village was reached, the foe fighting sword in hand to the last. Similarly, on their left, Valiant led an equally successful attack against a no less fierce resistance, the enemy falling where they fought, and rallying repeatedly.

Wright then advanced direct upon the main position at Chonda, Valiant being ordered to pass by his rear on the village of Shikarpore (and so to emerge ultimately on his left). Here he found the enemy occupying a series of entrenched positions, which were carried one after another by hard fighting; the 39th losing two commanding officers in succession, while they were admirably supported by the 2nd Grenadiers, and the 16th under Colonel McLaran, who subsequently distinguished himself greatly both at Ferozeshah and at Sobraon, where he fell. Scott's Cavalry Brigade also rendered good service; the 10th Light Cavalry, under Colonel Pope, delivering some effective charges.

Meantime, Wright's Brigade, covered by the batteries, advanced on Chonda; and on nearing the position, charged and captured the enemy's guns, the latter making a last desperate stand by an earthwork on the left of their position, which was finally carried by a charge of the Grenadier company of the 39th, under Captain Campbell, supported by a wing of the 56th Native Infantry, under Major Philips. This brought the battle to a conclusion; the Mahrattas having now been driven from all their positions, with the loss of all their guns and immense numbers of men. The nature of the ground prevented a cavalry pursuit, but this was of the less consequence, inasmuch as the rout was already complete and irretrievable. The Mahratta force had numbered from 10,000 to 12,000 men, with 56 guns; while the British had 30 available to bring into action. Our total loss was, 6 officers and 100 men killed; 34 officers and 650 men wounded.

On the same day, General Grey advancing northwards from the Jhansi neighbourhood, fought and vanquished a second Mahratta army at Puniar.

He had marched from his camp at Simmersea on the 28th. Reaching Puniar on the following day, he was attacked at about 4 o'clock in the afternoon by the enemy, who were occupying some heights close to the neighbouring fortified village of Mangore. Grey at once resolved to take the offensive. Finding that the nature of the ground made cavalry useless, he sent forward the 3rd Buffs with the 39th Native Infantry and a company of sappers to drive the enemy out of the strong position occupied by their centre and left. The Buffs attacked the centre; the Native Infantry moved to the crest of a hill commanding the flank. Both regiments rapidly carried the opposing positions in spite of a galling fire; and the remainder of Grey's troops—H.M.'s 50th, with the 50th and 58th Native Infantry coming up, the enemy were promptly put to flight with the loss of 24 guns. The total British loss was 35 killed and 182 wounded.

These two engagements destroyed the Gwalior army, putting any further resistance entirely out of the question. Within forty-eight hours of the first definitely hostile movement, the whole affair was at an end.

To dwell further on the effect would be superfluous. It is enough to remark that if the fight had been protracted, the Sikhs would almost certainly have crossed the Sutlej at once, instead of waiting two years. Had the war been deferred, the Gwalior men would probably have risen in the rear of the British force advancing on Ferozepore. Even as it was, there came a moment when the outcome of the Sutlej campaign was uncertain—and it is difficult to overestimate the dangers of the crisis which could have arisen if the Gwalior army had then been able to take the field.

APPENDIX II.

TABLES OF TROOPS

A.—*Troops available for a Multan Campaign: May* 8, 1848.

The abstract of a memorandum giving the details of the forces which might with safety be collected in a month—from "Umballa, Subattoo, Kussowlie, Loodaanah, Ferozepore, Jullundur, and Lahore"—shows the immensity of the risk which would have been incurred by such a movement in the event of a general rising.

	Guns.	Men.
6 troops Horse Artillery	36 ...	420
2 light Field-batteries	12 ...	120
6 reserve Companies Foot Artillery ...	...	360
1 company Pioneers	...	80
2 regiments Light Dragoons	...	900
3 „ Native Light Cavalry ...	...	900
2 „ Irregular Cavalry	...	800
5 „ European Infantry ...	...	3,500
6 „ Native Infantry	...	3,000
Total	48 ...	10,080

B.—*Troops desired for a Decisive Campaign : May* 11.

The following is the list drawn up by Lord Gough on May 11th, and submitted to the Governor-General :—

50 pieces of siege.
7 troops Horse Artillery }
6 light Field-batteries } 78 field guns.
3 regiments British Dragoons.
6 companies Sappers.
7 reserve companies Artillery.
5 regiments Light Cavalry.
5 „ Irregular Cavalry.
5 „ European Infantry.
18 „ Native Infantry.

Making up 24,000 of all arms: *besides* a strong column from Scinde.

Lord Gough at the same time recommended raising the strength of the Native Infantry regiments to 1000 each.

The Governor-General replied (through Mr. Elliot, 10th June), that "he had fully resolved on assembling a force calculated to inflict the fullest punishment, and exact ample reparation. He is persuaded that the force proposed by His Excellency is larger than is necessary. . . . The Governor-General feels himself precluded from sanctioning an increase of the army."

The force named, however, corresponds closely to the army finally assembled at Gujerat.

C.—Troops, Trans-Sutlej, fit for Service: Jan. 1, 1849.

(i.) *Beyond the Chenab.*

(*a*) *At Heylah.*

	Officers and men. Native.	European.
6 troops Horse Artillery	268	544
7 companies Foot Artillery ... ... (4 light field-batteries)	352	399
4 companies Pioneers	268	10
European Dragoons, 3rd		583
(3 regiments) 9th		628
14th		501
Light Cavalry, 1st	474	18
(4 regiments) 5th	423	16
6th	424	19
8th	469	14
Irregular Cavalry, 3rd	499	4
(3 regiments) 9th	585	4
12th	559	4
European Infantry, H.M.'s 24th		1066
(4 regiments) „ 29th		896
„ 61st		836
H.C.'s 2nd		648
Native Infantry, 15th	961	19
(13 regiments) 20th	857	19
25th	769	18
30th	908	20
31st	892	20
36th	889	19
45th	919	18
46th	844	18
56th	863	18
69th	904	15
70th	961	22

(b) *At Ramnuggur.*	Officers and men. Native.	Officers and men. European.
Native Infantry, 13th	873	22
22nd	933	19

Total of officers and men at Lord Gough's camp: Europeans, 6396; natives, 14,008.

(ii.) *At Lahore.*

1 troop Horse Artillery	33	98
3 companies Foot Artillery	168	143
1 company Pioneers	111	4
Irregular Cavalry, 13th and 14th	652	7
Native Infantry, 18th, 37th, 50th, 53rd, 73rd...	4243	78

(iii.) *With Wheeler.*

Horse Artillery	27	99
Foot Artillery	102	95
Light Cavalry, 7th	426	15
Irregular Cavalry, 2nd and 15th	969	4
Native Infantry, 3rd and 4th	1897	40
At Govindgurh.		
Horse Artillery	14	42
Native Infantry, 1st	1004	16

(iv.) *In the Jalandhar Doab.*

At Jalandhar.	
Horse Artillery, 2 guns, ...	42 men
Light Cavalry	214 "
Native Infantry	1045 "
At Hosheearpur.	
Horse Artillery, 4 guns, ...	100 "
Irregular Cavalry	141 "
Native Infantry	719 "

At Boodee Pind.

2 guns and 900 men Native Infantry; and distributed among 7 stations, 2744 Native Infantry.

(v.) *At Multan.*

Whish's Division and the Bombay column—European Infantry, 4 regiments; Native Infantry, 9 regiments; Cavalry, 5 regiments; 3 troops Horse Artillery; 7 companies Sappers; 8 companies Foot Artillery; 67 siege, and 30 field-guns.

APPENDIX III.

CHILLIANWALLA

A.—*Extract from Lord Gough's Diary.*

The following extract from Lord Gough's private diary shows what his intentions were conclusively.

"*Jan.* 11.—Preparations to march to Dingree [*sic*].

"*Jan.* 12.—Marched to Dingree—Made arrangements for attacking the enemy at Rassool—Lullianwallah—Futteh Shah ke Chuk—Lucknawalla and Moong to-morrow, except I find it more convenient to halt at Chillianwalla.

"*Jan.* 13.—Moved on Chillianwalla with the view to reconnoitre or to fall across the Sikhs should they attempt flight. As we approached we found a strong advanced post of Cavalry, whom a mound gave a very commanding view of the country, which we soon and easily dislodged, and had a very good view of the enemy's position about 3 miles in the front, with his right towards Futteh Shah ke Chuk, and his left upon the southern part of the low range of hills over Russool. As it was one o'clock before I fully satisfied myself of his position, I determined to postpone the attack until the following morning, and the Quarter-Master-General was in the act of arranging the formation of the camp when the enemy brought forward some guns to bear upon Chillianwalla. This induced me to order forward the heavy guns to dislodge them, which opened about half-past one. Their fire was almost immediately returned from nearly their whole line, evidently thrown much in front of their different positions. Conscious from this that the position was *new and not entrenched*, I decided at once upon attacking him."

The above extracts make it clear that (1) the move direct on Chillianwalla, not (as has been said) a route more to the right, was the original intention; there was no sudden change of plan; (2) the fact that the Sikhs had advanced beyond their entrenched position was the cause of the immediate engagement.

B.—*Note on the Cavalry Lesson.*

The disaster to the cavalry at Chillianwalla is painful to dwell upon, but conveys a never-to-be-forgotten lesson which cannot be passed over without additional comment.

To no arm of the service is the combination of cool judgment with resolute leading more essential. For a charge, even if successful, must lead to temporary disorganisation, if anything like severe opposition takes place. Flung at speed into a hot contest, officers and men become involved in desperate hand-to-hand combats. Suddenly, in a flash, as it were, success becomes apparent; the enemy, if cavalry, are disappearing; if infantry, are broken and dispersed. At that moment, the successful horsemen, elated with the triumph of victory, but already thrown into some disorder by the struggle, may easily be led away into an imprudent pursuit. Now is the time when the cool judgment of an experienced leader sees and acts upon the necessity for rallying and re-forming his men. Supports, therefore, to rally on are an imperative necessity for confirming and following up a success; they are no less imperative for checking and retrieving a temporary repulse; and no cavalry commander worthy the name will commit his men to a serious combat without supports ready at hand for either event. Thus it was that when on the left Thackwell's first line met with a check, no disaster ensued, because the 5th Cavalry were able to rally at once and with perfect steadiness, on the 8th. But on the right, Brigadier Pope neglected this elementary principle; his whole force advanced in one line with no supports; a check became a retreat; and the retreat, with no point to rally on, rapidly developed into a flight—with the disastrous consequences already narrated. Yet the troops which failed so lamentably were old soldiers, two-thirds of them British Dragoons, whose valour had already been put to the proof. Their conduct, indeed, cannot be excused; but it can be accounted for in part by the flagrant mismanagement of the brigadier. It may safely be affirmed that, with a competent officer in command, the disaster would never have occurred.

C.—Loss of Life.

The loss of life in Lord Gough's campaigns is generally compared with that which is normally to be looked for in contests with Oriental armies. Even then, it may be observed that Wellington lost all but one-third of his force, in killed and wounded, in the battle of Assaye, against the Mahrattas. Compare his letter, quoted at p. 107.

The proportion of losses for which the greatest European commanders have been responsible suggests that this is scarcely a conclusive method of passing judgment. In killed and wounded—

Marlborough	at	Blenheim	lost	23	per cent.	of his force.
"	"	Malplaquet	"	19	"	"
Wellington	"	Talavera	"	25	"	"
"	"	Assaye	"	31	"	"
Frederick II.	"	Kolin	"	24	"	"
"	"	Leuthen	"	20	"	"
"	"	Zorndorf	"	36	"	"

Whereas Gough never touched the lowest of these figures.

APPENDIX IV.

A SERGEANT ON THE COMMANDER-IN-CHIEF

THE following true copy of a letter written from Peshawur, 14th November, 1850, by a sergeant of the Bengal Artillery, who served under Lord Gough in the Punjab Campaign, is interesting as giving a trustworthy estimation of the opinion held by soldiers in the ranks of their leader's character and military qualities.

"I have just been thinking, on looking over some old newspapers, that you must have been led to believe that Lord Gough stood very low in the estimation of the troops as a commander. But if such be the case, depend upon it, you were never more deceived, for the very reverse of this was the case, for there was no danger, no matter how great, nor any undertaking, however desperate it might be, but they would have attempted it under him; indeed, *when he was present, they looked upon success as being certain*, and it was not as a commander alone that he was respected, but as a kind-feeling and good-hearted old man, who took a lively interest in the welfare of all those who were under him, and who took a pleasure in seeing every one around him as comfortable as circumstances would permit. For the officers and native troops I cannot speak, although I have every reason to think that they and us were alike in that respect. But as for the European soldiers, cavalry, infantry, and artillery, I don't think that men ever could have been more attached to any commander than they were to old Gough, and considering his kind and humane disposition, and the attention he always paid to the sick and wounded, there is little wonder that he was looked upon as a father more than as a military superior. I can never forget the reception he got from the troops as he rode along the front of our line just after we had been withdrawn out of the jungle on the evening of the Battle of Chillianwalla, I happened also to be at the General Hospital where the wounded and the dying were lying in hundreds, and as soon as they caught sight of his venerable white head, there was such a cheer burst forth that the dullest observer could not have misunderstood for a moment; ay, and that from many a poor fellow who had scarcely a head left upon his shoulders to shout with—it said, as plainly as ever cheer could say, 'You will never find us wanting when you require us.' And afterwards his attention to the wounded and sick was such as to gain the esteem and affection of every one. I used to see him in that hospital daily myself kindly inquiring after those who were recovering, and cheering up and consoling those who were bad; and, believe me, those who think that soldiers are incapable of appreciating these attentions on the part of a commander are woefully out in their calculations. May Gough long live to enjoy whatever rewards he may have got, for he is well worthy of them."—P. KEAY.

INDEX

INDEX.